Gender Inequality in Screenwriting Work

Natalie Wreyford

Gender Inequality in Screenwriting Work

palgrave
macmillan

Natalie Wreyford
University of Southampton
Southampton, UK

ISBN 978-3-319-95731-9   ISBN 978-3-319-95732-6   (eBook)
https://doi.org/10.1007/978-3-319-95732-6

Library of Congress Control Number: 2018951790

Cover illustration: Gen Sadakane / EyeEm / Getty Images
Cover design: Fatima Jamadar

This Palgrave Macmillan imprint is published by the registered company Springer Nature Switzerland AG
The registered company address is: Gewerbestrasse 11, 6330 Cham, Switzerland

For Honor & Seth

Acknowledgements

I am very grateful to all my research participants who gave their time and thoughts so generously. Your honesty and insights surpassed anything I could have hoped to get from my interviews. I would also like to say a huge thank you to my PhD supervisors, Dr Christina Scharff, whose wisdom and insight guided me through the majority of my research, and Dr Bridget Conor, who gallantly took the reins with much needed expertise and encouragement in my final stages. Both of them have shown me such generosity and support and truly exemplify how rewarding it can be to work with feminist academics. I am very grateful to you both for your continued advice and friendship, and sincerely hope we can find ways to work together in the future. My thanks also to Professor Ros Gill for her early supervision and continued support and interest in my work.

I am also very grateful to my examiners, Professor Mark Banks and Dr Stephanie Taylor, both of whose work was extremely influential on my thinking and whose wise feedback was invaluable. Thanks especially to Mark for your continued guidance. Thank you to Dr Shelley Cobb and Professor Linda Ruth Williams, who gave me my first full-time academic job on their project 'Calling the Shots: Women and Contemporary Film Culture in the UK' and allowed me to work from home so that I could be both a mother and an academic. You have both been incredibly supportive and generous and the time has flown by. I hope this year won't be the end of our working together, or our friendships. Thank you to my editor Lina Aboujieb for her support and guidance and to Ellie Freedman for always having the answers and reassurance I needed. Finally, thanks to King's College London and in particular to the department of Culture, Media and Creative Industries for providing a stimulating context and perfect home for my research and to my fellow PhD candidates who provided friendship, support, and debate that enriched my work and my experience, in particular Rachel O'Neill, Sara de Benedictis, Stefania Marghitu and Scarlett Brown.

Writing this book would not have been possible without the support of my family. In particular, I want to thank my mum, Sheenagh Wreyford, who put me up to it in the first place and who has been inexhaustibly supportive and inspirational my whole life, and my dad, Brian Wreyford, who brought me up to question authority and fight for the underdog. Thanks to my husband, Nathan Williams, for his love, for going out to work every day and navigating the sudden intrusion of feminist academic thinking in his life. Enormous love and gratitude to my children, Honor and Seth, who are my sunshine and my bedrock and have shown me first-hand the ridiculousness of gender stereotypes as well as the dangers; and thanks to my step-daughter Ellie for the many feminist discussions about film and life in general. Lots of love and admiration to my sister Catherine and my niece Kiri—two women who have endured far more than their fair share of adversity in life and deserve some peace and happiness.

I am very grateful to both SAGE Publications and *Studies in the Maternal* for allowing me to include in this book extracts from previously published articles:

- Wreyford, Natalie. "Birds of a feather: informal recruitment practices and gendered outcomes for screenwriting work in the UK film industry." The Sociological Review 63, no. 1_suppl: 84–96. Copyright © 2015. (SAGE Publications). Reprinted by permission of SAGE Publications.
- Wreyford, Natalie. 2013. "The Real Cost of Childcare; Motherhood and Flexible Creative Labour in the UK Film Industry-Review Essay." Studies in the Maternal 5, no. 2 (2013): 1–22. The article can be accessed here: https://www.mamsie.bbk.ac.uk/articles/abstract/10.16995/sim.26/.

This book is dedicated to women screenwriters everywhere, especially those who have never written a word.

CONTENTS

ABOUT THE AUTHOR

Natalie Wreyford is Research Fellow on 'Calling the Shots: Women and contemporary UK film culture' at the University of Southampton. She completed her PhD thesis on women screenwriters at King's College London. Prior to that, she worked for many years in screenplay development in the UK film industry, including as a Senior Development Executive at the UK Film Council and at Granada Film.

Abbreviations

ALCS   Authors' Licensing and Collecting Society
BAME   Black, Asian, and Minority Ethnic
BBC   British Broadcasting Corporation
BFI   British Film Institute
CTS   Calling the Shots: Women and Contemporary UK Film Culture
DCMS   Department for Culture, Media and Sport
EWA   European Women's Audiovisual Network
SIWG   Screen Idea Work Group
SPWG   Semi-permanent Work Group
UKFC   UK Film Council
WFTV   Women in Film and Television
WGGB   Writer's Guild of Great Britain

CHAPTER 1

Introduction: The Extent of Gender Inequality in Film Screenwriting Work

If I was a female writer now I'd think there was no opportunity. If I was a female writer and looked at the stats and looked at the stats again, at what're the chances of getting your projects into production? You'd almost want to give up there and then. I mean what are your chances? You may as well play the lottery. (Colin, employer)

I open with this evocative quote from one of my research participants as it so clearly illustrates the situation that inspired this book. Women still stand far less a chance than men of becoming the screenwriter of a film. The numbers are so dismal, and seem so stubbornly averse to change, that the women who succeed feel as rare and exceptional as lottery winners. I first became aware of the disparity in 2005 when I was working as Senior Development Executive for the UK Film Council (UKFC), then the UK government's strategic and funding body for the film industry. All the concern and effort to 'diversify' the film workforce at that time was focused on race and disability—inequalities that are no less of a problem today. But when I raised the issue of gender inequality, I was confronted with a post-feminist discourse from some of the senior management, suggesting that women had equal opportunities to men and no longer faced any barriers at work. In the years since then, the position of women in film has now become widely recognized as unfair and unequal. A still developing global conversation is happening in which issues like unequal pay, unconscious bias, and sexual harassment in the film labour market have become headline news, backed up by numbers showing the entrenched nature of gender inequality

© The Author(s) 2018
N. Wreyford, *Gender Inequality in Screenwriting Work*,
https://doi.org/10.1007/978-3-319-95732-6_1

1

in many key filmmaking roles. This has happened, in no small part, due to various campaigners and data gatherers worldwide, but—and partly in response to this—in the film labour market, gender inequality is still often discounted or presumed to be improving, as it was in my interviews:

> I feel like it's less of a kind of situation than it was five or ten or certainly twenty years ago. (Vanessa, Employer)

This attitude is typical of a 'progress narrative', identified by Christine Everingham, Deborah Stevenson, and Penny Warner-Smith (2007). It describes a common assumption in discussions of gender inequality that 'things are changing', as actor Annette Bening claimed at the opening of the 2017 Venice Film Festival, despite there being only one film directed by a woman in competition at the festival (Keslassy 2017). With so much attention on the subject, and high-profile pressure, why have so many schemes and gendered opportunities failed to shift the overall inclusion of women in filmmaking? This book seeks to address this problem and dig deep into the causes of gender inequality in screenwriting work, giving scholars, decision makers, and campaigners the tools to ensure that future action is based on profound knowledge of the film labour market and, therefore, make real change a possibility.

There are now plenty of data to indicate substantial and continued underemployment of everyone except white, able-bodied, cis-presenting men in film work. The data are patchy, and until very recently, as part of the work I'm doing with Shelley Cobb and Linda Ruth Williams at Southampton University (which I will detail later), the data have been mainly Hollywood facing. So let's start with the numbers that we have, since they provide a clear and undeniably grim overview of what women are up against. Ann Oakley (1999) has argued that without quantitative data, 'It is difficult to distinguish between personal experience and collective oppression. Only large-scale comparative data can determine to what extent the situations of men and women are structurally differentiated.' This has been particularly helpful in garnering support for the cause of gender inequality in film work, as Shelley Cobb and I (Wreyford and Cobb 2017) have argued elsewhere.

New data from the project 'Calling the Shots: Women and Contemporary UK Film Culture, 2000–2015'[1] (CTS) (Cobb et al. 2016) show that women made up 20 per cent of the screenwriters of British films in production in 2015. Just 13 per cent of all 203 films qualifying as British in

2015 had a woman screenwriter, and less than 2 per cent of all the screen-writers in 2015 were women of colour. The percentage of women working as screenwriters of British films in production has only increased two points since 2003—the first year for which project partner, the British Film Institute (BFI), could provide us with a list of qualifying films. Even this tiny increase may be misleading. Across all the categories we are researching and throughout the intervening years, the inclusion of women goes up or down slightly year on year, but always hovers around the same percentage (Cobb et al. 2018).

In May 2018, the Writer's Guild of Great Britain (WGGB) published a report on screenwriters in film and television work, in association with The Author's Licensing and Collecting Society (ALCS) (Kreager and Follows 2018). Looking at films and television programmes between 2005 and 2016, the report found that only 15 per cent of films had a woman screen-writer, while just 11 per cent of films were written predominantly by women, and in television, only 28 per cent of episodes were written by women. They also found that women screenwriters were less likely to have sustainable careers, with men 39 per cent more likely than women to write a second feature film and just 8 per cent of writers with four or more film credits being women.

The data that we compiled for CTS closely (and deliberately) echo the work done by Martha M. Lauzen (2018), at the Center for the Study of Women in Television and Film, San Diego State University. In her 'Celluloid Ceiling' reports, she has been looking at the presence of women behind the 250 highest grossing films every year since 1998 and in doing so has built up a much-needed body of evidence that not only are women under-represented in most key professions in film but that the situation is not changing. Slight increases in the percentages of writers, directors, pro-ducers, and other key roles in any year are all too often followed by slight decreases the following year, and overall, there is a sense that one or two successful women can alter the results in any given year, but in general, the industry is not ready to make changes to the level of women's involve-ment. Table 1.1 highlights some of the data from both projects. These comparisons show how little movement there is in the numbers in both studies. The slightly higher numbers from CTS reflect the fact that these data are based on films in production, whereas the Celluloid Ceiling report focuses on films that have been released. There is very likely a drop-off for women screenwriters between production and distribution, just as there is between development and production (Sinclair et al. 2006).

Table 1.1 Historical comparison of percentages of women employed in key behind-the-scene roles taken from the Celluloid Ceiling reports on the top 250 films and Calling the Shots reports on women working on British qualifying films

	2017	2015	2005	2003	1998
Calling the Shots reports					
% Women writers	n/a	20	20	18	n/a
% Women producers	n/a	27	29	24	n/a
% Women executive producers	n/a	18	17	18	n/a
% Women directors	n/a	13	12	11	n/a
The Celluloid Ceiling reports					
% Women writers	11	11	11	13	13
% Women producers	25	26	26	25	24
% Women executive producers	19	20	16	14	18
% Women directors	11	9	7	6	9

The rest of the data in Table 1.1 detail the participation of decision makers who employ writers and select which scripts to pursue to production. It is difficult to be optimistic about future prospects for women screenwriters whilst these numbers also remain low for women. Less than 30 per cent of producers are women, less than 20 per cent of executive producers, and in the UK, the percentage of women directors has only risen above 13 per cent three times in the last 12 years (Cobb et al. 2018). Recent reports commissioned by Directors UK (Follows et al. 2016) and the European Women's Audiovisual Network (EWA) (Aylett 2016) have also shown continued underemployment of women *directors* throughout Europe. Prior to the data provided by CTS, the main sources of data about women screenwriters in the UK were the BFI and the now defunct UKFC, with some contribution from Creative Skillset. In 2006, whilst I was employed at the UKFC, I commissioned a Scoping Study (Sinclair et al. 2006) to investigate the extent of the disparity of employment for women screenwriters in the UK. It was the first time such a systematic appraisal of gender inequality had been compiled on UK film workers and prompted the UKFC's Research and Statistics Unit to start including data on the percentages of women screenwriters and directors in their annual Statistical Yearbook. The BFI (2017) continues to collect and publish these data since it took over responsibilities from the UKFC. The Scoping Study confirmed my suspicions that women were under-represented in screenwriting on British films. The report provided some evidence to disperse within the UK film industry in order to prompt a change. As I have described earlier, this hasn't yet happened, which compels the argument to move on and address *why* change is not happening. The stagnation is at the heart of my research, and the desire to understand why change is so difficult is the main question that this book endeavours to answer. It has become clear that numbers on their own, whilst hugely important in revealing 'a pattern of inequality that must be addressed' (Wreyford and Cobb 2017), cannot provide the tools to make change a real possibility.

Although the Scoping Study did include some exploratory questions to try to understand possible reasons for the gender inequality, the report failed to acknowledge that all the interviewees are working in the UK film industry and therefore may have, to a greater or lesser extent, already accepted and taken on the dominant discourses of the industry in order to succeed. Contradictory opinions and ideas are very clearly missing from the study as well as any questioning of assumptions or discourse analysis. The Scoping Study was followed by another UKFC commission (Rogers 2007) to establish who actually writes the films that are certified as British by the Department for Culture, Media and Sport (DCMS) under Schedule 1 of the Film Act (1985). Looking at films released between 2004 and 2005, Susan Rogers discovered that 98 per cent of the writers were white, 82.5 per cent were men, 66 per cent were over the age of 46, and 61 per cent were not British. By talking to 63 screenwriters credited on these films, Rogers also discovered that half of them had a previous working relationship and nearly as many (42 per cent) had a previous *personal* relationship with the commission producer, director, or production company, supporting the infamous saying that it's 'who you know' that is most important in securing film work—something I unpack in great detail in this book.

Screenwriters exist in the shadow of directors. Even now, in this moment where the world seems to be finally awakening to the extent of gender inequality in film (and other) industries, most public and academic focus has remained firmly on directors and actors as the primary interest and focus for change. Angela McRobbie has described 'the illegible and invisible characteristics' (2002a, p. 105) of many jobs in the creative industries, since they often operate outside conventional office environments with flexible hours and hidden periods of underemployment. Screenwriting exemplifies this 'invisible' labour. The writers are mostly unknown to the public, even in an industry that is highly observable, heavily promoted, and discussed in all forms of media. Unlike professional writers in other media, such as television writers and novelists, screenwriters are not usually considered to be the principal author of the product they are creating. Film is very much viewed as 'the director's medium', despite the fact that screenwriters are 'primary creative personnel', to use David Hesmondhalgh's term (2007, p. 64). Screenwriters often originate the idea for the film and may work for several years on a film project before a director is even recruited. However, there is frequently more than one writer on a film and they can work in collaboration or sequence, producing many drafts or just one. As a consequence, an individual's final contribution is often difficult to assess and frequently subject to arbitration.

Screenwriters' work happens outside the concentrated and contained world of the production of the film. It takes place in private offices and private homes, and most often in isolation. It is difficult to even talk of the screenwriting 'career' since 'creative labourers don't have a career, they have informal, insecure and discontinuous employment' (Gill and Pratt 2008, p. 2). Bridget Conor (2010, p. 33) illustrates the affective contradictions felt by screenwriters towards their work and how many 'experienced their labour as highly intensive and personal; individualized and collaborative; competitive and hierarchized; marginalized and elite.' Screenwriters are not employees of any companies and often work for free, at the beginning of their careers, or at the beginning of each new project, so that it is difficult to find accurate records of where and when screenwriters are actually working. In addition, most screenplays are never fully realized as films. This means that a significant percentage of many screenwriters' work is never seen by more than a handful of people. What then of those who don't even make it into the identifiable pool of workers known as screenwriters? How is it possible to critically examine those who are not even present? Those who have been excluded or who have excluded themselves from this profession? I hope to provide some answers in this book.

Research on work in the film industries has so far tended to focus on film production as this stage provides more easily identifiable, finite, and readily available data sets. Far less scrutinized is the area that I am interested in—the messy, fractured, interminable, and often unpaid work that happens prior to the 'green-light'.[2] However, by the time 'action' has been called on the film set, most of the key decisions about the film's content would have already been made. In addition, during the development process, prior to beginning production, a film project will acquire most of the key personnel, including but not limited to, the screenwriter(s), producer(s), director(s), executive producer(s), and at a later stage, many heads of department, including the cinematographer, production designer, and costume designer. My book focuses on the very origin of a film project: the initial selection of the screenwriter and screenplay subject by the producer.

> You're working, you're doing a job and I think it's quite key to remember it all starts with the script and you're the first person on any film. (Emily, screenwriter)

Decisions made at this point can affect not only the on-screen roles written into the story but who is likely to take up these other key production roles, as I will demonstrate. It is therefore imperative to understand this seemingly impenetrable world and start to interrogate its power structures, means of access, and conditions of employment, not only in order to understand inequality in screenwriting work but if we are ever going to understand how inequality remains entrenched in the whole filmmaking process. By studying screenwriters' working lives and the recruitment processes to which they are subject, I am able to explore how women can become excluded right from the genesis of film projects.

I have found the work of Stephanie Taylor (2011) and her collaborations with Karen Littleton (2006, 2016) extremely useful in problematizing the idea that responsibility for a creative product can be attributed to one individual. Drawing on the work of Howard Becker (1982), Teresa Amabile (1983), and Vera John-Steiner (2000), as well as their own extensive empirical research, Taylor and Littleton explore 'the possibilities and constraints and conflicts around a creative identification' (2016, p. 4) and illustrate how creativity is a process that arises from social interaction. These are important ideas that I will come back to in more detail in Chap. 2. For now, I would just like to acknowledge that their writing has been critical to my understanding of how judgements about creative ability and worth are subject to historical contexts, discursive constraints, and individual identity work. When considering who writes films, it is important to remember Taylor and Littleton's claim that 'ownership of the output cannot appropriately be attributed to any particular individual, even though social conventions may dictate otherwise' (Ibid., p. 15).

I conducted interviews with screenwriters and employers of screenwriters. The 'employers' range from individual producers working as sole traders, to the senior personnel of large production companies, distribution companies, public financiers, and broadcasters, all of whom have some authority in the hiring of screenwriters. The screenwriters had, at the time of our conversations, experience ranging from no produced features to more than 12 feature film credits. My participants included 34 white British or British-resident individuals, three of South Asian background, two describing themselves as African black British, and one who was brought up in England, having been born in Jamaica. My sample was deliberately weighted to include a higher percentage of women than is found in the UK film industry generally, as I really wanted to hear their stories and opinions. The men screenwriters were included to make gendered comparison possible. All the participants' identities are protected in the book by the use of pseudonyms and I have not provided any demographic information when quoting from the interview transcripts. However, if a particular feature of someone's identity is relevant, I highlight it in the text. This is important in order to capture aspects of intersectional experience, but unfortunately, it runs the risk of reproducing patterns where whiteness is normalized.

Throughout my research and the writing of this book, it was important to me to be attentive to matters of intersectionality (Crenshaw 1989) and to recognize my own privileges as a middle-class, able-bodied, straight white woman and the limits of my comprehension of the benefits I may have that others lack. However, I aim to examine the case of women screenwriters following Herminia Ibarra in that my 'focus here is on the commonalities, rather than the difference between women and racial [and other] minorities' (1993, p. 65). These commonalities include under-representation 'within societal and organizational power elites' (Ibid., p. 63), being stereotyped negatively, and having embodied characteristics and habitus that have a 'lower status in this society' (Ibid., p. 66). I am also drawing on the work done by David Corsun and Wanda Costen (2001) in the field of management studies. They suggest that the explanations offered for women and non-white 'career stallings' may well apply to anyone who does not fit the dominant able-bodied, heterosexual white male model. Thus, whilst my focus is particularly on gender inequality—and I do not claim to have given sufficient attention to other forms of inequality—I believe and hope that my research has the potential to open up further discussions across multiple axes. I wish to improve the odds for anyone who wants to write screenplays, particularly those who do not see themselves reflected in the current demographic in any great number.

I had a very high response rate to my requests for participants. I was able to include individuals that might prove more difficult to identify for 'outsider' researchers without my knowledge and access to film labour market networks. For example, I spoke to unproduced screenwriters who had worked for a substantial number of years and were well known in the British industry despite having no screen credits. In contrast to Vicky Mayer (2008) and Sherry Ortner's (2010) observations about access to film industry figures, I was also able to include in my sample some of the most senior and experienced members of the UK film industry. In particular, I was able to speak to *employers* and not just the screenwriters themselves—something that makes my research particularly unique. Conversely, I was able to interview producers who work independently and under frequent changes to the name of their company.

Work in the film industry offers an exemplary case study for post-Fordist labour and, therefore, is an excellent place to start critically examining how inequality in creative careers is upheld, in particular by interrogating the role of those selecting who is considered creative and talented enough. According to Pierre Bourdieu (1996, p. 167) 'the principal obstacle to a rigorous science of the production of the value of cultural goods' is the 'charismatic ideology of "creation"'. Charismatic ideology 'directs the gaze towards the apparent producer and prevents us from asking who has created this "creator" and the magic power of transubstantiation with which the "creator" is endowed' (Ibid.). I consider how the 'creator' is conceived and acknowledged and by whom, and who is simultaneously found lacking by the very same judgements.

Susan Christopherson (2008) shows how creative project work is frequently organized by a 'key intermediary' who plays a significant role negotiating between the artists and the market. This is very similar to Pierre Bourdieu's (1984) term 'cultural intermediaries', which is slightly less concretely defined and can refer to the critics of art and culture such as journalists who review artistic endeavours and offer their opinion to help audiences decide which exhibitions, productions, and performances they would like to spend time and money going to see. Keith Negus (2002, p. 119) suggests that Bourdieu's cultural intermediaries can also be viewed as closer to Christopherson's term—occupying a position between artist and audience and 'operating across and exerting influence within a nexus of social relationships'. Key intermediaries play a crucial role in managing and coordinating creative people in many cultural industries. For example, Negus examines the role of A&R directors in the music industry as 'the point at which cultural judgments are converted into business decisions and vice versa' ((Negus 1998) quoted in

Scase and Davis, p. 67). In the film industry, this role is taken up by that of the film producer. James Curran and Vincent Porter (1983, pp. 179–180) argue that understanding a producer's role:

> ...lies in appreciating his or her ability to manipulate creatively the complex and interlocking relationship between four key factors: an understanding of public taste – of what subjects and genres could attract a broad audience; the ability to obtain adequate production finance; the understanding of who to use in the key creative roles and on what terms; and the effectiveness of her or his overall control of the production process.

A film producer will attempt to increase the value of a new film project for potential finance sources and distributors by employing key creatives with a demonstrable track record, which makes it difficult to diversify the existing pool of working writers (and directors). Nevertheless new writers emerge in the pool each year, so this doesn't explain why the gender (and other) inequalities persist. As I will demonstrate, senior and influential film producers are, like Negus's key decision makers in the music industry, 'drawn from a very particular class background and habitus' (2002, p. 120), which informs their decision making:

> ...what often appear to be fundamentally economic or commercial decisions (which artists to sign/how much to invest in them/how to market them) are based on a series of historically specific cultural values, beliefs and prejudices. (Ibid., p. 116)

In addition, and of vital importance for my own research, is how the film producer is 'critical to interpreting how incentives move from conglomerate distributor to the workforce' (Christopherson 2008, p. 80). The producer makes decisions about whom to hire based on their perception of the demands and tastes of the distributors and the cinema audience. I will examine whether this is a critical point at which discriminatory ideologies are reawakened and reinforced. If the audience is imagined as predominantly men, for example, as Christopherson asserts, does the distribution sector demand of the producer that the product be designed for men, and does this lead to a favouring of men writers and directors who demonstrate the corresponding tastes, and indeed, in Bourdieusian terms, the right habitus, or 'feel for the game' (Bourdieu and Wacquant 1992)?

Mark Deuze (2011, p. 1) describes the 'hourglass structure' of creative industries where a handful of companies interact with many individuals in creative roles and also a large audience. It is these companies, these managers, these intermediaries who play a crucial role in deciding whose work is allowed through to address the audience. Deuze argues, '[M]ore attention needs to be given to understanding professional values, idiosyncrasies of talent and people management issues like hiring and retention policies' (Ibid., p. 2), which is what I do in this book. Producers as creative managers, key intermediaries, and indeed gatekeepers to finance and production play a key role in upholding gender disparities as will become clear.

There is no doubt that the UK film industry employs disproportionately low numbers of women in key creative roles, including as screenwriters, or that the availability of statistical evidence has resulted in little change. The work done by screenwriters is often 'invisible', to return to McRobbie (2002b)—hidden away from public eyes and the theatre of production, the majority of their work only ever read by a handful of people and their authorship often attributed to others such as rewriters and actors, but most of all to directors. The women who do this work are even less visible: far less likely than men to see their words make it to the screen. As a passionate activist and advocate for women screenwriters, I came to view my fieldwork as a way to have impact by raising consciousness of the issue and indeed presenting people with data and statistics that make them question their own assumptions:

> I just think it's, the more I hear myself [laughs] or talk to you, I just think it's completely male dominated. I mean I don't know, but it is isn't it? (Gillian, employer)

This book aims to cast a spotlight on the women who are missing from a profession that is itself under-examined by academics and undervalued by media focused on celebrity actors and 'auteur' directors.[3] In Chap. 2, I will drill down into the ways that professions become gendered, how dominant film industry discourses about screenwriting make it harder for some to take up the position of screenwriter, and why women may be socialized into taking up alternative jobs in the film industry. I then develop this in Chap. 3, to consider what film workers indicate are the requirements of a career in film and how to get that important first break. In particular, I look at why this might be harder for some than others. Chapter 4 closely examines the employment processes and working practices that uphold multiple axes of inequality in screenwriting work and leads on to how Pierre Bourdieu's concept of habitus can help us understand some of the barriers women face in building a screenwriting career. Chapter 5 examines the impact of motherhood, and indeed maternal assumption on women screenwriters, and Chap. 6 considers what it is like for women to always be in the minority, especially when it comes to attaching a director to a film project. I end with a discussion of gendered taste in Chap. 7, clearly demonstrating how power becomes unevenly distributed in the socialized construction of identities and the outcome in real terms for those participating in creative work. My conclusion clarifies the usefulness of my research for making screenwriting work more accessible for women and other marginalized groups and offers some ideas as to how this might be achieved.

In analysing my data, I found certain theoretical approaches more helpful than others. Pierre Bourdieu's theories (1977, 1984, and Bourdieu and Wacquant 1992) were particularly useful because of his focus on cultural production and consumption. But more crucially, for the way that he makes visible—and therefore, discussable—how characteristics of individuals that are widely understood to be naturally occurring and inevitable have actually been socially constructed. His dissection of scholastic measurements, judgements of taste and aesthetics, and the way that the dominant classes are able to position their own achievements and dispositions as having more value than those of the dominated, have all been extremely useful to me in understanding how, in the film industry, subjective choices are able to be positioned as market-driven or meritocratic. Bourdieu has been heavily criticized for his position on women, so I will clarify why his theories are so useful despite—and sometimes because of—this. I will discuss both how Bourdieu is useful for an analysis of creative work and can be 'appropriated' (Moi 1991) for a deeper understanding of gendered inequality.

Doing gender and doing work are 'empirically intertwined' (Fenstermaker et al. 2002, p. 38) and a growing body of research—to which this book makes a contribution—examines the way in which the two work together to maintain inequalities. Unless we can deconstruct this process, what hope is there of more women being able to take centre stage and share their creative vision with the world as original creators such as screenwriters rather than simply nurturers, caretakers, assistants, agents, and editors of male screenwriters. To see women's stories in all their variety and complexity is to contribute to the disintegration of the homogeneous category of 'women' and to share women's experiences with a variety of men in ways that might help them understand that we are not so different after all. Therein lies the possibility of change, crisis, trouble, and the disruption of gender: in the creative work of women. As De Lauretis proposes: 'to make up one's story, the possibility to speak as subject of discourse, which means also to be listened to, to be granted authorship and authori-tiy over the story' is extremely attractive (De Lauretis 1987, p. 113) and quite possibly revolutionary.

Notes

1. Calling the Shots is funded by the Arts and Humanities Research Council (UK) for the period of 2014–2018. You can find out more about the project on the following website: https://www.southampton.ac.uk/cswf/index. page
2. A film is considered to have a 'green-light' when all the financing is committed and the project can move from the development phase to pre-production and production.
3. '*Auteur*' is the French word for 'author' and '*auteur* theory' argues that in spite of the collaborative and industrial nature of filmmaking, the director's creative voice is strong enough to be able to attribute the authorship of the film to him or her alone.

References

Amabile, Teresa M. 1983. The social psychology of creativity: A componential conceptualization. *Journal of Personality and Social Psychology* 45 (2): 357.

Aylett, Holly. 2016. Where are the woman directors? Report on gender equality for directors in the European film industry 2006–2013. European Women's Audiovisual Network. http://www.ewawomen.com/uploads/files/MERGED_Press-2016.pdf. Accessed 26 Mar 2018.

Becker, Howard Saul. 1982. *Art worlds*. Berkeley: University of California Press.

BFI Statistical Yearbook. 2017. British Film Institute. http://www.bfi.org.uk/sites/bfi.org.uk/files/downloads/bfi-statistical-yearbook-2017.pdf. Accessed 26 Mar 2018.

Bourdieu, Pierre. 1977. *Outline of a theory of practice*. Vol. 16. Cambridge, UK: Cambridge University Press.

———. 1984. *Distinction: A social critique of the judgment of taste*. Cambridge, MA: Harvard University Press.

———. 1996. *The rules of art: Genesis and structure of the literary field*. Stanford: Stanford University Press.

Bourdieu, Pierre, and Loïc Wacquant. 1992. *An invitation to reflexive sociology*. Chicago: University of Chicago Press.

Christopherson, Susan. 2008. Beyond the self-expressive creative worker: An industry perspective on entertainment media. *Theory, Culture & Society* 25 (7–8): 73–95.

Cobb, Shelley, Linda Ruth Williams, and Natalie Wreyford. 2016. *Calling the Shots: Women working in key roles on UK films in production during 2015*. https://www.southampton.ac.uk/cswf/project/number_tracking.page. Accessed 26 Mar 2018.

———. 2018. *Calling the Shots: Women directors and cinematographers on British Films since 2003*. https://s25407.pcdn.co/wp-content/uploads/2018/02/Calling-the-Shots-Report-Feb-2018-Women-directors-and-cinematographers.pdf. Accessed 26 Mar 2018.

Conor, Bridget. 2010. Everybody's a writer theorizing screenwriting as creative labour. *Journal of Screenwriting* 1 (1): 27–43.

Corsun, David L., and Wanda M. Costen. 2001. Is the glass ceiling unbreakable? Habitus, fields, and the stalling of women and minorities in management. *Journal of Management Inquiry* 10 (1): 16–25.

Crenshaw, Kimberle. 1989. Demarginalizing the intersection of race and sex: A black feminist critique of antidiscrimination doctrine, feminist theory and anti-racist politics. *University of Chicago Legal Forum* 1989 (1), Article 8: 139–167.

Curran, James, and Vincent Porter. 1983. *British cinema history*. London: Weidenfeld & Nicolson.

De Lauretis, Teresa. 1987. *Technologies of gender: Essays on theory, film, and fiction*. Bloomington: Indiana University Press.

Deuze, Mark. 2011. *Managing media work*. Thousand Oaks: Sage.

Everingham, Christine, Deborah Stevenson, and Penny Warner-Smith. 2007. 'Things are getting better all the time'? Challenging the narrative of women's progress from a generational perspective. *Sociology* 41 (3): 419–437.

Fenstermaker, Sarah, Candace West, and Don Zimmerman. 2002. Gender inequality: New conceptual terrain. In *Doing gender, doing difference: Inequality, power, and institutional change*, ed. Sarah Fenstermaker and Candace West, vol. 2013, 25–39. New York: Routledge.

Film Act. 1985. HM Government. https://www.legislation.gov.uk/ukpga/1985/21. Accessed 26 Mar 2018.

Follows, Stephen, Alexis Kreager, and Eleanor Gomes. 2016. *Cut out of the picture: A study of gender inequality amongst film directors in the UK film industry*. Directors UK. https://d29dqxe14uxvcr.cloudfront.net/uploads%2F1461930983739-erk37ak82v20lnpl-0dacf96122678073f64e99c9b75e90bf%2FCut+Out+of+The+Picture+-+Report.pdf. Accessed 26 Mar 2018.

Gill, Rosalind, and Andy Pratt. 2008. In the social factory? Immaterial labour, precariousness and cultural work. *Theory, Culture & Society* 25 (7–8): 1–30.

Hesmondhalgh, David. 2007. *The cultural industries*. Los Angeles: SAGE Publishing.

Ibarra, Herminia. 1993. Personal networks of women and minorities in management: A conceptual framework. *Academy of Management Review* 18 (1): 56–87.

John-Steiner, Vera. 2000. *Creative collaboration*. Oxford: Oxford University Press.

Keslassy, Elsa. 2017. Annette Bening addresses lack of female directors at Venice: 'Things are changing'. *Variety*. http://variety.com/2017/film/news/annette-bening-venice-film-festival-female-directors-sharp-shrewd-creative-1202542606/. Accessed 26 Mar 2018.

Kreager, Alexis, and Stephen Follows. 2018. Gender inequality and screenwriters. A study of the impact of gender on equality of opportunity for screenwriters and key creatives in the UK film and television industries. *The Writers Guild of Great Britain*. https://writersguild.org.uk/wp-content/uploads/2018/05/Gender-Inequality-and-Screenwriters.pdf. Accessed 13 June 2018.

Lauzen, Martha M. 2018. *The Celluloid Ceiling: behind-the-scenes employment of women on the top 100, 250, and 500 Films of 2017*. San Diego State University. https://womenintvfilm.sdsu.edu/wp-content/uploads/2018/01/2017_Celluloid_Ceiling_Report.pdf. Accessed 26 Mar 2018.

Mayer, Vicki. 2008. Studying up and f**cking up: Ethnographic interviewing in production studies. *Cinema Journal* 47 (2): 141–148.

McRobbie, Angela. 2002a. Holloway to Hollywood: Happiness at work in the cultural economy. In *Cultural economy: Cultural analysis and commercial life*, ed. Paul Du Gay and Michael Pryke, 97–114. London: Sage.

———. 2002b. Clubs to companies: Notes on the decline of political culture in speeded up creative worlds. *Cultural Studies* 16 (4): 516–531.

Moi, Toril. 1991. Appropriating Bourdieu: Feminist theory and Pierre Bourdieu's sociology of culture. *New Literary History* 22 (4): 1017–1049.

Negus, Keith. 1998. Cultural production and the corporation: Musical genres and the strategic management of creativity in the US recording industry. *Media, Culture & Society* 20 (3): 359–379.

———. 2002. The work of cultural intermediaries and the enduring distance between production and consumption. *Cultural Studies* 16 (4): 501–515.

Oakley, Ann. 1999. Paradigm wars: Some thoughts on a personal and public trajectory. *International Journal of Social Research Methodology* 2 (3): 247–254.

Ortner, Sherry B. 2010. Access: Reflections on studying up in Hollywood. *Ethnography* 11 (2): 211–233.

Rogers, Susan. 2007. *British films: Who writes British films and how they are recruited*. UK Film Council. http://www.bfi.org.uk/sites/bfi.org.uk/files/downloads/uk-film-council-writing-british-films-who-writes-british-films-and-how-they-are-recruited.pdf. Accessed 26 Mar 2018.

Scase, Richard, and Howard H. Davis. 2000. *Managing creativity: The dynamics of work and organization*. Buckingham: Open University Press.

Sinclair, Alice, Emma Pollard, and Helen Wolfe. 2006. *Scoping study into the lack of women screenwriters in the UK*. A report presented to the UK Film Council. UK Film Council. http://www.bfi.org.uk/sites/bfi.org.uk/files/downloads/uk-film-council-women-screenwriters-scoping-study.pdf. Accessed 26 Mar 2018.

Taylor, Stephanie. 2011. Negotiating oppositions and uncertainties: Gendered conflicts in creative identity work. *Feminism & Psychology* 21 (3): 354–371.

Taylor, Stephanie, and Karen Littleton. 2006. Biographies in talk: A narrative-discursive research approach. *Qualitative Sociology Review* 2 (1): 22–38.

———. 2016. *Contemporary identities of creativity and creative work*. London/New York: Routledge.

Wreyford, Natalie, and Shelley Cobb. 2017. Data and responsibility: Toward a feminist methodology for producing historical data on women in the contemporary UK film industry. *Feminist Media Histories* 3 (3): 107–132.

CHAPTER 2

Gendering the Screenwriter

I always think of it like being a prop forward in rugby, you have to keep getting up and go on to the next scrum because that's what it's about. (Patrick, screenwriter)

In this opening quote, Patrick is describing his work as a screenwriter, making an analogy to a front-line position in a game that is still widely viewed as predominantly a man's sport: boisterous and unruly and including repeated and violent bodily contact, some of the hallmarks of a masculinized identity. It's unlikely to be the first comparison that would spring to mind for most people thinking about a writer's work. It's a singular image, but looking across all 40 of the interviews that I conducted with screenwriters and their employers, it is an example of a widespread underlying assumption of screenwriting as a gendered profession. In this chapter, in order to demonstrate how men are subtly positioned as more suited to screenwriting, I will identify recurring patterns in the way UK film workers talk about screenwriters. A close examination of these discursive patterns reveals how individuals working in the UK film industry make use of shared ideas about screenwriting labour to identify those they consider suitable for the work and—more importantly—how this can also keep other people out. I will demonstrate how the subject position of a screenwriter is constructed discursively and how this might result in disadvantages for women.

The discourses that I reveal are so deeply embedded in the way that employers think about screenwriters that they are widely accepted as

© The Author(s) 2018   17
N. Wreyford, *Gender Inequality in Screenwriting Work*,
https://doi.org/10.1007/978-3-319-95732-6_2

common sense or universal truths, even by the screenwriters themselves. If we are to understand the power and utility of these dominant ideas, Margaret Wetherell (1998) suggests that there is a need to 'render strange usual or habitual ways of making sense'. It is particularly important to the process of unpacking how people might be excluded by this sense-making. The discourses I identify form the context for how far individuals can position themselves as suitable subjects (or otherwise) for screenwriting work and are utilized in a way that assumes these ideas to have 'pre-existed an individual speaker's talk' (Taylor and Littleton 2006, p. 29) and are therefore very difficult for an individual screenwriter to challenge.

As with the quotation at the start of this chapter, screenwriting work was repeatedly discussed in masculine terms by the workers that I spoke to. For example, it was proposed that for screenwriter Lucinda Coxon, working with director Guillermo del Toro on *Pacific Rim* (del Toro 2013) would give her more 'muscle'. Others suggested that a screenwriter needed to be 'tough', 'a good carpenter' or an architect 'creating a blueprint', referencing professions and attributes which, like rugby, are traditionally associated with men. One employer considered that screenwriting was 'like very fine drawing, very elegant, whether it's Leonardo da Vinci or Henry Moore'—a slightly different take, but firmly making an association between creativity and men. In addition, there were several comparisons to screenwriting and film production being like the military or prison, a comment about the 'brutality of the [film] world', and multiple references to the writer as 'king' (never queen).

However, in this chapter, I go beyond obviously gendered comparisons to reveal new ways of understanding how disadvantage happens in creative work. Ros Gill (2014) has argued that sexism is 'increasingly dynamic, mobile and agile, requiring more nuanced vocabularies of critique'. I will address Gill's appeal here. To properly understand how the screenwriter subject is constructed as male, I have identified key discourses that on first glance are not obviously gendered but which on closer inspection reveal entrenched attitudes that make it harder for women to embody the role. Screenwriter Patrick also told me that employers view screenwriting work as 'some sort of magic that you go and do' (magicians having further gender connotations: see Nardi 2010). This is characteristic of the way that screenwriting was described by many of my employer participants. So often notions of the need for writers to develop skills or learn the craft were disparaged in favour of a discourse of an intangible, special innate ability, a little like magic. By contrast, the screenwriters themselves predominantly discussed how they discovered an *interest* in screenwriting that motivated them to pursue a career, and to attain the necessary skills and experience. Whilst this is not at first glance an obviously sexist dynamic, this disjuncture is at the heart of this chapter, which demonstrates the ways that the screenwriter subject is discursively restricted in subtle ways that uphold the very gendered status quo.

Stephanie Taylor and Karen Littleton (2006, p. 23) have argued that identities are socially constructed 'because they are resourced and constrained by larger understandings which prevail in the speaker's social and cultural context'. By focusing in this chapter on how discourse shapes and constrains the ideal screenwriter subject position, I will demonstrate how this limits which people can take up the screenwriter identity. In order to show this happening in the UK film community, I first manifest the entrenched belief that creativity is an innate quality of certain special individuals (see Banks 2017 for a full discussion of the idea of innate talent), and then show how the film industry is presented as a meritocracy where these special individuals can expect to be 'discovered' and enjoy the rewards of their talents, if they remain committed. This raises questions about why most of those identified and discovered as screenwriters continue to be white men. In order to challenge and undermine these discourses, I will then go on to reveal how the talk of film workers can be shown to contain counter—but no less prevalent—discourses: discourses that directly challenge the supremacy of the ideas of the special creative individual and the film industry as a meritocracy, and open up the screenwriter subject position to be occupied by others. I contend that there is a need to disrupt accepted beliefs about screenwriting in order to find a way to a more inclusive workforce. Following Wetherell's argument for the importance of 'investigation of the social and political consequences of discursive patterning' (1998, p. 405), I unpack the ways in which these contradictory discourses are drawn upon, and demonstrate the consequences for gender equality in screenwriting labour.

In the final section, I reflect on why certain ideas about screenwriting continue to dominate in the UK industry, whilst others go unacknowledged. I demonstrate how the prevalent view that 'it's getting better' actually works to allow speakers to do nothing to redress gender inequality. Blind optimism was such a common way that gender inequality was disregarded by film workers in my research that this discourse presented itself as an urgent site for my interrogation, especially when contrasted with the static figures about gender inequality as outlined in my introduction. Throughout this chapter, I am drawing on Jonathan Potter and Margaret Wetherell's argument that social discourses such as those which happen in an interview 'do not just describe things; they *do* things. And being active, they have social and political implications' (1987, p. 6). I am also influenced by Ros Gill's (2000) interrogation of how the gender inequality of radio DJs is justified by radio stations, because I wish to unpack the practical ideologies through which continued gender imbalance is accepted by those who employ screenwriters, and by the screenwriters themselves.

CREATIVITY AND MERIT

Two ideas were repeatedly drawn upon by those that I interviewed: the special creative individual and the film industry as meritocracy. Both were presented as ungendered and were therefore used with confidence and conviction, reinforcing how normalized they are in the context of UK film workers' talk. These discourses emerged at different points in our conversations, sometimes as answers to questions that I asked all my participants, such as what they thought made a good screenwriter, or what was expected from a screenwriter, including hours worked, recruitment practices, and expected remuneration. Other evidence of these discursive patterns arose from more general discussions on topics such as their own biography, working with directors, and their views on the diversity of the UK film workforce. Both notions draw on wider discourses found in other creative industries and professions (see Littler (2017) for a comprehensive history of meritocracy and Banks (2017) on the way certain individuals are deemed to have innate talent in music professions). Nigel Edley and Margaret Wetherell (2001, p. 190) describe how people can make choices in the language they use, but 'the options aren't always equal. Some constructions or formulations will be more 'available' than others and they are easier to say.' This availability reflects which ways of understanding the world have become dominant or hegemonic. By drawing on dominant discourses in their talk, my participants were able to present certain arguments and practices as 'common sense' and, as a consequence, acceptable and unproblematic—something I challenge in this chapter.

Screenwriting was unquestionably deemed to be a creative profession by my participants, and the notion of creativity as an innate quality possessed by certain individuals was repeatedly drawn upon to identify candidates who could fulfil such a screenwriting role. For example:

...there's some sort of innate quality there, it just happens easily for some people. (Robert, screenwriter)

...[Employers] still behave as though you're hiring some unlockable capsule of genius that you can snap open at will and sort of sprinkle on the goodies and it will become genius. (Freddie, screenwriter)

You can learn and study the craft and the function and the layout and for-matting of writing but that sparkle and wit and unique voice cannot be taught and that's the illusive thing you're always hoping for. (Nick, employer)

Howard Becker (1982) has shown how the romantic idea of 'the artist' is particular to Western societies of the late nineteenth and twentieth centu-ries and that the dominant tradition in Sociology of Art 'takes the artist and art work, rather than the network of cooperation, as central to the analysis of art as a social phenomenon' (Ibid., p. xi). Even critical sociolo-gists who see through excessively positive assessments of creative work often do not question the individualized, 'gifted' nature of creative work, so established is this idea in our culture. However, even within this cus-tomary framework, it is perhaps surprising that screenwriting is perceived as requiring such a unique, innate talent. Bridget Conor (2010, p. 29) has convincingly demonstrated that screenwriting is often viewed as the *least* creative form of writing 'because of its unashamed rigidity of form, its unapologetic commercial obligations, its inherent collectivity which downplays and denies claims to individual creative authorship and its lim-inality in terms of claims to literary status'. Generally screenplays are judged as inferior or imperfect art or craft forms, little more than a 'blue-print' for the final film or a document for raising money.

Screenwriting is a fascinating art form because it is an art form but you're making a blueprint really, you know you're selling a blueprint that some-body else is going to build. (Frankie, screenwriter)

Indeed, one of my employer participants articulated a common and rather disparaging longing in the industry which illustrates how screenwriting is both held up to impossible standards and simultaneously judged as failing: 'I crave the day I read a script and it blows me away. I've never had it yet' (Colin, employer).

Despite this very critical appraisal of their work, screenwriters were still celebrated as gifted individuals in my interviews. As part of this discourse, it was commonly argued that screenwriters could be recognized by an almost obsessive drive to write that takes precedence over other aspects of a more 'normal' life, such as having a family, a social life, or indeed sleeping and eating. The screenwriters talked about working through the night, getting up at 5:30 in the morning to work before the rest of their household woke, giving up holidays to write, even writing while they are actually in their 'day job'.

> Oh my god, I work all the time. When I can. I keep saying to myself, I just want to take Friday off and just do stuff that needs doing around the house, you know? (Emma, screenwriter)

> I tend to do my best writing work sitting at the computer writing between ten at night and three in the morning. (Esther, screenwriter)

> I was writing in my office on the secret and we would write at the weekend, pretty much from Friday night to Sunday. (Patrick, screenwriter)

Indeed, there was evidence that a screenwriter may be expected to continue to exhibit this devotion to their art even in extreme circumstances:

> You know, I worked with somebody recently their mum died, then their dad died, and then another something happened…another writer had somebody tried to kill themselves. Somebody very close to them and so on and you just end up in a situation where you're "Of course, you take all the time you need here" and things just last forever, options on books are running out and stuff like this. Come on! (Frank, employer)

> You can pick up people are just not quite committed for some reason. Which could be anything. It could be too busy, could be family stuff, could be other stuff going on in their life, you don't know. I think you can pick up their ambivalence a bit. (Gillian, employer)

In these examples, there is a clear subtext that perhaps these screenwriters are not up to the job. It was a very common to find the linked idea that success or failure in screenwriting is heavily influenced by 'how much you want it', that is, your ambition, commitment, and priorities. In this way, a creative personality was also to be recognized as someone unable to ignore this calling:

I think if I haven't done it maybe it doesn't mean enough to you. It has to be something that is so compulsive that you have no choice but to make it, you have no choice but to put yourself in that place where whatever you put on that page as being judged and exposed. (Eloise, employer)

You just wouldn't do it unless you felt so committed and so hungry and so, aside from being any good and having a bit of talent, those are the most important qualifications. (Jack, screenwriter)

I think it's about a burning ambition to express something and I think if you've got a burning ambition to express something you'll find a way somehow. (Martha, employer)

This all-consuming, obsessive notion of the creative individual, functions to exclude anyone with other responsibilities or demands on their time. Feminists have long argued that women are limited by having more restrictions on their time due to expectations around childcare and homemaking (see, for example Franks 1999; Kelan 2008) and are expected to be other-oriented (Taylor 2011). Commonly in my interviews, the low numbers of women in creative roles such as screenwriting was framed as women having more important things to do:

I'm not saying women aren't committed but we've got all this other stuff going on and as you get older you do have children. I think also women sort of get 'you know this industry is bullshit, I'm going to do something else'. (Emily, screenwriter)

So...'I will not waste my time on this slightly fruitless pastime when I could be looking after the kids', that's quite conceivable. (Frank, employer)

This can be challenged in a number of ways, not least by questioning why the pressures of parenting still fall predominantly on mothers and how the division of labour between man as breadwinner and woman as caregiver remains the ideal organization of production (Kelan 2008). I will return to look in detail at the challenges of maternal assumption in Chap. 5. For my purposes here, it is important to recognize that the positioning of women as more rational, and work in the film industry as less important than raising children, wards off potential criticism of sexism. It does this by positioning women as somehow more sensible than men and functions as a sort of disclaimer to the idea that there is a problem that requires remedy. It is perhaps worth considering that if childcare is so very important, why are so few men acting as primary carers? By refusing to acknowledge that some people (frequently women) have more demands on their time, the notion of 'how much you want it' conceals a real and gendered barrier. It also neatly sidesteps the evidence that creative workers such as screenwriters may struggle for years to make a living from their work (McRobbie 2002). This might make the profession off-putting for those unable to rely on family or partners to support them. Black women, for example, have been shown to more frequently bear the burden of being both breadwinner and primary caregiver (Yanick and Feagin 2015).

Crucially, though, failing to recognize that some people may not have the luxury of being able to follow their dreams also obscures possible reasons why screenwriting continues to be dominated by white, middle- and upper-class men. Suggesting they are the only ones sufficiently foolish enough to want to be screenwriters, whilst everyone else gets on with more important tasks, white male privilege is simultaneously concealed and reinforced:

> So there's this kind of at a certain point they must think it's too tiresome and if you're a smart person you must think why am I being stupid? Whereas I think men find it easier to be pig-headed about things. (Freddie, screenwriter)

By positioning creativity as a quality of an individual, over which they themselves have limited control, and by further describing men as innately 'pig-headed' and driven whilst women are naturally more nurturing and common-sensical, the suggestion is that men are more inherently suited to screenwriting work—a subtle form of sexism which permeates through the talk of my participants. There is no need for anyone to be openly and explicitly disparaging of women when they are able to draw on these gendered constructions to justify their lack of inclusion.

Although there were some occasional acknowledgements to the roles of opportunity, encouragement, and perseverance, this did not ever appear to override the notion that to be a screenwriter, you need to be born with that magic ingredient that marks you out as 'talented'.

> There's experience, but there's also that level of talent, and some very, very talented people may not have to work as hard (laughs) to get things done. (Paul, employer)

My mum used to teach singing ... And she would say she could teach anyone to sing, her line would be anyone can have a voice and it might just take
time to relax them. You know people would say 'what about I'm off key'
and my mum would say 'enough lessons I can get you to sing in tune'. It's
just about confidence and breathing and all these things, it's about technique. And I suppose you could argue that maybe you could make the same
parallel with writing. I'm not sure you can. (Martha, employer)

I think there has to be an aptitude exists in the pupil for the teacher to be
able to learn their stuff. (Richard, employer)

Indeed, opportunity and perseverance were often discounted completely.
Writing was construed by the employers as something that can be done
anywhere and by anyone, even the least advantaged, if you had the drive
to be creative within you:

You could say technically if J.K Rowling[1] could write a book in a café as a
single mother then everybody could do it but clearly for her it was compulsive, it was probably a way to escape her life and it came from within, you
know. (Eloise, employer)

However, in contrast, the screenwriters would often express notions of
creativity as being something they were 'drawn to' (Patrick, screenwriter),
a preference, or an interest as opposed to an ability that you are born with.
For example:

I think people can be creative in lots of different ways, but in terms of what
we're doing, I just think specifically you're just either that way inclined or
you're not. (Patrick, screenwriter)

I think one of the key characteristics a writer has to have is curiosity and
about everybody that's around you, or the world that's going on around
you, or what's going on in the world, or just being able to sponge things up
really and then to be able to feed that into a processor and hope that some
drama comes out at the end of it. (Natasha, screenwriter)

I didn't have a notebook aged 6 that said when I grow up I want to be a
screenwriter. That said, my brother and I would watch – I'm sure other
children do this – but we would watch films obsessively and quote them
obsessively and deconstruct them obsessively and so that kind of process was
bubbling away from quite an early age. (Will, screenwriter)

The screenwriters also recognized the profession as one requiring craft skills and believed that this aspect of screenwriting labour, at least, could be taught, or learnt through practice, and indeed might make all the difference:

> You can come up with a great premise or a good character and write it down on the back of a napkin and think you're brilliant but actually crafting it is just so difficult. (Emma, screenwriter)

> I think writing for film and television and all of them, even radio, is more akin to being an architect than anything approaching being an artist. You know, seeing the shape, seeing the structures that hold the story up, the place and time where you place things. I think it is a craft, it's not an art. (Tony, screenwriter)

There was also much talk of practical necessity which conflicts with the idea of natural ability, or indeed even lifelong attraction to the profession:

> So in order to get to direct the kind of stories I want to direct almost always involved rewriting as well, but it's always been in that order, pragmatically, rather than... I never thought I want to be a writer. (Frankie, screenwriter)

> When I was at drama school I wrote a full-length play and I decided I wanted to do that more than act because I'd fallen out of love with acting. (Tony, screenwriter)

However, despite these hints at a possible alternative way of talking about screenwriting careers as being created through personal choice and opportunity, most participants drew upon the culturally established idea of a special, talented individual artist-genius and therefore presented the ideal screenwriter as a person who is driven to write screenplays at the expense of other aspects of their life. When doing this, they also connected to another prevalent discourse that was drawn on by many of my participants: that of the film industry as a meritocracy. It is unsurprising that those who are already working in the film industry have a vested interest in claiming that success is based on merit. However, it is important to understand the implications this has for those trying to build a career in a profession where most of those who succeed are rich, white, and men.

THE MYTH OF MERITOCRACY

In my conversations, the notion of the film industry as a meritocracy was drawn upon many times, with employers eager to stress that they don't care who the writer is; it's simply the story, the script, and the quality of writing that they are interested in:

> We are so craving for good stories for something they can go and make so if it's written by a man or woman I don't think they care less. I really do. (Eloise, employer)

> The good thing about being a writer, I think, particularly here, is you don't need to be accredited, I mean if there's just a fabulous script, you're in. No-one cares who wrote it. (Pete, employer)

> I don't care whether they are women or men. I care if they're good. (Ian, employer)

In 2009, Creative Skillset produced a report with Women in Film and Television UK, called 'Why her?' (2009). The women that they spoke to had found success in film and television and these women expressed a belief that they worked in meritocratic industries: 'It's more about whether you can do a good job rather than what sex you are' (Ibid., Industry Culture and Attitudes). Those interviewed suggested the under-representation of women might be due to a lack of awareness on the behalf of young girls that they can do it. This perhaps in turn suggests a lack of awareness amongst those working in creative industries of the barriers that women might face.

The idea that if you are any good as a screenwriter, your talent will eventually be 'discovered' and success will follow, is firmly entrenched in the film industry, as in other creative industries (see, for example Nixon (2003) on the advertising industry and Taylor and Littleton (2012) on the art world). Taylor and Littleton call this the 'big break' narrative, and demonstrate that from the creative worker's point of view, it functions to validate their continued commitment to their chosen career, even if they've had little success. I argue that it is drawing on a wider discourse, firmly established and available to be used by speakers, that the recognition of artistic ability is purely meritocratic.

> ...you could be an absolute outsider, think about Whatshername, you know famously the woman who got an Academy Award and had been a prostitute

in her last job. Diablo Cody[2]. She is an amazing [sic] good writer. Wrote an amazing script and it got made. Who cares what she did before? (Pete, employer)

Diablo Cody is one of only four women to have single-handedly won the Academy Award for Best Original Screenplay, and one of only two of those who wasn't also the director. She first became known for her candid biography of her years as a stripper (not as a prostitute, as Pete suggests), something that may well have actually given her visibility and therefore access to Hollywood. She is, in many ways then, exceptional, and by using her as an example of what is possible, Pete avoids acknowledging the barriers that most women may face. Cody's is not a career path that many could follow.

The employers I spoke to expressed confidence in their systems for finding writers and their own ability to judge screenwriters' work, for example:

If there were women, they would be in the room. That's what I think. If I looked at a sample and it was good enough they would be there. (Gillian, employer)

The quality of writing, that's probably the best way to put it, the quality of writing and writer is the most important factor. (Ian, employer)

They were also able to draw on notions of the free market as an argument against introducing conscious measures to redress the imbalance, suggesting that it is the audiences, not the employers (producers, financiers), who ultimately dictate which films get made:

I don't think there will ever be a really self-conscious 'oh we really, really need to be favouring...' you know, I don't think we'll get to a point, because there's a commercial imperative, so I don't think there will ever be a place of active, positive discrimination. (Nick, employer)

There's a side of me that also feels very irritated by people who say there should be more women, there should be 50/50, because for me it has to be ultimately based on merit. (Eloise, employer)

This continued assertion of meritocracy in the film industry is a form of symbolic violence (Bourdieu and Wacquant 1992) which reinforces the dominance of white, male, heterosexual, able-bodied creativity, in a way that is accepted and seen as both natural and legitimate, even by those whose interests are not served. Indeed, some of my participants articulated their discomfort with the notion that there is any discrimination in their industry, particularly the women employers:

> I can't imagine for one second that women would be discriminated against because they are women if they come up with a great story. (Eloise, employer)

> I suppose what I think is that less women set out to do it. I cannot believe that they are less good. So I believe if there were the same amount doing it they would be getting the same commissions. (Laura, employer)

> I hate to think it's the industry that's prejudiced. I don't feel as a woman that I'm never employed because I'm a woman. I've never felt that, ever. Maybe I'm sometimes employed because I'm a woman. You know, maybe (Producer) would rather have a girl assistant because I'll look after him more. Make him tea without grumbling. (Pippa, employer)

As this last example indicates, it was repeatedly suggested to me that it was in fact men who were at a disadvantage, some men even believing there is positive discrimination towards women in the UK film industry:

> A lot of them got picked up because people were desperate to find people who ticked all the boxes 'oh god yes we've found a woman, and she's black and she's a lesbian and she can write' or direct or whatever it was. Fantastic! (Freddie, screenwriter)

> Natalie: Do you think it would have made any difference to your career if you were a woman?
> Tony: Er….at the beginning I think it would have helped it.
> Natalie: Why do you think that?
> Tony: Because start of careers usually involves backing from government, or it used to.

Howard Becker (1982) argues that it is simply implausible to believe that all possible candidates can 'come to the attention of 'everyone whose opinion affects the formation of reputations''. Following on from this, Taylor and Littleton (2012) deduce that it is important to consider what methods prevail for gaining the attention of significant decision makers and opinion formers, as I will be considering in some length in the next chapter.

More critically, for this chapter's analysis of how the work of screenwriters is understood by the film industry, these discourses of meritocracy and individual creative ability fail to recognize the social, educational, and environmental dimensions of creativity (Amabile 1983; Banks 2017), let alone how these might disadvantage women screenwriters. It assumes an equal playing field for all who wish to enter. Richard Florida argues (2002, p. 78), 'by papering over the causes of cultural and educational advantage, meritocracy may subtly perpetuate the very prejudices it claims to renounce'. In the next section, I will consider how my participants discussed their working practices and relationships in a way that reinforces Becker's argument about creative work being a product of collaboration rather than being a property of an individual and, crucially, how a better understanding of 'creativity' could point the way to finding the women who might be missing from the screenwriting profession.

Disrupting Dominant Perceptions of Screenwriting Work

Although participants talked about individual creative genius, they also discussed the importance of collaboration. Without questioning the meritocratic nature of the film industry, they also revealed the pervasive tendency of people to work with others who were most 'like' them. By considering these contrasting perceptions about screenwriting work, it is possible to disrupt and problematize the accepted discourses that I have shown function to uphold gender inequality. The contradictions in my participants' talk reveal ideological dilemmas (Billig et al. 1988), opening up the possibility of different understandings of creative screenwriting work and, more importantly, broadening the possible subject positions available for individuals to take up as screenwriters.

It was universally accepted by my participants that screenwriters must work in collaboration with others, such as script editors, producers, and directors, accepting comments and criticisms of their writing as part of the job:

> ...if you're a writer specifically, as opposed to a writer/director, you have to roll with the punches, you have to be flexible and adaptable in the development of a project. (Nick, employer)

So keeping your own spirits up when you're constantly being told 'do this' 'do that', or what have you 'oh no, no change that', 'oh no we don't like that' or 'we don't like this'. And you can go into a meeting one day and be told we need a table, you go away and write the table and you bring it back and they say 'oh no we asked for a biscuit' and you say 'oh no you asked for a table' and they say 'I don't think we did' and so I think that's tricky. (Catherine, screenwriter)

Screenwriters must navigate conflicting job requirements, such as being able to generate confidence in their skills and 'vision' for a new project whilst being able to accommodate the opinions and objectives of others. A growing body of work, following Becker—and particularly in Social Psychology—is successfully demonstrating the limitations of an understanding of creativity as a personality trait of certain individuals. Teresa Amabile contends that anyone can be creative to a greater or lesser extent, although not everyone's output may be recognized as 'historically significant' (1983, p. 361). I will return to a discussion of how and by whom film projects are deemed culturally important and worthwhile in Chap. 7, but in this section, I want to further examine the discourse of collaboration, and how it serves as a contrast to the idea of a special creative individual. Amabile's work suggests that assigning creative status to certain people may indeed be a way of obscuring social inequalities. Similarly, in direct opposition to the discourse of the exceptional individual, Stephanie Taylor and Karen Littleton argue that 'creative activity is collaborative, emerging from the interactions and relationships between people' (2012, p. 11), suggesting that it is in the relationships and the process where creative work is generated.

Collaboration is widely recognized as a key dimension of film production and was accepted by my screenwriter participants as a necessary and even appealing part of their job:

…you're writing drama for people to act out and for a lot of other people to collaborate on and I think that's the part of writing that's always excited me, so I can't imagine myself ever writing a novel for example, because I think I'd find it quite lonely. (Natasha, screenwriter)

It's exciting when you're collaborating and being creative and yeah. (Usma, screenwriter)

I love that feeling, there's a small group of people, the producer, the director, me, or maybe two producers, the director, me and we're all working together on the project, I love that feeling. (Robert, screenwriter)

Indeed, the employers, despite their reliance on the notion of a creative individual, all recognized collaboration as an important part of a screenwriter's job:

> ...in film particularly it's a very collaborative process and... there aren't many auteurs out there (Nick, employer)

> But what's really interesting is that even the really high level of writers do want to collaborate. (Ian, employer)

There was talk of how tricky it can be to find the right person to collaborate with, which also reveals that relationships are regarded as vital to producing good work. For example:

> I think you can't be the kind of writer who likes high concepts and big films or slightly quirky but still all about the entertainment and then you've got a producer who wants to make *Fish Tank*.[3] It's not going to work. (Emily, screenwriter)

> Screenwriting may take more because – I believe it's like meeting the person you're going to marry. You have to find the person, the company or people who 'get' what you're trying to do in that script, get it and see the audience for it. (Rob, employer)

In addition, screenwriter Rachel expressed how the collaborative nature of film could result in complications around authorship and credit:

> ...that can be a strange experience when you see your director being interviewed about how they had this idea and why they made these decisions and so on and well, they didn't! (laughs) they weren't there! (Rachel, screenwriter)

Debates about authorship in film production are not new, but to continue to favour an approach that recognizes only one person as having consummate creative credit has multiple implications for women. In my conversations, collaboration was presented as a process that doesn't always result in positive outcomes for everyone involved.

> On the other hand it's very difficult because you may have an absolutely delightful relationship with the writer who's become a very good friend and

it's incredibly awkward and probably we're not quite as good when it's appropriate at firing the writer and moving on. (Pete, employer)

I like writers who respond to things I'm saying, I work with some writers who, for different reasons, don't like to contribute much in a room, and sort of stare slightly blankly, which, well it really pisses you off, because you're giving feedback on the work and they just look at you… (Frank, employer)

However, neither Pete nor Frank's comments suggest that this in any way diminishes the importance of collaboration. Indeed, the dominant attitude to collaboration amongst my participants was a positive one, with recognition of the results as seen in successful teams working across multiple projects:

Clearly between Danny Boyle[4] and Frank Cotterall Boyce[5] there was an affinity. Clearly different forces at play because I would argue Danny is a lot more linear and likes more tangible things whereas Frank Cotterall Boyce likes to go off at a tangent but there was an affinity in terms of the tone they were going for and the vibe they were going for. (Eloise, employer)

What is interesting about Eloise's observation is that both of these men have worked more frequently with other men, suggesting that her comment is less about the particular relationship and betrays a strongly held trust in creative partnerships, here involving all men: Danny Boyle and John Hodge, Frank Cotterall Boyce and Michael Winterbottom, Danny Boyle and Frank Cotterall Boyce. Tessa commented on another type of creative collaboration, where a director becomes known for working with the same actors on multiple projects:

Yeah, which is why you understand why people like David O. Russell[6], they find a team of people, a team of actors, a team of producers and they stick with those people because it works and to everybody else it seems like elitism but to people in the industry you know it's because they've found the magic formula where everyone gets on and everyone can argue and scream at each other and still come away with something that everyone's happy with at the end. (Tessa, screenwriter)

On closer inspection, what is exposed by these two conflicting discourses of the creative individual and the power of successful collaborating is that some roles are viewed as more significant than others. Within collaboration, some work is considered to be 'requiring the special gift or sensibility of an artist' (Becker 1974). In the film world, at least, it would seem that this is often gendered in a way that roles frequently held by women, such as the producer or the script editor, are not recognized as quite as creative nor are the individuals that hold those positions regarded as being as special as the men they work with:

> You know the producer is the enabler; you're the really nice to everyone who gets the best work out of people. But having been doing it for twenty years, you know I'm fucking fed up with these men. I make men look good. That's what I do. (Nicola, employer)

> There's lots of female producers. I think that could be neck and neck. I think we're seen as people who care. You know, I think the stereotype also works for us, favours us in terms of 'they'll get it done' and 'they can multi-task' and 'charming' and sort of things 'connected', 'might know that person', 'maybe sleeping with the director'. (Vicky, employer)

So even though the ideas of the special individual and creative collaboration exist in competition with each other, the tension produced maps onto constructions of what work is considered more special, and these constructions themselves are gendered. In order to illustrate this further, I want to now offer a consideration of the role of other jobs that play a part in the screenwriting process.

'Collaborwriting': When Does Collaboration Become Co-creation?

Heads of development, development executives, script editors, and story editors are all employed predominantly to work with the screenwriter, developing their script over many drafts to improve it and support the screenwriting process. Those with 'Development' in their job title tend to work across several projects for one company and be in more permanent employment or longer contracts than script editors, story editors, and script consultants who are generally freelance and often seen as having lower status. They will work with or for a producer, who also frequently plays a role in the discussions about the screenplay, but often have a closer working relationship with the screenwriter due to the producers' other responsibilities. The role is heavily gendered, as acknowledged by my participants:

And developers. I mean what about the whole 'D-girl' thing? That's what they call it in America don't they? Which is hideous. (Gillian, employer)

...most script editors are young women and quite a lot of male TV writers end up married to script editors... (Usma, screenwriter)

Robin Leidner (1991, p. 155) argues that 'When jobholders are all of one gender, it appears that people of that gender must be especially well suited to the work, even if at other times and places, the other gender does the same work.' Screenplay development was frequently regarded as a nurturing role by those that I spoke to and as such was seen as a natural fit for women:

Women tend to be quite good at nurturing. If you're interested in writing and you're not a writer yourself or you're interested in writing but you might be more prone to be in positions where you can be an editor, where you can be a development person, you can help people find their vision. (Eloise, employer)

Is there a nurturing aspect to this development side and women can feel drawn to that? Nursing a baby through production. I've had such good notes from development executives, I've often wondered why they aren't writing. They're so good. Why aren't they writing scripts? It's a question you might direct to them. (Jack, screenwriter)

It is easy to see from these examples that development is being closely associated with writing, but is not considered to be actual writing. Eloise uses a very convoluted linguistic formation to propose that development jobs might be good if 'you're interested in writing but you might be more prone to be in positions where you can be an editor' without discussing why someone might be 'more prone' to be in these positions despite their interest in writing. Jack goes further: 'They're so good. Why aren't they writing scripts?' As a screenwriter himself, he recognizes their ability. Emma, who had previously worked for many years in a development role before becoming a screenwriter, articulates that it is often difficult to pinpoint exactly who is responsible for what:

Well I've always come up with ideas and always given those ideas away to screenwriters... (Emma, screenwriter)

This observation is backed up by one of the men employers, echoing Rachel's earlier comment about directors and creative authorship:

And what's really funny is, I've heard [man screenwriter and director] say lots of times how he came up with the ending and I think 'oh yeah? That was the [woman] development executive that came up with that!' (Pete, employer)

Nick, an employer working in a senior development role—who was also attempting screenwriting in his spare time—referred to the development process as 'collaborwriting', pushing the idea of the collaborative develop-ment relationship from one of nurturing the writer closer to one of co-writing. It is perhaps worth noting that he is one of a few men working in a development role and may find it easier to assert his equality with the screenwriter than women development workers might. He also works for one of the small number of large, established film production employers. Men who hold development jobs can frequently be found in these well-paid, more prestige positions, echoing research on nurses (Porter 1992) and waiting staff (Hall 1993).

Of my 20 employers, 11 admitted that they either had considered or were actively attempting some screenwriting, and of those who said they had not, two of the women said they would consider other forms of writ-ing. In addition, four of the screenwriters I spoke to had previously worked in development roles. It is not hard, therefore, to see that there is a close relationship between the work of screenwriters and those who work with screenwriters in development. Although clearly, the assigned 'screenwriter' will most likely be the person who sits at a keyboard and types words onto a page, it is worth considering why this person is more often a man than a woman. Throughout my conversations, a lack of confidence was repeat-edly suggested as a key reason why women might not put themselves for-ward as screenwriters as frequently as men:

Women are more self-doubting (Lance, screenwriter)

My understanding is that women respond to rejection less well than men respond to it and quite often don't pursue their careers. (Frank, employer)

I don't know whether it's true but I think women do sometimes need a sup-port network round them and I think that's why women theatre writers do well because they come out of those new writer schemes and you see them on Twitter they're all friends with each other, they're very supportive of each other and give each other a lot of comfort and read each other's scripts, that sort of stuff, back each other up. (Kate, employer)

This discourse puts the blame and responsibility at the feet of wannabe women screenwriters and offers the all-too-common need for confidence and assertiveness training for women (Gill and Orgad 2015). Although this explanation treats women as though they are all the same and is again individualizing the problem, some of the women screenwriters were able to articulate a sense that women might face different challenges than men:

> I think men are, just because at school they're encouraged to come out and be counted. Girls are taught to think before they speak. I think it's a lot to do with how you look. Girls don't want to look stupid and I think boys don't care about looking stupid generally. (Emily, screenwriter)

> So if you were a young woman who was passionate about film and you want to be a filmmaker, you would have to be so passionate to cope with the genuine hostility that you're likely to meet until you prove yourself. (Hannah, screenwriter)

These women have had a degree of success securing paid screenwriting work and yet recognize that girls are socialized to put themselves forward less impulsively than men. Hannah was one of a few that spoke about open 'hostility' from men whilst at work, and indicates that women may have good reason for not pushing themselves forward as forcefully as men.

The work of Rosalind Gill (2007), Angela McRobbie (2007), and Christina Scharff (2012) has been essential to informing my comprehension of gender in a 'post-feminist' world. Their work provides a feminist perspective on 'a grammar of individualism' (Gill 2007, p. 153) found in the talk of my research participants, and helps understand why many of them found it hard to even recognize inequalities. Neoliberal discourses, which position the modern British woman as self-responsible, do not take into account wider structural inequalities and exclusions that might help explain why some people have more success than others. However, lack of confidence or reticence to be on the receiving end of hostility does not offer the full explanation for why women are more likely to be found supporting and 'nurturing' men without getting equal creative credit. It does, on the other hand, suggest an answer to the question of why there are less women than men entering screenwriting and other film roles. I contend that this challenge to the 'special creative individual', highlighted by the discourse of creative collaboration, may provide a clue to where at least some of the missing women screenwriters might be found.

Gendered expectations and a lack of role models might lead women who may otherwise consider a career as a screenwriter to take jobs in development working with writers as a way to be part of the screenwriting process without having to identify themselves as the special creative individual, 'being judged and exposed' as Eloise suggested earlier, in the process. Women participants who had been—or still were—in development roles, reflected on their lack of encouragement or suitability to take up creative roles:

> I think about directors and I've stood next to directors and thought 'fucking hell I could do that!' but nobody said to me, and I went to St. Paul's[7] and Oxford, which is the pushiest schooling you can have but no one really said to me – 'hold on, but you could be a director. You could do that'. (Nicola, employer)

> I think I struggle cos I think I'm not very creative. So that's why I wouldn't write. I wouldn't dare because I think I'm not creative. Now maybe that's a message I've had? As a woman? Do other women feel like that? I don't know. But I definitely feel I'm not creative. I'm really good at telling you what works and doesn't work, you know, absolutely. (Gillian, employer)

Although there is some fluidity between roles in the industry, most of those who make it from a supportive role in development to a successful career as a screenwriter are men. In an observation that echoes recent discussions of the apparent ease with which men film directors move from low-budget independent films to big-budget studio pictures (Silverstein 2014), Emma describes how she has observed this gendered aspect to successful movement from script editor to script writer:

> When I look at people who have crossed over from my world, from the development world: [Screenwriter], Okay? The guy who used to work for [film financier] who's now he's writing [film script], he was script editor on [film script].... [Screenwriter/director] you know was at [production company] for a long time.... All men. ...They get big commissions; they are completely embraced by the industry. (Emma, screenwriter)

This of course suggests that simply recognizing development roles as creative is not the whole solution, since it is likely to lead to more men development personnel getting screenwriting work but less so women. However, it is further evidence that the screenwriting role is very gendered.

Continued reliance on the discourse of the identifiable creative individual is to deny the importance of collaboration and indeed 'other people' in creating well-received screenplays (and indeed films). If screenplays emerge, not from the unique imagination of one person, but through the work of creative teams, it might suggest that there are more potential screenwriters than can be recognized by the 'creative individual' criteria, and this raises questions about why they are not finding access to work or success.

My research participants worked hard to suggest that successful collaborations are found through some kind of intangible, elusive, and often unpredictable process, as with Tessa's suggestion that 'they've found the magic formula' (see earlier quote). This echoes the meritocratic discourse that allows those working in the film industry to believe that their processes are fair and open. However, on analysis of my interviews, it became apparent that collaboration was often happening along the lines of homophily. Homophily is the tendency of individuals to associate and bond with similar others (Ibarra 1992).

Natalie: What makes for a good working relationship?
Paul: Shared sensibility. For starters. I think. (Paul, employer)

The similarity of partners in creative collaboration could be found along the lines of class, age, background, race, and gender. Here is Eloise, talking about working with screenwriters who are in the same age bracket as herself:

> By and large I realize I feel more comfortable personally with my peers or younger because I feel you can be a lot more yourself, you know you can say exactly what you want. You are the same generation. You are the same level roughly so there's no sort of tension. (Eloise, employer)

Esther is a black screenwriter who was born in the UK but educated in Jamaica. She was given her first job as a screenwriter by a British production company run by a successful black actor. She expressed her difficulty finding people who understood her cultural references and background:

> One of the biggest frustrations for me on jobs that aren't going right is that we don't have a common language to talk about a piece. (Esther, screenwriter)

Hannah found both her class and gender to be an issue when finding collaborators:

> ...when you're meeting some Exec, that you just know, they might be the same gender but you know they are a different class and you're trying to joyfully express your idea and you can see them going 'ooh that sounds so tacky'. (Hannah, screenwriter)

Since my sample was weighted to include a much higher percentage of women than are found in the industry, I heard many examples of women working productively with other women. Here are a few examples:

> All three of my feature films were directed by women. All three produced by women. (Catherine, screenwriter)

> I'm pretty sure that the fact that she could rely on my instincts, coming from a similar – we're not, we don't have a similar background or anything but the fact that we both have a female sensibility and the same idea about what sort of risks we wanted to take with the material (Jo, employer)

> ...she's a story editor if you like and she talks to me and we discuss plot points and things, and my first assistant director is a woman and we three girls, we are so safe with each other, we are so secure with each other, and it's so creative. (Hannah, screenwriter)

> I think I've been drawn to working with the female directors I've worked with because I got the impression that they would be more collaborative and it would be a more equal partnership and I wouldn't be subjected to someone who thought that they were right all the time. (Natasha, screenwriter)

This presents a happy picture for women in film, but with men continuing to far outnumber women as producers, executive producers, and directors of films (Lauzen 2018; Cobb et al. 2016), and whilst the numbers for black, Asian, and minority ethnic people (BAME) are even lower (Cobb et al. 2018), the reality is that all women and BAME men are likely to have a tougher time finding productive collaborative relationships in the film industry.

Certainly, there was talk of these difficulties in my conversations with women screenwriters:

> I really dream of finding that magic partnership, like a director always works with a certain writer or something and you understand why directors try and write because trying to get that relationship is really, really difficult. (Tessa, screenwriter)

> I don't have a relationship with a director like that and I wish I did. (Catherine, screenwriter)

Although none of them appeared to have considered that their gender might have been a factor in this, some of the women participants talked about difficulties they had experienced working in creative collaboration with men:

> I definitely know that many of the men I've worked with would have been more comfortable with a guy that they could lad around with and probably feel like they have to be a bit more on their best behaviour with a woman. (Usma, screenwriter)

Emily expressed frustration when discussing women characters with men collaborators such as directors and producers:

> Of course, once we get onto the female roles and I'm going 'no, no, no, she wouldn't say that' and they're going 'why not, but that's my fantasy woman' and I'm saying 'but that's really disgusting and I'm not going to put it in my script' (Emily, screenwriter)

Gillian recalled an experience with a man screenwriter who ignored her throughout a meeting, despite the fact that she was the person who had invited him to come onto the project and indeed despite her potential power to refuse him employment:

> That's something I was really surprised at and I'll come out and say 'did you notice how he just talked to you all the time?' And now I've got a bit of a thing with this guy. I'm like, is he going to do that again? You know, and he didn't do it the second time. But I really felt he did the first meeting it was really bizarre and it almost put me off. I could have said 'no, we're not having him.' (Gillian, employer)

Similarly, Vicky, a black British producer, expressed a sense of being unlike those she had go to for film finance, and suggested that some of her competitors may have an advantage that she didn't:

Yeah right 'tennis on Friday? Golf?' I'm not that world. I don't want to play tennis and golf with you. I want you to fund my film because you like it and you think it's going to make you money! (Vicky, employer)

Indeed, the interviews were peppered with references to the very sociable nature of the film business, which perhaps helps explain the strongly felt need for homophily in creative collaborative work. Jo tries to explain the usefulness of informality when building a creative relationship:

It can be pretty hard at the beginning when you don't really know somebody and both sides are finding their way and the relationship can feel quite formal and actually it's a really informal relationship and it's not best served by a formal structure. It's better served by being able to relax with somebody and chat over a cup of coffee (Jo, employer)

Here, Vicky suggests that this provides a good approach even once the work is underway:

I'm checking in. I'm checking in without checking if you know what I mean. I'm not saying "So, tell me what the character said today. Are you actually writing? Are you actually working?" It's more of the level "How's it going? Do you want to have coffee?" and keeping that relationship going. "You know you can talk to me if you want. You know I'm here to problem-solve. You know this is a project we're doing together." (Vicky, employer)

Vanessa articulates why the film industry might be particularly susceptible to reliance on personal relationships as much as skills or experience:

I guess it's a lot about communication and personality, you know, making film is really hard, and so if you set out on that journey with somebody who you just don't quite get on with, or who is difficult to deal with, then it can make it so much more painful. (Vanessa, employer)

But whilst these may be genuine ways to manage working relationships, creative homophily also serves to uphold existing inequalities. More importantly, it raises questions about why there appears to be a common belief that we can socialize and work better with those who are more like us along gender, race, age, and other lines. The most recurrent answer that men and women screenwriters gave to my question 'What makes for a good working relationship with directors, producers and other collaborators?' was 'respect'. Here, one employer talks about fixing a script that has 'gone wrong' by bringing in a script editor to collaborate with the writer:

> It's a fuck up and what we've done is we've given, we've strongly recommended that they need to get a script editor in the mix. We've recommended someone who is old school, who is the same age as the writer, because the writer is of a certain age and stature, and you know, there'll be respect and they actually it transpires, they knew each other twenty years ago. (Martha, employer)

Interestingly, Martha's example also illustrates how reliance on homophily might uphold the status quo by the fact that her writer and script editor already knew each other. However, the answer seems to be more complex for gender. A few women screenwriters suggested that the spectre of sex (always depicted as heteronormative) presented problems:

> ...you know when you're starting to work on projects, you know, guys, into your 30s most people have a partner or are married so it's easier for guys to hang out with other guys than it is to hang out with other women, in the evening or going on trips. (Frankie, screenwriter)

> But I was really conscious that in order for us to be, you know, I would spend many hours alone in a room with one man working on a film and it would not be comfortable for either of us if sex was an issue for us. So I went to considerable lengths to not make that an issue and be...not exactly be one of the blokes, I didn't exactly hang around swearing and drinking beer and so on but I definitely didn't dress in any way that could be sexy or attractive or anything like that. I dressed in a plain, non-descript, it doesn't matter who I am sort of way. (Rachel, screenwriter)

> Another male writer friend of mine ended up in this very intense intellectual collaboration with his script editor and was sort of wondering if he was really in love with her and he were all going 'no, no, no, you're not in love with her, you're married, you've got two kids' but you can see that dynamic and it's very exciting for both parties but you can't have that with a, that's not going to happen with two women. (Usma, screenwriter)

Sean Nixon (2003) has shown how all-men creative partnerships in advertising diffuse the homoerotic associations of such a close form of creative collaboration. His study indicates that around 80 per cent of

creative teams were all men, and the relationship between the art directors and copywriters was often referred to, even by the men themselves,
as a 'marriage'. This was deemed fitting because of the long hours working together and the sense of a long-lasting commitment, which relied on
trust and teamwork. However, Sean Nixon also argues that:

> ...comparing the partnerships to an intimate relationship like marriage,
> journalists and practitioners were able to both give public expression to
> these homosocial desires, while diffusing the homoerotic associations of this
> intimacy by routing it through a heterosexual form...and fixing their identi-
> ties (in the case of the practitioners) as robustly heterosexual. (Ibid., p. 118)

My data clearly resonate with Sean Nixon's findings, but his argument is
that men's creative 'marriages' are less about being uncomfortable with
women in the creative partnerships because of the spectre of sex but
indeed a way of justifying, or accounting for, their absence. Therefore,
questions still stand as to why the intimacy of creative collaboration still
works to exclude women. My research suggests one possible answer. There
was considerable talk about men and women not being interested in the
same projects and so more naturally working with those of the same
gender:

> [Women screenwriter] is writing [film title] so...you know, and that's got a
> female director and it's a female-driven project and that's, that's a good fit
> there, (Nick, employer)

> It would make sense, wouldn't it? If most directors are men, they respond
> to – loosely – male themed stories. (Paul, employer)

I will return to a detailed examination of this notion of gendered tastes in
Chap. 7 and I will argue that it is central to continued gender inequality
in screenwriting. For now it is clear that creative homophily is widely
understood by the UK film industry as a path to successful collaboration,
and since the numbers of able-bodied, middle- and upper-class white men
far outweigh anyone else, it is very likely that a view of the industry as a
meritocracy may not be entirely well founded. Even though all this talk of
both collaboration and homophily seems to challenge the doctrine of the
talented individual discovered through meritocracy, there was a failure to
acknowledge that collaboration is esteemed less than creativity, and that

homophily works to disadvantage women and other marginalized people in the film industry.

Clearly, some interpretations of success are more hegemonic, and by looking at the work done by film workers' repeated assertions that gender inequality is no longer a concern, that it is on its way to being solved, and is certainly 'getting better', it is possible to understand the reasons for this.

I expect it not to stay the same for very long (Yvonne, employer)

Certainly for me I think things have shifted in the last few years. (Frank, employer)

I think it is changing. That would be my argument for you. (Vanessa, employer)

These are just some of the examples from my fieldwork where participants tried to suggest that gender inequality in the UK film industry was no longer an issue. This is a common discourse, frequently noted in feminist research (see, for example, Edley and Wetherell 2001; Kelan 2009; Scharff 2012) and typical of a 'progress narrative' (Everignham et al. 2007) as discussed in my introduction. Many of my men employer participants were keen to name-check women screenwriters that they were either working with, or desired to work with in the future, and to present themselves as having either no bias, or even having a bias towards women screenwriters.

I have a slight prejudice myself, which is generally speaking I prefer working with women and generally speaking I prefer women. (Pete, employer)

If I was to try to find the top thirty screenwriters in the UK that we wanted to make a film with, I'd be surprised, well I don't think it would be as low as 25%, I think it would be...perhaps 40%? (Ian, employer)

Nick works for a large production company and said they have 'about 50 projects on the British slate and that's supplemented by say 20 on the American slate'. He claimed that: 'we're probably working with more female writers than we are male writers at the moment.' Even allowing for some writers to be working across more than one script that is still a huge number of women screenwriters for one company to be working with given the numbers in employment each year. In our conversation, he only mentioned five women screenwriters, and all of them after I asked specifically about gender. He voluntarily mentioned 12 men writers by name throughout the interview. Indeed, throughout all my interviews, I repeatedly heard the same five or six women screenwriters' names, those who were currently in high demand. On one occasion, I arrived at an interview to find the employer hurriedly writing a list of women screenwriters. Mentioning these women accomplishes a rhetorical function of giving the impression that equality has been achieved. By noting the same handful of names being repeated across my data, I observed how tokenistic this is in reality. Actress Geena Davis, who has campaigned for many years for gender equality in film and television, argues that there are data to show that men tend to overestimate the percentage of women:

> In a group if there's 17 per cent women, men think it's balanced. If there's 33 per cent women, they think there's more women than men. (Geena Davis, quoted in Rosenberg 2013)

There were discursive attempts by some employers to provide a reason for the perceived increase in women:

> What I've been encouraged by really is there are a lot of interesting female playwrights coming through and starting to move into screenwriting and you feel like 'ooh, okay'. I do definitely feel like something's shifted in the last few years. (Vanessa, employer)

> I think again, one of the great things about our team at the moment is that we are very aware of gender issues and it's the make up of the team, we take it very seriously, we question it, and that's therefore it is a vivid part of our conversations. (Martha, employer)

Others suggested that even though there are only a few examples so far, this would encourage other women to follow in their footsteps:

> And you imagine the more female screenwriters there are or the more female playwrights or people writing for the first time are going to think oh yeah- (Robert, screenwriter)

> If you had two times Jane Goldman, writing what she's writing, genre films, very well, one or two of them become successful, that would also act as inspiration to other people, who would think 'I can do it as well' (Rob, employer)

These statements indicate an ignorance or forgetfulness of the history of women screenwriters, who were in the majority in the early film period (Francke 1994) and the many critical and commercial accomplishments of women screenwriters since, including on some of the highest grossing movies ever made, including the *Lord of the Rings* Trilogy, *The Empire Strikes Back* and *The Hunger Games* franchise.

As I outlined in the introduction, the data I have gathered for the 'Calling the Shots' project at Southampton University and the continuing annual reports from Centre for the Study of Women in Television and Film at San Diego State University show variations year by year in the percentage of women in key creative positions in feature films, but little change overall. Why then, do those within the industry suggest that there are noticeable improvements? A narrative of progress is not exclusive to the film industry, and it has been shown to be common in discussions of gender inequality (Everingham et al. 2007). In post-feminist contexts, equal opportunities policies are often described in gender-neutral terms as if gender inequality were a thing of the past, thus masking the persistence of discrimination and inequality (Liff and Cameron 1997). However, more than that, such disavowing on the part of screenwriters' employers allows them to ignore the need to take action to achieve change, or to question their own contribution to the problem of gender inequality. Whilst those in a position to employ screenwriters interpret the presence of a few women screenwriters in current employment as representing an end to inequality, they may overlook the evidence that suggests more needs to be done. This of course also functions to distance the speakers from any allegations of wrongdoing whilst at the same time avoiding any responsibility to take steps to improve the situation for women.

In the last few years, there has been an unprecedented upsurge in interest in the subject of gender equality in film, everything from on-screen representation (Butterly 2014) to who is working creatively behind the camera (Rosser 2014), and from sexist red carpet questions (Nianias 2015) to who gets recognized with award nominations (Karlin 2015). Despite this, there is still no evidence that the level of participation by women in key creative roles such as screenwriting is improving. Indeed, it's possible that all the public noise about gender equality adds fire to the flames of the 'it's getting better' discourse, as everyone assumes someone else is solving the problem and creative women who are already working in film enjoy enhanced publicity. In this chapter I have highlighted three separate discourses that are consciously drawn upon by film workers—the special creative individual, meritocracy, and things are getting better. They serve to justify the continued gender imbalance, and to allow those in a position to change the situation to do nothing. It is a strong indication of why the statistics are not changing year after year.

By continuing to utilize these three myths, without acknowledging the equally persuasive evidence of creative collaboration and homophily, workers in the UK film industry reinforce perceptions of screenwriting labour that allow the continued predominance of wealthy white men to be seen as unproblematic. The very existence of contradictory ways of encouraging screenwriting success opens up the possibility of questioning these entrenched principles about screenwriting labour. All five of these discourses are available to and drawn on by my participants, suggesting tensions exist in the way that screenwriting labour is understood by those most familiar with it. At these points of contention, it is possible to challenge the hegemonic beliefs. As I have shown, currently, the 'special creative individual' is recognized in the film industry by characteristics that make it harder for women to take up that subject position. That collaboration is less recognized as an essential creative element results in certain roles predominantly held by women to be devalued as less creative. The failure to recognize the role of homophily in creative work disadvantages both women and other minority communities, who are subtly othered through talk of meritocracy (homophily is a key theme that I will return to throughout this book).

There is a clear persistence of shared understandings of screenwriting work that suit some people more than others. Although these are not explicitly sexist, they still fulfil the rhetorical function of justifying inequalities and contribute to the upholding of the gender imbalance. My analysis here addresses Ros Gill's call for more nuanced vocabularies of critique to better understand how contemporary sexism works. Reliance on these gendered understandings of the screenwriter and their work has real outcomes for women seeking employment as screenwriters. By analysing some of the more informal and subtle ways in which inequalities are discursively legitimized, I have demonstrated one key mechanism through which gender inequality is upheld in the UK film industry. In the next chapter, I will begin my fine grain analysis of the informal recruitment practices that screenwriters are subject to and how they make it more difficult for women to occupy the role.

NOTES

1. Joanne Rowling is the author of the hugely successful 'Harry Potter' novels (Rowling, J. K. 1997. *Harry Potter and the Philosopher's Stone*, London, Bloomsbury).
2. Diablo Cody is the screenwriter of films including *Juno* and *Young Adult* (both directed by Jason Reitman 2007 and 2011, respectively).
3. *Fish Tank* is a multiple-award-winning, low-budget, coming-of-age story written and directed by British filmmaker Andrea Arnold (2009).
4. Danny Boyle is the director of films such as *Trainspotting* (1996), *Slumdog Millionaire* (2008), and *28 Days Later* (2002).
5. Frank Cotterall Boyce is the screenwriter of films such as *Welcome to Sarajevo* (1997) and *The Claim* (2000, both directed by Michael Winterbottom), and *Hilary and Jackie* (directed by Anand Tucker 1998). He worked with Danny Boyle on *Millions* (2004) and the London 2012 Olympic Games Opening Ceremony.
6. David O. Russell is an American writer-director. His films include *American Hustle* (2013), *Silver Lining's Playbook* (2012), and *Joy* (2015).
7. St Paul's Girls School is an independent school in West London. Fees are currently between £7000 and £9000 per term. Their website is www.spgs.org

REFERENCES

Amabile, Teresa M. 1983. The social psychology of creativity: A componential conceptualization. *Journal of Personality and Social Psychology* 45 (2): 357.

Arnold, Andrea. 2009. Director Fish Tank. Screenwriter: Andrea Arnold: IFC Films.

Banks, Mark. 2017. *Creative justice: Cultural industries, work and inequality.* London: Pickering & Chatto Publishers.

Becker, Howard Saul. 1974. Art as collective action. *American Sociological Review* 39 (6): 767–776.

———. 1982. *Art worlds.* London: University of California Press.

Billig, Michael, Susan Condor, Derek Edwards, Mike Gane, David Middleton, and Alan Radley, eds. 1988. *Ideological dilemmas: A social psychology of everyday thinking.* London: Sage.

Bourdieu, Pierre, and Loïc Wacquant. 1992. *An invitation to reflexive sociology.* Chicago: University of Chicago Press.

Boyle, Danny. 1996. Director. Trainspotting. Screenwriter: John Hodge: Film 4.

———. 2002. Director. 28 Days Later. Screenwriter: Alex Garland: 20th Century Fox.

———. 2004. Director. Millions. Screenwriter: Frank Cottrell Boyce: Fox Searchlight.

———. 2008. Director. Slumdog Millionaire. Screenwriter: Simon Beaufoy: Warner Bros, Film 4.

———. 2012. Director. London 2012 Olympic Opening Ceremony: Isles of wonder. Screenwriters: Danny Boyle, Frank Cottrell Boyce: BBC.

Butterly, A. 2014. Hollywood: Too few women on screen, new study finds. *BBC*. http://www.bbc.co.uk/newsbeat/26528206. Accessed 2 Apr 2018.

Cobb, Shelley, Linda Ruth Williams, and Natalie Wreyford. 2016. *Calling the shots: Women working in key roles on UK films in production during 2015*. https://www.southampton.ac.uk/cswf/project/number_tracking.page. Accessed 26 Mar 2018.

———. 2018. *Calling the shots: Women directors and cinematographers on British Films since 2003*. https://s25407.pcdn.co/wp-content/uploads/2018/02/Calling-the-Shots-Report-Feb-2018-Women-directors-and-cinematographers.pdf. Accessed 26 Mar 2018.

Conor, Bridget. 2010. Everybody's a writer theorizing screenwriting as creative labour. *Journal of Screenwriting* 1 (1): 27–43.

Creative Skillset and Women in Film and Television. 2009. *Why her? Report: Factors that have influenced successful women in Film and TV*. http://publications.skillset.org/index.php?id=57. Accessed 2012. The report is no longer available online but details can be found here: http://creativeskillset.org/assets/0000/6249/Women_in_the_Creative_Media_Industries_report_-_Sept_2010.pdf. Accessed 27 Mar 2018.

Del Toro, Guillermo. 2013. Director Pacific Rim. Screenwriters: Travis Beacham, Guillermo del Toro. Warner Brothers.

Edley, Nigel, and Margaret Wetherell. 2001. Jekyll and Hyde: Men's constructions of feminism and feminists. *Feminism & Psychology* 11: 439–457.

Everingham, Christine, Deborah Stevenson, and Penny Warner-Smith. 2007. 'Things are getting better all the time'? Challenging the narrative of women's progress from a generational perspective. *Sociology* 41 (3): 419–437.

Florida, Richard. 2002. *The rise of the creative class*. New York: Basic Books.

Francke, Lizzie. 1994. *Script girls: Women screenwriters in Hollywood*. London: British Film Institute.

Franks, Suzanne. 1999. *Having none of it: Women, men and the future of work*. London: Granta.

Gill, Rosalind. 2000. Justifying injustice: Broadcasters' accounts of inequality in radio. In *Discourse analytic research*, ed. E. Burman and I. Parker. London: Routledge.

———. 2007. Postfeminist media culture: Elements of a sensibility. *European Journal of Cultural Studies* 10 (2): 147–166.

————. 2014. Unspeakable inequalities: Post feminism, entrepreneurial subjectivity, and the repudiation of sexism among cultural workers. *Social Politics* 21 (4): 509–528.

Gill, Rosalind, and Shani Orgad. 2015. The confidence cult(ure). *Australian Feminist Studies* 30 (86): 324–344.

Hall, Elaine. 1993. Waitering/waitressing. *Gender & Society* 7: 329–346.

Ibarra, Herminia. 1992. Homophily and differential returns: Sex differences in network structure and access in an advertising firm. *Administrative Science Quarterly* 37: 422–447.

Karlin, Lily. 2015. The 2015 Oscars will be terrible for women, as usual. *The Huffington Post.* https://www.huffingtonpost.co.uk/entry/2015-oscars-terrible-women_n_6727088. Accessed 2 Apr 2018.

Kelan, Elisabeth. 2008. Gender, risk and employment insecurity: The masculine breadwinner subtext. *Human Relations* 61: 1171–1202.

————. 2009. *Performing gender at work.* Hampshire: Palgrave Macmillan.

Lauzen, Martha M. 2018. The Celluloid Ceiling: Behind-the-scenes employment of women on the top 100, 250, and 500 films of 2017. San Diego State University. https://womenintvfilm.sdsu.edu/wp-content/uploads/2018/01/2017_Celluloid_Ceiling_Report.pdf. Accessed 26 Mar 2018.

Leidner, Robin. 1991. Serving hamburgers and selling insurance: Gender, work, and identity in interactive service jobs. *Gender & Society* 5 (2): 154–177.

Liff, Sonia, and Ivy Cameron. 1997. Changing equality cultures to move beyond 'women's problems'. *Gender, Work & Organization* 4 (1): 35–46.

Littler, Jo. 2017. *Against meritocracy: Culture, power and myths of mobility.* Oxfordshire: Routledge.

McRobbie, Angela. 2002. Holloway to Hollywood: Happiness at work in the cultural economy. In *Cultural economy: Cultural analysis and commercial life*, ed. Paul Du Gay and Michael Pryke, 97–114. London: Sage.

————. 2007. Top girls? Young women and the post-feminist sexual contract. *Cultural Studies* 21 (4–5): 718–737.

Nardi, Peter M. 2010. Why have women magicians vanished? *Pacific Standard.* https://psmag.com/social-justice/why-have-women-magicians-vanished-8369. Accessed 3 Apr 2018.

Nianias, Helen. 2015. 'Ask better questions': Amy Poehler's inspired feminist Golden Globes campaign against the awards show gender divide. *The Independent.* https://www.independent.co.uk/news/people/ask-better-questions-amy-poehlers-inspired-feminist-golden-globes-campaign-against-the-awards-show-9971748.html. Accessed 3 Apr 2018.

Nixon, Sean. 2003. *Advertising cultures: Gender, commerce, creativity.* London: Sage.

Porter, Sam. 1992. Women in a women's job: The gendered experience of nurses. *Sociology of Health & Illness* 14: 510–527.

Potter, Jonathan, and Margaret Wetherell. 1987. *Discourse and social psychology: Beyond attitudes and behaviour*. London: Sage.

Reitman, Jason. 2007. Director: Juno. Screenwriter: Diablo Cody: Fox Searchlight.

———. 2011. Director: Young Adult. Screenwriter: Diablo Cody: Paramount Pictures.

Rosenberg, Alyssa. 2013. At the MPAA, Geena Davis says raising awareness key to change ratio on women in movies. *Think Progress*. https://thinkprogress.org/at-the-mpaa-geena-davis-says-raising-awareness-key-to-change-the-ratio-on-women-in-movies-c8318a547659/. Accessed 26 Apr 2018.

Rosser, Michael. 2014. Only 16.3% of European films directed by women. Women in Film and Television UK. https://wftv.org.uk/only-16-3-of-european-films-directed-by-women/. Accessed 4 Apr 2018.

Rowling, J.K. 1997. *Harry Potter and the philosopher's stone*. London: Bloomsbury.

Russell, David O. 2012. Director. Silver Linings Playbook. 2012. Screenwriter: David O. Russell: Weinstein Company.

———. 2013. Director. American Hustle. Screenwriters: Eric Warren Singer, David O. Russell: Columbia Pictures.

———. 2015. Director. Joy. 2015. Screenwriter: David O. Russell: Fox 2000 Pictures.

Scharff, Christina. 2012. *Repudiating feminism: Young women in a neoliberal world*. Surrey: Ashgate Publishing, Ltd.

Silverstein, Melissa. 2014. *The unbelievable privilege of being a male director*. Women and Hollywood Blog. http://blogs.indiewire.com/womenandhollywood/the-unbelievable-privilege-of-being-a-male-director. Accessed 4 Apr 2018.

St Jean, Yanick, and Joe R. Feagin. 2015. *Double burden: Black women and everyday racism*. London/New York: Routledge.

Taylor, Stephanie. 2011. Negotiating oppositions and uncertainties: Gendered conflicts in creative identity work. *Feminism & Psychology* 21 (3): 354–371.

Taylor, Stephanie, and Karen Littleton. 2006. Biographies in talk: A narrative-discursive research approach. *Qualitative Sociology Review* 2 (1): 22–38.

———. 2012. *Contemporary identities of creativity and creative work*. Oxfordshire: Routledge.

Tucker, Anand. 1998. Director. Hilary and Jackie. Screenwriter: Frank Cottrell Boyce: Film 4.

Wetherell, Margaret. 1998. Positioning and interpretative repertoires: Conversation analysis and post-structuralism in dialogue. *Discourse & Society* 9 (3): 387–412.

Winterbottom, Michael. 1997. Director Welcome to Sarajevo. Screenwriter: Frank Cottrell Boyce: Miramax.

———. 2000. Director. The Claim. 2000. Screenwriter: Frank Cottrell Boyce: BBC Films.

CHAPTER 3

Gender, Capital, and Getting In

Well I think I had an incredibly fortunate transition but of course your fortune is partly because you know people and you're in the right place and
you've done the right thing. (Rachel, screenwriter)

To succeed in a creative profession is now one of the most sought-after
goals in the UK labour market, particularly for younger generations.
Angela McRobbie (2002, p. 109) contends that "creativity/talent' has
recently come to represent the most desired of human qualities, expressive
of, indeed synonymous with, an 'inner self' and hence a mark of unique-
ness.' She describes a growing expectation, especially amongst the middle
classes, for a sense of fulfilment and even happiness from work. More
recently, McRobbie (2016) has criticized the neoliberal promise of self-
actualizing rewards in creative work and believes it acts as a way for the
state to relinquish responsibility for welfare and wage security. Bolstered
by the positive framing of success stories in the wider media, the desire to
work entrepreneurially in a creative role is still ubiquitous amongst young
people, despite widespread economic decline and increased unemploy-
ment (Ibid.). The potential rewards remain seductive, if not remunerative,
even though there are far more losers than winners (Banks 2007).

Although, and indeed, *because* it is still widely considered one of the
most glamorous and desirable of careers, the film industry is notoriously
hard to break into (Randle and Culkin 2009). For any available work,
there are huge numbers of candidates. However, traditional formal recruitment practices, such as job advertisements, evidence of recognized

© The Author(s) 2018
N. Wreyford, *Gender Inequality in Screenwriting Work*,
https://Doi.org/10.1007/978-3-319-95732-6_3

qualifications, and interview panels are rarely used, particularly for what are viewed as the most key creative positions, of which the screenwriter is one. Indeed, the first challenge for a screenwriter is to find out when and where opportunities to be paid might arise. The structure of film work, with companies being formed for the duration of a project, and much of the workforce being freelance, means very little public data of the type available from firms in other industries is available (Christopherson 2008). With the exception of the broadcasters in the UK, the big studios in the United States, and a handful of more successful companies, film labour is mostly carried out in small or micro business run by producers who may employ an assistant or development executive (often these roles are combined) on a full-time contract and employ all other personnel, including screenwriters, as and when required on a project-by-project basis (Jones 1996).

The unpredictable nature of creative projects means that it is more economical for producers to employ workers on a flexible basis for the duration that they are required. Project-based employment, such as being contracted to one film at a time, means that 'freelance workers are increasingly having to rely on developing their own strategies for acquiring skills, finding work and making careers' (Randle and Culkin 2009, p. 98). As one film production labourer accurately articulates:

> Doing the work is fun. Finding the work is the job. (Margery, Script Supervisor, quoted in Ibid., p. 101)

As I described in the previous chapter, creative work like screenwriting is frequently perceived within the UK film industry as an innate quality of a special individual; a mysterious and unquantifiable talent which some even referred to as being like magic. Such ambiguity surrounding requisite characteristics and skills makes for difficulty in identifying capable screenwriting candidates:

> It's a delicate one though to know how hard they're writing and how competent they are. And sometimes it's very difficult to know that. How talented are they? (Paul, employer)

Creative work such as filmmaking is regarded as a high-risk, speculative endeavour, since the product is often made before it is clear who the audience is, how large that audience is, and indeed whether profit will be possible for the product at all. It is within this context that judgements are made about which film projects are worth pursuing and which individuals are worth employing. Even where previous work is available to be assessed, Denise Bielby's research on gender inequality has shown that there is a lack of consensus in the film industry on how to assess or account for an individual's input:

[M]easuring the specific contributions of individual artists to the quality of an aesthetic object is inherently ambiguous, and in commercialized mass culture industries there is little consensus about what constitutes competence among creative personnel. (Bielby 2009, p. 240)

A career in film, if we can even call it that, shares the characteristics of other creative labour as described by critical sociologists. Screenwriting is precarious, discontinuous, and requires much free labour on the part of the individual to create work, build a portfolio, and develop connections with other people that might help them to get paid work. This chapter and the next contribute to the growing body of research on inequality in creative professions by exploring the gendered dynamics of informal and networked recruitment processes. It is informed by key thinking from the fields of creative industries, cultural studies, and gender and work, but by introducing new empirical data from interviews with screenwriters and their employers, I am able to trace some of the ways that inequality of opportunity is sustained through structural and subjective mechanisms that are not held accountable through equal opportunities policies (Jones and Pringle 2015).

It's impossible to know exactly how many people are actively seeking screenwriting work at any given time. The numbers are hard to come by for the same reasons that this area is under-researched: the freelance, project-based, often unpaid nature of this work, undertaken by small and micro business. Data on screenwriters are conspicuous by their absence from Creative Skillset's many censuses and labour force digests. However, the UK Film Council's (UKFC) final annual report (2010) states that they had 1720 applications in the period March 2009 to March 2010.[1] Even though a few of these may have had the same writer attached, this figure helps to give a sense of the number of film projects circulating in the UK at any given time. In addition, the UKFC recorded 517 applications to the training body Skillset and 1487 applications to the nine Regional Screen Agencies (Ibid., p. 12). The UKFC's 'Scoping Study into the lack of

Women Screenwriters in the UK' (Sinclair et al. 2006, p. 73) also references the number of projects applying for development funding between 2004 and 2005 (statistics from the UKFC's own database)—a total of 1173 of the total 1646 applications for that financial year were for script development (as opposed to production finance). One of my participants who worked for a large film financier discussed their capacity to read screenplays:

> All our projects are sent via agents or production companies because we receive so many anyway and we're such a tiny team that we can't possibly read more than about fifty projects a week. (Yvonne, employer)

The smaller companies are even more selective:

> We don't look at any unsolicited material at all. (Ian, employer)

Bearing in mind that in the UK people go to the cinema on average less than three times a year and that American films take 59 per cent of the box office (BFI 2017), it is clear that in screenwriting work, supply greatly outstrips demand.

Great riches of fame and fortune are apparently available to those who succeed in creative professions, although this perception has helped to obscure the reality of poor pay and conditions suffered by the majority of creative workers. But the desire to work creatively cannot be explained in financial terms alone. As Angela McRobbie observes:

> In the cultural sector, those up to the age of approximately 40 now normatively self-exploit themselves by working hours no employer could legally enforce; they also do without all the protection afforded by employee status including sickness benefits; they are largely non-unionized; they are expected to take out private pension plans (which many cannot afford to do); they are unable to claim benefits for non-work time between jobs or 'projects' and they also cover their own workspace and equipment costs. (McRobbie 2002, p. 101)

McRobbie references the apparent rags-to-riches stories of successful creative workers such as radio presenter Chris Evans and novelist J. K. Rowling. Implied in these folklores is a discourse of entrepreneurship. 'Anyone can do it' if they have the talent and drive. No specialist training or expensive equipment is required for careers like screenwriting. However, these broad-brush stroke myths hide the real truth that many are facing different barriers and consequent levels of success. So what makes it so endlessly attractive as a career choice?

Richard Florida makes a convincing argument for how the developed world has moved from an industrial economy populated by 'Organization Man' to one where:

> People are still striving to be themselves, to find meaningful work, and to live in communities that let them validate their identities and live as complete people. (2002, p. xix)

He argues that the traditional forms of identity creation—for example, family, church, neighbourhoods, companies—are no longer so relevant and 'a fundamental characteristic of life today is that we strive to create our own identities...defining our identities along the varied dimensions of our creativity' (Ibid., p. 7). David Hesmondhalgh (2007, p. 207) believes that 'the willingness of so many hundreds of thousands of people to take their place in the reservoir of cultural labour is the consequence of a commitment to doing creative work of which they can be proud' and 'the glamour surrounding these worlds'. To this, we can probably add Mark Deuze's (2011) reference to 'making cool stuff', McKinlay and Smith's (2009) argument that 'prestige, status and glamour are attached to many creative occupations in public perception', and Mark Bank's (2007) 'cultural work, it seems, is hardly like work at all'. In fact, creativity and financial success are often seen as poles apart. David Hesmondhalgh traces this back to the Romantic movement of the nineteenth century:

> The influences of the Romantic Movement and modernism have been profound and helped establish a widespread view in the West that symbolic creativity can only flourish if it is far away from commerce as possible. This view is embodied in prevailing myths about great artists. We often think of the greatest symbol creators as either being unrecognized, having little or no commercial success in their lifetime (such as Van Gogh) or being driven to despair by the superficiality of the commercial world they came to inhabit (Kurt Cobain for example). (2007, p. 69)

It seems that in a developed and post-Fordist society, being a creative professional is often perceived as proof of your own worth and importance and perhaps helps to attain a degree of self-actualization.[2]

On the other hand, Bridget Conor (2014, p. 1) claims that 'screenwriting is often framed and represented as the least creative form of writing.' Why, then, is it so attractive as a potential career? Following a Marxist tradition, I contend that—though artistic work is 'not so different from other kinds of labour' (Hesmondhalgh 2007, p. 4)—the idea that 'artists' are, in some way, special and marked out from the rest of us is central to the way that screenwriters self-exploit and accept difficult conditions of employment. It is also central to the film workers' justifications of inequalities of access to screenwriting employment along gender, race, class, and other lines, on the basis that employment decisions are made solely on assessment of talent and experience. The fact that making a living wage by screenwriting is extremely difficult does not seem to deter a great many people, but it may have a significant role to play in understanding why some do not succeed or even try and why women, black, Asian, and minority ethnic (BAME) people and the working classes are significantly under-represented in the profession. The tension between creativity and commerce may be one of the most important in understanding cultural and creative industries and those who work within them, and yet 'surprisingly little attention has been paid in sociology to the means of, and barriers to entry' in creative work (Hesmondhalgh 2007, p. 71).

To overcome gender inequality, 'we will need to understand the mechanisms by which it is sustained in institutional social arrangements' (Fenstermaker et al. 2002, p. 38). I will be doing exactly this and start by analysing the way my participants talk about how they got that first elusive job in the film industry. I outline the importance of social capital and other signifiers of belonging over formal qualifications, and highlight some of the gendered experiences of my participants. In the next chapter, I will look at the consequences for women of an employment market based predominantly on networking and demonstrate how my research sheds light on the precise ways in which networking for work has gendered outcomes. Throughout both, I will also explore how my participants talk about these practices and inequalities more generally, and how they are navigated and understood by those working in the UK film industry.

Formal qualifications have limited use for screenwriters and indeed can be a disadvantage. Pierre Bourdieu found that many believe the teaching of art to be 'a contradiction in terms for some, who hold that beauty is neither taught nor learnt but is a grace transmitted from invested masters to predestined disciples' (1984, p. 67). This is clearly problematic when the result is that the majority of those who are apparently 'predestined' are white, wealthy men. Bourdieu observed that the perceived differences between a scholar (someone who has studied to gain cultural capital) and a 'worldly gentleman'[3] (someone who inherits and subsumes cultural capital through upbringing and social class) are firmly entrenched in discussions of perceived due dominance in creative and cultural work. He argues that the latter's 'status-derived capital' is legitimated by being embodied by the upper classes. Bourdieu's theories of the habitus and embodied capital (1977, 1986) are particularly useful in accounting for why men might be perceived to have more worthwhile ideas and more valuable stories than women. He offers a model of social strata of power operating through the accumulation of various forms of capital, which in turn have different values in particular social 'fields'. *Economic* capital, which takes the form of money, or possessions that can be converted into money, can be understood as an individual's financial assets. *Social* capital is the actual and potential value of a person's connections with others. It is accumulated through birth, relationships with others and membership of certain groups and clubs, all of which are of course related to each other. *Cultural* capital is found in the acquiring of cultural goods and in the sum of a person's embodied competencies and institutionalized knowledges such as educational qualifications and familiarity with various art forms. All of these capitals can function as *symbolic* capital because of their ability to give the individual a certain status or recognition within a particular field.

A person's capital and the resulting dispositions, skills, and tastes (see Chap. 7) form their capacities for action within a particular field. People are predisposed to act in certain ways due to their 'habitus'—the embodied and subconscious capacities of a person's socialized dispositions:

> Different conditions of existence produce different habitus. (Bourdieu 1984, p. 166)

For Bourdieu, each field is a structured system of social positions within which takes place a competitive game to get power and control the legitimacy of other participants. Without the right capital, as embodied and also recognized in the habitus, it may be hard for an individual to take part—let alone dominate—in a field.

Individuals surround themselves with manifestations of their habitus—through their appearance, property, interests, and tastes. Bourdieu claims that these classificatory schemes act as 'countless pieces of information a person consciously or unconsciously imparts endlessly' (Ibid., p. 169) and through which people are able to identify those most like themselves.

> The spontaneous decoding of one habitus by another is the basis of the
> immediate affinities which orient social encounters, discouraging socially
> discordant relationships. (Ibid., p. 239)

In the film industries, where employment is mostly done through informal
and social methods, such signifiers of a person's habitus are important
identifiers of belonging (or not belonging) in the field. The habitus offers
a way to account for why some individuals feel more welcome, and more
comfortable, in film labour markets than others. Those with the dominant
habitus in a field are thus both the holders of symbolic capital and consequently those with the power. They are able to make *their* views and tastes
appear to have more value and to marginalize the participation of others:

> Subordinated groups are 'marked' thus we talk about 'women writers' but
> not 'men writers', 'Black politicians' but not 'white politicians', 'gay TV
> personalities' but not 'straight TV personalities'. Dominant groups, on the
> other hand, are 'unmarked': to be white/male/straight is the default stan-
> dard for being human. (Cameron and Kulick 2003, p. 153)

Bourdieu offers a particularly helpful approach to understanding how the
dynamic of gendered socialization can result in the suppression of women
and other social groups ('aesthetic intolerance can be terribly violent'
(1984, p. 56)), despite his apparent lack of attention to gender in the
majority of his work, which predominantly focuses on class differences.
Toril Moi, who thanks Bourdieu himself for helping her develop 'a
productive feminist perspective on his theories', (1991, p. 1043) offers a
way to use Bourdieu to 'reconceptualise gender as a social category' (Ibid.,
p. 1019).

Using Bourdieu's theories, Moi (Ibid., p. 1030) outlines how 'to produce a gender habitus requires an extremely elaborate social process' and:

> [E]ven such basic activities as teaching children how to move, dress and eat
> are thoroughly political, in that they impose on them an unspoken under-
> standing of legitimate ways to (re)present their body to themselves and
> others.

She argues that gender has much in common with Bourdieu's concept of
class: it is perceived as natural and self-evident, and it is historically reproduced, embodied, and makes an individual open to judgement. Bourdieu
never looks at class as a field in its own right but sees it as part of the

'whole social field', and Moi argues that gender should be similarly considered, with the added advantage of facilitating an intersectional framework where there is no 'fixed and unchangeable hierarchy' (Ibid., p. 1035) between the effects of gender and class on a person's habitus and life experiences.

Bourdieu's theories are useful to explain why and how women's voices might be excluded from a field like the film industry:

> [A]ny field is necessarily structured by a series of unspoken and unspeakable rules for what can legitimately be said – or perceived within the field. (Ibid., p. 1022)

In this sense, Bourdieu writes, the whole field functions as a form of censorship. However, despite his efforts to conceptualize bodily dispositions as also shaping the fields in which they operate, critics of Bourdieu have found his theories less helpful in accounting for the possibility of change (Lovell 2000). For me this is actually one of the strengths of Bourdieu's work. In my 12 years of investigating the lack of women screenwriters, I have seen almost no change in the position of women in film, as Calling the Shots (CTS) (Cobb et al. 2018) and Martha Lauzen's (2018) annual reports testify. Bev Skeggs's (1997) interviews with working-class women demonstrated how even the smallest amounts of capital can be used by possessors to leverage their position as much as possible, but the same individuals are ultimately constrained by social structures. An individual on their own can certainly do little to change the rules of the field beyond their own experience. Those who dominate get to make the rules.

Therefore, although the dominant classes simply use different modes of capital acquisition, by naturalizing the apparent gifts of those who *don't* have to study the rules of screenwriting in a scholastic environment, the dominant class is able to dismiss others as lacking what they apparently naturally possess. This theory is useful in understanding the UK film industry's contemptuous judgement of those with formal screenwriting qualifications. The 'gentleman' is positioned as having instinctive taste and ability, perhaps honed during trips to the theatre or participation in stage performances at school or university. Only unrefined persons who lack such instincts are reduced to trying to 'learn' this by enrolling on screenwriting courses or—the lowest regarded of all—media studies. In this way, the status quo is upheld, as those who already belong to the dominant group are perceived to be naturally talented, and anyone different is considered lacking.

In the UK film industry, the dominant discourse is that if you have to be taught it, you obviously don't 'have it'.

> I don't really believe in the 'you teach structure in these ways'. I think it is something innate. (Kate, employer)

> I think structure is an art that you can learn or you can be helped with, you know I could structure, as you could, you've worked in it so much, it's quite easy to put the building blocks in place in a sense, but I think the actual talent is writing character and dialogue that is believable and moving and doesn't feel on the nose and clumsy. (Nicola, employer)

> What makes a person creative? I don't know. I think you've either got it or you don't in some ways. I read something the other day that made me think and it was somebody talking about modern art and art schools and saying the problem with art schools now is that they don't teach you the thing that they could teach you which is form, and they try and teach you the thing that they can't teach you which is how to have ideas. (Patrick, screenwriter)

Apparent in these examples from my participants is an ideological dilemma (Billig et al. 1988)—a tension between whether some aspects of screenwriting, and indeed which aspects, it might be possible to learn. More critically, there is a gap between these possible learnable elements and the more intangible demonstratives of some kind of natural genius. So, a script may be well written, but the idea at its heart can still be considered not good enough. The story structure might fit a traditional film model, but the writer can still be judged as demonstrating insufficient insight into human behaviour. The previously discussed discourse of innate talent promotes the apparently natural ability of those who apparently do have 'it'. In the case of screenwriting, 'it' would likely be considered to be marketable ideas and cinematic writing ability—disputed concepts at best.

Recognition of these attributes is dependent on more nebulous and subjective criteria that cannot be formally measured. Aspirant screenwriters who are unable to gain this subjective recognition of their ability or ideas are therefore also unable to prove themselves through the acquisition of qualifications either, since qualifications are considered the antithesis of being born with an innate ability. This of course helps to preserve the status of those who *are* judged as having the right ability. It is particularly important therefore to unpack the way that these subjective assessments happen, and to identify any potential sites where inequalities may be reinforced. Bourdieu's research is focused on socio-economic class differ-ence, but I shall show how his theories can also be applied to unpack the gendered aspects of cultural dominance.

GETTING IN

Natalie: What would you say are the greatest difficulties for you as a
             working screenwriter?
Catherine: Well, I think for a lot of people it's getting started frankly.

I asked all my participants to tell me about their own journey into the UK film industry and, in particular, how they got their first paid job. It is difficult to draw too many wide conclusions from such a small sample, but my findings clearly indicate that there is more than one route into a cre-ative career in film. For the screenwriters, work in television and theatre was the most common career prior to securing film work. Four men and two women screenwriters had previously worked in television and two men and two women screenwriters had written for the stage. However, rarely was success in one of these media cited as a direct path to a film screenwriting commission, and indeed even when it was, some found the transition between media a less than straightforward one:

> It's a bit like going up to someone you've heard is a really good plumber and saying 'I've heard you're a really good plumber, would you like to come and landscape my garden?' and it's like 'Why would you think I'd be good at that? I'm a plumber!' sort of thing. (Natasha, screenwriter)

Four of the women screenwriters had been actresses, although none of the men screenwriters mentioned having done any paid acting work. The pop-ularity of this background for women may be due to the lack of work for older actresses:

> If I'd been a man I might not have got to the point in my mid-thirties where I was frustrated by my acting career, because there may have been more opportunities for me as an actor. So therefore I may not have had the need to find something else to do. (Catherine, screenwriter)

Other previous careers and creative experience mentioned by the screen-writers included novel writing, being musicians in bands, working in film development (see Chap. 1), and making short films. Four screenwriters specifically mentioned getting help from friends that they already knew within the film industry. The employers had even more diverse backgrounds. Four had previously worked in television, three had been to film school, two started off on the bottom rung as runners, two had been talent agents, two had worked in art-house cinemas, one had worked in radio, one in film production, and one in music video production. Three mentioned getting a foot in the door with help from friends that they knew in a personal context.

The variety of backgrounds exhibited by both screenwriters and their employers confirms that in the film industry, specific qualification or previous experience is not necessary to begin a career (Grugulis and Stoyanova 2009). In a collaborative media such as film, television, or theatre, it can be difficult to attribute the success or failure of a product to one person. In which case, employers often rely on more than their own review of a candidate's body of work. Reputation is key for screenwriters, most commonly in the form of personal recommendation from a trusted source, or evidence of employment with a number of significant employers leading to the perception that everyone is relying on 'established talent' and trying to hire the same few names.

> [M]y list of writers that I know are likely to get a commission is tiny. It's really small. (Laura, employer)

> We had a writer and we needed to find somebody else, and so we got a list. And the list is – it's not a list tailored to this project – it's a list of A List writers. And they're all very good but some of them are so obviously not suited, you know because as I said they need to have a comedic element or, and some of those guys are really serious, which doesn't mean they're not good but nevertheless they haven't written up to this point anything comedic. And they're just being mentioned because they're big names and they've had success and won awards and therefore they are good. (Eloise, employer)

In this second quotation, Eloise describes how a list of suitable candidates was given to her by her financiers, who appear to be more concerned with a screenwriter's volume of produced work than their suitability for the job. It is perhaps worth noting that she refers to the screenwriters as 'guys', a term which is most often used to refer to men. However, she also acknowledged that this same validation by reputation can be applied to those who are new to screenwriting:

I heard this person that everybody respects loves this new writer, so it can only mean that they're great. (Eloise, employer)

Despite this reliance on track record and reputation, many of the employers I spoke to conveyed confidence in their ability to read and assess screenplays for creative and commercial potential. There was a shared sense that good writing is objectively recognizable. For example:

With a producer, if somebody's hiring me, you can't tell if a producer is good until you hire them really. If you read a script [that] is good that person can't argue with it. (Pippa, employer)

The quality of writing, that's probably the best way to put it, the quality of writing and writer is the most important factor. (Ian, employer)

In this way, an individual's subjective opinion of a writer or screenplay is framed as an objective, incontestable assessment. This, as I have shown, is tied into the belief that the industry is a meritocracy and talented individuals will find their way to success. However, there was also evidence of conflicting opinions about what makes a good screenplay:

[R]elatable characters, people you care about. (Jack, screenwriter)

[S]creenplays, it seems to me, are all about the structure. (Natasha, screenwriter)

I sort of think dialogue is more important than structure. (Nicola, employer)

[T]here's so many different, there's so many different facets to it, I think and there's so many different kinds of screenwriting. (Robert, screenwriter)

These kinds of debates over screenplay content can give the impression that careful consideration is being given as to which individuals and projects are most worthwhile of investment, but they can also be used to detract from questions of fairness and equality of access. Discussions about addressing inequalities were notably scarce in my participants' descriptions of how they assess screenwriters and screenplays, although Vicky did recognize how access can be easier for some who have the right demographic attributes, as opposed to a strong track record:

Vicky: Yeah. 'He's like us'. It's more golf club and 'he's a bit like my
            son'. You know I hear that a lot 'he reminds me of my son'. Wow.
            Gosh.
Natalie: Daughters?
Vicky: I've not heard anybody say it. So it is like: 'we can have a conversa-
            tion with him'. 'He's a good guy' I think I've heard. There are so
            many things you hear and then you're like 'oh that's what that
            means!' I mean he might be a good guy, I don't know, but based
            on what we know so far I don't think he's better than anyone else.
            You kind of realize other people don't need to say: 'this is what
            I've done before'. Because it's taken as read that you'll be fine.

Irena Grugulis and Dimitrinka Stoyanova (2009, p. 139) have shown
how the film industry teaches workers through 'participation in a community of fellows'. Learning is done 'on the job', and entrance is not
reliant on formal qualifications. Vicky's comments above suggest that the
right habitus—that of being like those already working the industry—can
possibly be more significant than qualifications, ability, or experience
when it comes to getting in and getting on. I will return to explore how
Bourdieu's concept of habitus can help with an understanding of how
people are excluded from the UK film industry in Chap. 6, but it is worth
noting here that once again, we have two prevailing discourses that are at
odds with one another. There is talk of a reliance on reputation on the
one hand and a belief in the objective assessment of a writer's work on the
other. As I have shown, a closer look at the latter reveals that it is quite
contested in and of itself and there is little consensus as to what constitutes a good script. Much discursive work has to be done to make sense
of these dichotomies, and indeed, much labour is done within the industry too:

[W]e discuss everything in a weekly three-hour development meeting. So
the whole development team meet and talk about what they've read and the
theatre they've seen and the books they've read, the television they've
watched, etc. (Yvonne, employer)

[O]bviously we talk to all the agents. We have a one-page concept. Who've
you got that would be good for this? We get suggestions in from all the
agents, you know. And then we sit and discuss them and read samples of
their writing, and then meet them and get their take on the film. (Colin,
employer)

In order to have an up-to-date knowledge of screenwriters' reputations, employers have to be in a constant state of consultation with each other, creating a hierarchy of networks (Grugulis and Stoyanova 2012) and opinions, as I shall unpack in more detail in the next chapter. Through these networked conversations, these discourses together function to allow individuals to justify subjective choices and to present opinions as facts. There is little room for recognition of taste as subjective, and where there is, a hierarchy of tastes is established where some tastes are better than others, as I shall unpack in Chap. 7. For the purposes of this chapter, it is important to note that in the constant buzz of information exchange between employers, a screenwriter's worth and consequent employability are crystalized, even in the ebb and flow as people fall into and out of favour depending on their most recent work or commission (Blair 2001).

It is important then, that we understand how these networked processes of assessment and judgement work in more detail. Before I turn to that, however, I will examine how my participants talked about getting into the industry in the first place. How does a person come to be in the position of being discussed, or of being a discusser? In the next sections, I will examine some common patterns of access to the film industry that can be identified through my interviews. I begin by highlighting the requirements that do seem to be necessary to start a career in the film industry: personal contacts and attendance at particular universities and schools.

Nepotism is 'the practice among those with power or influence of favouring relatives or friends, especially by giving them jobs' and derives from the French and Italian words for nephew (oxforddictionaries.com). Nepotism is a widely tolerated practice in the film industry (Blair et al. 2001; Grugulis and Stoyanova 2012), clearly recognizable through shared surnames and potentially creating a very small and closed network. My research data were peppered with references to early opportunities in film work established through personal contacts and family members, even in the biographies of the women. For example:

> And my husband looked at it and he said 'ooh, I think we should show this to (producer). (Producer) was the producer he'd just worked with and he gave it to her. (Catherine, screenwriter)

> My dad works in film, and my uncle and my godfather. (Kate, employer)

> The work experience was through a friend's mother. (Fiona, screenwriter)

> I heard about the job through a kind of friend of a friend of a friend and got the interview. (Vanessa, employer)

Indeed, Yvonne, one of the most experienced employers that I spoke to, admitted that someone without any personal connections would be likely to have a tough time getting a break:

> It's very, very hard to have no relationship to an organization and get your first full commission that way, but it doesn't *not* happen. (Yvonne, employer)

A few participants were keen to tell me that they had found their way in without having any contacts, which is tantamount to an acknowledgement of actually how rare this is:

> I didn't know anyone in the industry (Nick, employer)

> The old adage of 'it's not what you know, but who you know' but I didn't know anybody really. (Hannah, screenwriter)

The capital derived from social connections—social capital—is clearly evidenced here. Bourdieu (1984, p. 143) argues that social capital is particularly important in 'relatively unbureaucratized areas of social space (where social dispositions count for more than academically guaranteed 'competences')', as is the case in the UK film industry.

Some participants who clearly had contacts tried to discount their usefulness, perhaps in order to maintain a conviction that the industry is meritocratic, but also in order to argue that it was their own skills and abilities that got them to where they were:

> But then I didn't make it massively easy on myself because I did get a list of people to write to from my dad but then I didn't tell them that I was his daughter because I didn't want nepotism to come into play [laughs]. (Kate, employer)

> At the time the last thing I wanted to do was go into the film business because my family were all in the film business. (Pete, employer)

Statements such as these are particularly powerful since they reference the family connection, which can reinforce a sense of innate ability, but at the same time portray the individual as succeeding simply because they worked hard and demonstrated a personal suitability for the job. In particular, both employers do not appear to acknowledge the exceptional advantage they received from their familial connections, such as being handed a list of contacts, having an insider's viewpoint, or having a similarity of habitus (and of course that shared surname). I also encountered participants whom I knew well, who omitted details of personal contacts and close relationships with their employers from their biographies when talking to me, in favour of a narrative of having succeeded on their own merit. One participant had taken over the position that his wife previous held but didn't mention it when I asked how he got the job, despite mentioning her by first name later on in the interview because he was aware that I knew her from the time when she held his current job. Since these kinds of omissions happened in several of the interviews, it struck me as something noteworthy. It's not clear how conscious the speakers were in making these exclusions to their biographies, but it is arguable that discursive work was being done to establish their own personal aptitude, as this is generally a more acceptable way to describe their career success rather than referencing advantages derived from their social capital, such as nepotism.

In my conversations, there were mentions of nepotism, but mostly from participants referencing others rather than themselves:

[A]nd like, Ken Loach's[4] son was an assistant producer and he'd not even done half of what I'd done but he was allowed to direct. There was another girl there whose mother was one of the senior researchers and she'd brought her in. So there was a lot of that going on. (Jay, employer)

[Y]ou know, cos of his mother, you know, he was in the business. (Pippa, employer)

When I first went to the National Film School[5] I couldn't believe the elitism that was there, the nepotism and favouritism and 'let's all keep this industry to ourselves'. (Colin, employer)

In addition, there was an awareness of the advantage of having certain kinds of education. In particular, the predominance of those who had attended a private school:

The industry here, we know it's very matey, it's very nepotistic, it's very private school boys, let's be honest. (Emma, screenwriter)

> I dress like a nice, middle-class white girl and I know how to interact with
> all those nice, middle-class white men because I went to a nice private school
> and that's my world. (Pippa, employer)

The way that both Emma and Pippa talk about private schools here suggests that attendance at one is less about getting a good education and more about acquiring the right habitus and the social capital gained from those you might meet there.

There was also a clear discourse throughout my conversations that suggested that it was similarly advantageous to have attended university at Oxford, Cambridge, or Bristol:

> [A]t university I met a lot of ambitious people – I went to Cambridge –
> people whose parents worked in the industry and it started to seem a little
> more accessible to me. (Fiona, screenwriter)

> [A]nd then came back and went to Cambridge, so started directing stuff at
> Cambridge. (Frankie, screenwriter)

This was apparent in the talk of both those who attended one of these three universities, as well as those who had not:

> So you know it still happens through the Bristol set, the Oxbridge set, the
> dinner parties. A lot of that. Mostly that I would say. (Jay, employer)

> [W]hen we first started writing it was all men and they were all of a type, you
> know, Oxford, Cambridge, Bristol. (Patrick, screenwriter)

I didn't ask *any* of my participants where they went to university, or indeed *whether* they went to university. Eleven of the participants, more than one quarter of my sample, voluntarily told me that they had been to one of these three universities. Only one other university was mentioned by anyone, suggesting that if you went to one of these three, you know that it is worth revealing in conversation. It has been well documented that attendance at universities, and particularly gaining a place at Oxbridge colleges, is far easier for children who have attended private schools (Banks 2017; Pells 2017). This is a discourse that is as much about class and privilege as it is about education. Once again, the currency of attendance at one of these universities appears to be less clearly about the quality of their education than a signifier of the right habitus and considerable social capital in the UK film industry. Lauren Rivera (2011) has studied elite employers' use of educational credentials in the United States, and found that:

> Elite employers used education as a strong proxy of candidates' underlying abilities and sensibilities. However, it was not the length (e.g. the number of years of schooling- or content (e.g. degrees completed, coursework taken, skills acquired) of education that elite employers tended to use in making such assessment but its prestige. (p. 72)

Just like in the UK film industry, candidates from prestigious universities have an advantage because employers 'largely believed that the status of a candidate's educational affiliation was a reflection of his/her intellectual, social, and moral worth' (Ibid., p. 75), and consequently, they are fast-tracked over others with better qualifications.

As a side note, there were also signs that attendance at these universities could increase a person's confidence, partly through a sense of belonging to a community of insiders:

> I went to Cambridge University and you're surrounded by these kids who have everything. They went to these great private schools, their parents are politicians or great movie actors – it makes you want to do amazing things as well. (Tessa, screenwriter)

The notion of confidence was very gendered in my conversations (see Gill and Orgad 2015 for a full discussion of how confidence is used in post-feminist culture to individualize gender inequality), with it frequently being presented as a requirement of the job and consequently a key reason why women might have less success in screenwriting than men:

> It requires a level of assertion and pig-headedness that men are more able to call upon. Women are more self-doubting. (Lance, screenwriter)

Jack: There's a lot of women in development as Development Execs. I don't know if that's a role they feel more comfortable doing than writing, because of a confidence barrier you have to overcome to sit down and write.
Natalie: Why would men have more confidence than women?
Jack: Because women are cleverer that's why. Women are cleverer. Because they know. They know. They know how difficult it is, how hard it is and they undersell themselves.

There is clearly some discursive work being done in these examples to present men as less clever and more selfish and stubborn, disclaimers that the speakers use in order that they cannot be accused of making a sexist statement about women. However, in the context of recruitment, the repeated reference to women's lack of confidence also works to individualize the problem—it's not the industry's problem that there are so few women, it is down to the women to work on themselves to become more confident. Rather than suggesting changes to the industry, it places the onus on disadvantaged groups:

> I think it's up to women. I think it's up to them to get off their arses and make a film rather than go: 'Oh my god, woe is me, it's not fair, it's all really prejudiced, we should have this opportunity'. Why not work your butt off, get good, do what you need to do to get good? (Pippa, employer)

It is beyond the scope of this book to examine whether class, educational and related social capital can completely level the playing field for men and women. However, particularly amongst the more established of my screenwriter participants, my research does reinforce a significant observation on the final page of Marsha McCreadie's (2006) book of interviews with successful women screenwriters:

> Nearly every woman writer I interviewed was from what Americans prefer to call the upper middle class; really our upper class. They were all from privileged backgrounds, or had gone to exclusive undergraduate or graduate schools.

Six of my women screenwriters mentioned that they had been to one of the three named universities, and all of these were white women. This perhaps does suggest that men are less reliant than women on having gone to the right university or belonging to the right class, or perhaps have less need to bring it up in conversation. Incidentally, I was aware that one of the men employers went to Cambridge but did not bring it up in his interview with me.

It was common for my participants to seem comfortable discussing possible disadvantage in their industry in class terms:

> I'm always conscious of the fact that directing is a rich boy's game. You know, it's only rich kids that do it. (Ed, screenwriter)

So then you get into class and the whole thing about film producers just being trustafarians, people who have just come into the industry with money. And there is no one of my experience who goes against that. (Laura, employer)

I often think if you want to get exclusively into films I don't know how you do it these days apart from if you've got really rich parents and you're a trustafarian. (Patrick, screenwriter)

I think that it's quite an insecure profession that is quite often undertaken by trustafarians. (Pete, employer)

'Trustafarians' are mentioned by different participants. The term is a combination of 'trust fund' and 'Rastafarian' and refers to 'privileged white kids who subscribe to the hippie lifestyle (because they can) since they have no worries about money, a job etc.' (Urbandictionary.com 2003). It is clear that here the term has some discursive power and is most likely being used to refer to the pervasiveness in the UK film industry of 'rich kids…living out their "creative" fantasies that usually don't come to anything' (Ibid., 2006), able to do so because they seem to have no money worries, as (though) they had a trust fund from their parents. This class discourse was often connected to the acutely felt issue of low and irregular pay, and the recognition that film work can require a long period of apprenticeship or work experience (Siebert and Wilson 2013) for little financial reward:

It's back to a class thing. How on earth do you enter this industry at any level if you can't afford to live in your parents' house and get them to give you an allowance for three years? You know? It takes that long for people to take you seriously and pay you properly. (Kate, employer)

I think I worked for over fourteen, fifteen months doing work experience. (Laura, employer)

The application of this to screenwriting work is less obvious, since there are few opportunities for formal on-the-job training or work experience. For screenwriters, it reflects the requirement to self-fund your own training and improvement (Conor 2014) and possibly alludes to the length of time it takes to build up contacts and a reputation for good work:

I think in many ways I couldn't have survived my first year of being a writer if I hadn't been propped up by my parents so you know it was that background did have a part for me as well, you know they helped me financially because I just couldn't have done it otherwise. You're earning so little money that we would have just starved to death. (Patrick, screenwriter)

[S]o essentially unless you've got a rich uncle, a private income or another job. (Freddie, screenwriter)

I mean, I've got to the point now where I'm not going to write another script unless I'm being paid for it. I'm not writing another spec because I'm beyond, I've got a body of work, I've got a day job, I've got a family. My time is precious, I'm not going to sit down and write a spec script. (Jack, screenwriter)

Even experienced screenwriters are often asked to do work for free at the beginning of each project in order to secure a commission because of the high-risk nature of the commissioning process:

I think if there was more development money in this country I think there would just be more chances taken. More of kind of 'yes let's go with this idea and develop it up and maybe it will work or not'. (Fiona, screenwriter)

'Could you send me a treatment[6] and by the way we can't pay you' usually in one same breath. (Emily, screenwriter)

[Y]ou talk to a Development Exec or a Commissioner and they're interested in the idea, but you usually have to go and do a lot of work, you know, unpaid work to even get a kind of initial commission. (Usma, screenwriter)

Emily also believed that it might be more difficult for women to ask for money under these circumstances:

I think there's some truth in the fact that women aren't as good at going and asking for money. Saying 'actually I deserve to be paid'. I think that's a cultural thing. I don't think we're encouraged to behave like that. You see it in films – the cold bitch, that's what she does. She acts like a man and asks for money. She's a hard-core businesswoman and I think no, that's just basic humanity: I'm doing a job, I should be paid for it. But I've seen male colleagues and it's quite a natural thing for them whereas I have to gear myself up. (Emily, screenwriter)

This supports the view recently made popular by Sheryl Sandberg, the COO of Facebook that women just need to 'lean in' (Sandberg 2013), and according to former Sony Picture Chair Amy Pascal, 'know what they're worth' (Beaumont-Thomas 2015). However, a recent study found that women do ask for pay rises as often as men but do not receive them (Lartey 2016). There is also evidence to back up Emily's claims that women who ask for money are judged more harshly than men (Bowles et al. 2007), and this is a clear connection to Ros Gill and Shani Orgad's (2015) discussion of confidence and replacing discussions of systemic and structural sexism with a neoliberal demand for women to solve the problem through self-improvement. For women without another source of finance, it is potentially even more difficult to support themselves and sustain their career, particularly whilst they are still trying to establish their reputation.

Undoubtedly, there are gendered aspects to pay in the film industries as evidenced by the gendered pay gap revealed for A List actors in the Sony Pictures hacked documents (Lapidos 2015). In 2016, the Writer's Guild of America (Hunt 2016) reported that the pay gap for women film screen-writers had increased by 8.3 per cent to over $22,000. My research also indicates that women from lower class backgrounds may be doubly disadvantaged and have an even more difficult time gaining access to screen-writing work in the UK film industry. It is important to note that class appears to be an acceptable way that individuals can talk about degrees of advantage and disadvantage in accessing screenwriting work. These discourses of class and educational advantage might obscure evidence of gender and racial inequalities. Class is the predominant discourse of privilege in the film industry, even for those who clearly felt individually disadvantaged by their gender or skin colour. This can be seen in Pippa's comment earlier, where she describes herself as sounding like 'a nice, middle-class white girl'.

Pippa described her background as the 'usual, stereotypical immigrant story' and explained that her father had come from India with no money or education but had set up his own business and earned enough to send his children to 'good schools'. She uses her educational capital—'I went to a nice private school'—rather than address the differentness of her race or gender. Vicky, who describes herself as 'African', believed that dressing like the people with whom she is meeting would help to prevent her being perceived as different when pitching for film finances:

> I get that all the time. I walk into a room of investors, they're not expecting, they might not have clocked my name, they are not expecting 'Other' and

there is that kind of 'what have you done before?' or 'what school are you at?' you know? There is that sense of you're not going to be capable. And I have to be conscious of it. I'm aware that I can't, I love to have red hair and be really funky....But there is that thing, you walk into a room and you've got five minutes to impress and I guess it's just easier if you're a guy dressed the same as all the other guys that come in.

Vicky didn't highlight her gender as a disadvantage, but her use of the term 'guy' and 'all the other guys' suggests that she is aware of it. She went on to say, 'surely if I was a guy I could just go [adopts laid back pose] 'yeah' – cocksure.' Pippa, however, as I illustrated in the last chapter, was one of those who voiced a more dominant discourse that her gender was far from being a disadvantage and indeed was probably an advantage in gaining employment:

I hate to think it's the industry that's prejudiced. I don't feel as a woman that I'm never employed because I'm a woman. I've never felt that, ever. Maybe I'm sometimes employed *because* I'm a woman.

At the same time she was keen to disassociate herself from traditional femininity:

I'm not girly. I'm not a girly girl. I'm um...I'm a bit of a tomboy and I think I've got slightly more male genes that most people.

She did also recognize that she was expected to work to fit in:

I'm the one that's adapted in a way to make it work and they won't even think about it, you know, but they're comfortable because the film industry is so rich and so middle class. You speak a certain way, and you look a certain way and you know about social etiquette and how to kind of laugh at the right moments or whatever it may be. That's so much part of it. You fit in and you're accepted and therefore you're okay. But if I was [adopts cockney accent] 'all right, how's it going?' and I came in a sari or I was a really traditional Indian woman, I don't think I would fit in, who knows?

Her references to a sari and 'a traditional Indian woman' indicate that she, like Vicky, is aware of the gendered and racial aspects of what she is saying but avoids highlighting them, seemingly more comfortable talking about class. However, she does acknowledge that:

[I]t's just generally harder for women and women of colour to succeed because there's not very many of us and I think it's just a human instinct to work with people that you're comfortable with and you're used to having around.

In this way she accounts for any potential prejudice she may face as a natural human instinct and not as sexism or racism, without questioning the idea that employing people that you consider to be more like yourself, and therefore more trustworthy and familiar, is a form of sexism and racism. On a discursive level, the recourse to nature and instincts also allows her to solve the ideological dilemma between her statement that she's never felt disadvantaged and her observation that gender and race do matter.

Hannah explicitly argued that class was for her more clear-cut as an issue than her gender:

[I]t's harder to know what's going on with the male/female thing I think, it's harder to judge that because you just can't tell if it's because you're a woman. The class thing is easier for me, and I feel like very sure that those things are very clear and very difficult to get right, when you're meeting some Exec, that you just know, they might be the same gender but you know they are a different class and you're trying to joyfully express your idea and you can see them going 'ooh that sounds so tacky'. (Hannah, screenwriter)

Hannah's reference to 'some exec' finding her idea 'tacky' echoes Bourdieu's observation that the dominant classes find the tastes of the lower classes 'vulgar' (Bourdieu 1984, p. 171). This suggests that Hannah identifies as being from a less dominant (that is, a lower socio-economic) class than those she is applying to for work or money. However, across my participants, class talk wasn't limited to those in economically disadvantaged classes, possibly because working in the film industry was viewed repeatedly as requiring a substantial amount of money—see Laura's comment about 'trustafarian' producers earlier. Laura had worked in publishing for over a year after university without getting paid, suggesting that she was able to support herself financially during this time and therefore is perhaps not of a working-class background, although she still feels at a financial disadvantage compared to others.

Throughout my interviews, race and gender inequalities tended to be disarticulated more than class inequalities.

Yes, well this particular director I really enjoyed working with but then she, I'm not sure if it was because she was a woman, I think we just sort of clicked as people. I've not had a particularly rewarding time working with any of the male directors I've worked with. No, I mean, I wouldn't say that, you know, generally maybe with a couple of exceptions, I wouldn't say I had a great time. (Usma, screenwriter)

In fact, some seemed to notice disparities for the first time in response to me bringing up gender inequality as a topic of conversation. Patrick reflected that in his experience in radio comedy writing, he was more aware of class differences than very obvious gender inequalities:

Especially in comedy it seems to be that Oxbridge male set who tend to dominate. Especially Radio 4 when we first started writing it was all men and they were all of a type, you know, Oxford, Cambridge, Bristol. It was all that kind of type. And occasionally you would get a female writer in there and I, probably being young, never stopped to think 'gosh what's that like?' Like [woman writer] who was always there and she was always really, really funny and I never thought, 'wow, what's that like for her to be in a room full of fifteen blokes trying to get her ideas across?' but it never struck me because she was always very confident and funny and her ideas were better than mine (laughs).

Patrick discursively deals with any guilt he might feel about not considering the reasons for and consequences of being the only women in a room of men by complimenting the women writer. This echoes other discursive constructs around women's absence from screenwriting work that I have already discussed where women are positioned as more clever and/or sensible than men. However, I did encounter many examples of all-too-real gendered experiences working and seeking work within the film industry. For example, from Corrine, a screenwriter and director:

On my first film, the first shot was in the can. It was about 7am in the morning and one of the male crew comes up to me and says 'Why do women bleed?' and I'm all confused and I don't know what to say so he says 'because they're evil' and walks off laughing. It was just meant to destabilize me and put me off. (Corrine, screenwriter)

Or Emily talking about pitching her screenplay ideas:

I pitched this romantic comedy and it's 'lovely, lovely' and then I pitched this full on action film but it's fast and funny and she sat there and said 'women don't write actions films. Come on [Emily] you know this, you're not going to get anywhere with that sort of thing.'

Frankie described how she 'always dressed down because I don't want to be looked at as beautiful because that means objected [sic]', by which we could interpret that as a woman she is having to consciously work to present herself as agentic. When I picked up on the point that Gillian's boss was a man, she said 'it's a he. Yeah, it's always a he,' and Hannah noted that 'even my agent has a football team with all his writers and directors that I'll never be on'—noting the missed opportunity for networking as well as an awareness of difference.

Perhaps most remarkably, Lance gave me an extended metaphor where he explained that 'women are better nurturers, hard-wired to look after their offspring. Men are not hard-wired to hang around,' so therefore, men might find it easier to hand their screenplay 'baby' over to a director than a woman would. The idea was echoed by Jack, who suggested that women might be drawn to development work in order to 'nurse a baby through to production', suggesting by omission that his role as a screenwriter did not include the same level of commitment. The gendered experiences are sometimes subtle, sometimes overt, but—perhaps because of the isolation of screenwriters from others in the same position as them, and the limited number of women screenwriters—this generally had not built into a wider understanding of gender discrimination as part of the job market in the film industry.

Discussions would often leak into talking about film production rather than development because it was generally thought to be easier to account for the lack of women directors due to the continued predominance of childcare responsibilities falling on women's shoulders:

If you've got kids or family I don't know how women with young children direct, I just don't know how they do it. So you've either got to be single, or divorced or whatever, or have a really understanding mother, so just practically I think, it's trouble whereas for men it's just never an issue. (Pippa, employer)

I've asked this question of people 'Why are there so few female directors?' The answer to that might even strike a chord with you: 'They get married and have families and it's more than a full time job'. They take over all that and it's got to have an impact, I'm afraid. That doesn't completely explain the pitifully low number of female writers. (Rob, employer)

I will be thoroughly dissecting the notions of motherhood and employment in creative professions in detail in Chap. 5, but it's worth considering here that childcare was seen by many of my participants as an acceptable way to account for a continued lack of women—another way that their absence was individualized and therefore dismissed as not an industry problem. There was little or no discussion in my conversations as to whether childcare should be a woman's task or whether the film industry should adapt to accommodate such caring responsibilities. Ros Gill (2014, p. 511) has argued that these claims about women and childcare as explanation for the lack of women in creative industries 'have taken on an almost hegemonic status as the 'acceptable face of feminism'', leaving little room for other areas of critique. Despite the prevalence of women hair and make-up artists on film sets, many of whom are some of the first on set every day, it was presented to me as common sense that women having children explained their low inclusion in other roles, and negated the need to look for other reasons for continued inequality.

> Some female writers don't really start emerging until their kids have got to a certain age. (Frank, employer)

> I also think it's not conducive with having a family. I was incredibly ambitious and then I had kids. (Nicola, employer)

The difficulty in talking about sexism and gendered forms of discrimination in the post-feminist workplace has been well documented by feminist academics (Gill 2000; Kelan 2009). The women screenwriters I spoke to often played down the role their gender might play in their lack of success. Tessa gives a good example of this dynamic in her conversation with me:

> Like for me my peer is [man screenwriter] who's incredibly successful. He was a friend of mine at Cambridge, so I compare myself to him and he's won all these awards and blah, blah, blah, and I've never had anything made. So I make quite a lot of money and I get consistent work, which is, you know, brilliant and more than anyone could ask for and my husband's always yelling at me 'you need to be happier with where you are!' and stuff like that. But you constantly compare yourself, I dunno, I do anyway.

Tessa never mentions that gender might be a contributing factor in their comparative success and frames it as a very personal and individual story, but even though she's acknowledging her own achievements, she clearly feels a sense of unfairness. Like Pippa's disavowing of sexism as human nature seen earlier, Emma was also keen to suggest that people weren't discriminating consciously and therefore couldn't be 'blamed', suggesting they can't be held accountable to change their behaviour:

[I]t's unconscious even, I don't blame people, it's just there, they just don't know how to deal with women and that's why to be honest (Emma, screenwriter)

Fiona suggested that the film industry was just like any other industry. Her tone and laughter made it sound like she believed this was just the way life is and there's not much that can be done about it:

I mean you've got a lot of key women doing great things? And female producers. It's a male dominated world, isn't it (laughs)? I don't know because it shouldn't be the case but I think it's probably a case of women having children and men getting hired over women because that's what happens in every industry. (Fiona, screenwriter)

So, to draw together and conclude the arguments I have made in this chapter, clearly the old adage 'it's not what you know, it's who you know' is alive and thriving in the UK film industry. There is a culture of uncertainty and subjectivity and this leads to a reliance on similarities of habitus and cultural capital as a safety net for getting it wrong. Those working in the UK film industry find it difficult to talk about gender inequality in terms of access to work. The only accepted discourse is to uphold belief in a naturalized, biological instinct and drive that women are considered to have: to want to bear and nurture children rather than continue in the workplace. This talk works to individualize the unfair position of women screenwriters whilst freeing the speaker from any responsibility for challenging the situation. Gendered experiences and even examples of blatant sexism were described to me, but degrees of disadvantage in gaining screenwriting work are only comfortably discussed as a class problem.

Despite there being many routes into film work, it is clear that certain cultural and social capital derived from attending private school or one of three key universities carries more weight than any formal qualifications. Whilst there is an acknowledgement of the financial difficulties in starting and sustaining a screenwriting career, this is not translated into a concern for anyone from an economically challenged background. Indeed, there is an awareness amongst film workers of the substantial familial wealth that sustains the careers of many. Difficulties of fitting in caused by the gender or racial background of an individual are occasionally acknowledged but often buried in a more acceptable class discourse, leaving little room for a shared understanding of the barriers that may be faced by women or BAME screenwriters, particularly if they are also economically or educationally underprivileged. It is difficult for these individuals to talk about the discrimination and disadvantage they may face without access to discourses and understandings of the mechanisms at work. In this chapter, I have begun to unveil these mechanisms and allow them to be talked about. I have shown how the right habitus is a significant advantage to being recognized as capable in the UK film industry. Whilst my participants may predominantly acknowledge this in class terms, they also presented considerable evidence that this is also true for gender and race. In the next chapter, I will turn to look at how working screenwriters are required to sustain their careers through socialized employment practices and how this contributes to the upholding of gender and other inequalities.

NOTES

1. This is the last year for which the UKFC had responsibility for distributing public money. The British Film Institute (BFI) does not release similar data on its applicants in its annual reports.
2. Richard Florida quotes economist Paul Romer, for whom creativity is what distinguishes the human race from other species (Florida 2002, p. 36).
3. Bourdieu's word is 'the *mondain*, the effortlessly elegant' (1984, p. 62).
4. Ken Loach is a British film director with a long and illustrious career. See his list of credits at: http://www.imdb.com/name/nm0516360/
5. The National Film and Television School is highly respected and world-renowned. For more information, see their website: https://nfts.co.uk/
6. A screenplay treatment is a document of around five to ten pages that outlines the film's storyline and introduces the main characters. It is often used to secure finance for development and/or production.

REFERENCES

Banks, Mark. 2007. *The politics of cultural work*. Hampshire: Palgrave Macmillan.
Banks, Mark. 2017. *Creative justice: Cultural industries, work and inequality*. London: Pickering & Chatto Publishers.
Beaumont-Thomas, Ben. 2015. Ex-Sony Picture chief Amy Pascal opens up over hack: 'Angie didn't care'. *The Guardian*. https://www.theguardian.com/

film/2015/feb/12/sony-pictures-chief-amy-pascal-hack-interview. Accessed 14 Apr 2018.

BFI. 2017. BFI statistical yearbook 2017. http://www.bfi.org.uk/sites/bfi.org.uk/files/downloads/bfi-statistical-yearbook-2017.pdf. Accessed 4 Apr 2018.

Bielby, Denise D. 2009. Gender inequality in culture industries: Women and men writers in film and television. *Sociologie du travail* 51 (2): 237–252.

Billig, Michael, Susan Condor, Derek Edwards, Mike Gane, David Middleton, and Alan Radley. 1988. *Ideological dilemmas: A social psychology of everyday thinking*. London: Sage.

Blair, Helen. 2001. 'You're only as good as your last job': The relationship between labour market and labour process in the British film industry. *Work, Employment and Society* 15 (1): 149–169.

Blair, Helen, Nigel Culkin, and K.R. Randle. 2001. *From Hollywood to Borehamwood-Exploring nepotism and networking in US and UK freelance film careers*. Business School Working Papers, Film Industry Research Group Paper, vol. 7. University of Hertfordshire Business School.

Bourdieu, Pierre. 1977. *Outline of a theory of practice*. Vol. 16. Cambridge, UK: Cambridge University Press.

———. 1984. *Distinction: A social critique of the judgment of taste*. Cambridge, MA: Harvard University Press.

———. 1986. The forms of capital (1986). In *Cultural theory: An anthology*, ed. Imre Szeman and Timothy Kaposy, 81–93. West Sussex: Wiley., 2011.

Bowles, Hannah Riley, Linda Babcock, and Lei Lai. 2007. Social incentives for gender differences in the propensity to initiate negotiations: Sometimes it does hurt to ask. *Organizational Behavior and Human Decision Processes* 103 (1): 84–103.

Cameron, Deborah, and Don Kulick. 2003. *Language and sexuality*. Cambridge: Cambridge University Press.

Christopherson, Susan. 2008. Beyond the self-expressive creative worker: An industry perspective on entertainment media. *Theory, Culture & Society* 25 (7–8): 73–95.

Cobb, Shelley, Linda Ruth Williams and Natalie Wreyford. 2018. Calling the shots: Women directors and cinematographers on British Films since 2003. https://s25407.pcdn.co/wp-content/uploads/2018/02/Calling-the-Shots-Report-Feb-2018-Women-directors-and-cinematographers.pdf. Accessed 26 Mar 2018.

Conor, Bridget. 2014. *Screenwriting: Creative labor and professional practice*. Oxfordshire: Routledge.

Deuze, Mark. 2011. *Managing media work*. Thousand Oaks: Sage.

Fenstermaker, Sarah, Candace West, and Don Zimmerman. 2002. Gender inequality: New conceptual terrain. In *Doing gender, doing difference: Inequality, power, and institutional change*, ed. Sarah Fenstermaker and Candace West, vol. 2013, 25–39. New York, Routledge.

Florida, Richard. 2002. *The rise of the creative class*. New York: Basic Books.

Gill, Rosalind. 2000. Justifying injustice: Broadcasters' accounts of inequality in radio. In *Discourse analytic research*, ed. E. Burman and I. Parker. London: Routledge.

———. 2014. Unspeakable inequalities: Post feminism, entrepreneurial subjectivity, and the repudiation of sexism among cultural workers. *Social Politics: International Studies in Gender, State & Society* 21 (4): 509–528.

Gill, Rosalind, and Shani Orgad. 2015. The confidence cult (ure). *Australian Feminist Studies* 30 (86): 324–344.

Grugulis, Irena, and Dimitrinka Stoyanova. 2009. I don't know where you learn them': Skills in film and TV. In *Creative labour: Working in the creative industries*, ed. Alan McKinlay and Chris Smith, 135–155. Hampshire: Palgrave Macmillan.

———. 2012. Social capital and networks in film and TV: Jobs for the boys? *Organization Studies* 33 (10): 1311–1331.

Hesmondhalgh, David. 2007. *The cultural industries*. London: Sage Publishing.

Hunt, Darnell M. 2016. The 2016 Hollywood writers report: Renaissance in reverse? Writers Guild of America, West. http://www.wga.org/uploadedFiles/who_we_are/HWR16.pdf. Accessed 12 Apr 2018.

Jones, Candace. 1996. Careers in project networks: The case of the film industry. In *The boundaryless career: A new employment principle for a new organizational era*, ed. Michael B. Arthur and Denise M. Rousseau, 58–75. New York: Oxford University Press.

Jones, Deborah, and Judith K. Pringle. 2015. Unmanageable inequalities: Sexism in the film industry. *The Sociological Review* 63 (1_suppl): 37–49.

Kelan, Elisabeth. 2009. *Performing gender at work*. Hampshire: Palgrave Macmillan.

Lapidos, Juliet. 2015. The Sony hack and the gender pay gap. *The New York Times*. https://takingnote.blogs.nytimes.com/2015/01/12/the-sony-hack-and-the-gender-pay-gap/. Accessed 14 Apr 2018.

Lartey, Jamiles. 2016. Women ask for pay increases as often as men but receive them less, study says. *The Guardian*. https://www.theguardian.com/world/2016/sep/05/gender-wage-gap-women-pay-raise-men-study. Accessed April 12th 2018.

Lauzen, Martha M. 2018. *The celluloid ceiling: Behind-the-Scenes employment of women on the top 100, 250, and 500 films of 2017*. San Diego State University. https://womenintvfilm.sdsu.edu/wp-content/uploads/2018/01/2017_Celluloid_Ceiling_Report.pdf. Accessed 26 Mar 2018.

Lovell, Terry. 2000. Thinking feminism with and against Bourdieu. *Feminist Theory* 1 (1): 11–32.

McCreadie, Marsha. 2006. *Women screenwriters today: Their lives and words*. Connecticut: Praeger Publishing.

McKinlay, Alan, and Chris Smith, eds. 2009. *Creative labour: Working in the creative industries*. Hampshire: Palgrave Macmillan.

McRobbie, Angela. 2002. Holloway to Hollywood: Happiness at work in the cultural economy. In *Cultural economy: Cultural analysis and commercial life*, ed. Paul Du Gay and Michael Pryke, 97–114. London: Sage.

———. 2016. *Be creative: Making a living in the new culture industries*. Cambridge: Polity Press.

Moi, Toril. 1991. Appropriating Bourdieu: Feminist theory and Pierre Bourdieu's sociology of culture. *New Literary History* 22 (4): 1017–1049.

Oxforddictionaries.com. https://en.oxforddictionaries.com/definition/nepotism. Accessed 14 Apr 2008.

Pells, Rachel. 2017. State school pupils have 'reduced chance' of winning Oxbridge places as they apply to oversubscribed courses. *The Independent*. https://www.independent.co.uk/news/education/education-news/oxbridge-places-state-school-pupils-reduced-change-university-courses-oversubscribed-oxford-a7892101.html. Accessed 12 Apr 2018.

Randle, Keith, and Nigel Culkin. 2009. Getting in and getting on in Hollywood: Freelance careers in an uncertain industry. In *Creative labour*, ed. Alan McKinlay and Chris Smith. Hampshire: Palgrave Macmillan.

Rivera, Lauren A. 2011. Ives, extracurriculars, and exclusion: Elite employers' use of educational credentials. *Research in Social Stratification and Mobility* 29 (1): 71–90.

Sandberg, Sheryl. 2013. *Lean in: Women, work, and the will to lead*. New York: Random House.

Siebert, Sabina, and Fiona Wilson. 2013. All work and no pay: Consequences of unpaid work in the creative industries. *Work, Employment and Society* 27 (4): 711–721.

Sinclair, Alice, Emma Pollard, and Helen Wolfe. 2006. *Scoping study into the lack of women screenwriters in the UK*. A report presented to the UK Film Council. UK Film Council. http://www.bfi.org.uk/sites/bfi.org.uk/files/downloads/uk-film-council-women-screenwriters-scoping-study.pdf. Accessed 26 Mar 2018.

Skeggs, Beverley. 1997. *Formations of class & gender: Becoming respectable*. London: Sage.

UK Film Council. 2010. UK Film Council group and lottery annual report and financial statements for the year ended 31 March 2010. http://www.bfi.org.uk/sites/bfi.org.uk/files/downloads/uk-film-council-annual-report-and-accounts-2009-10.pdf. Accessed 4 Apr 2018.

Urbandictionary.com. 2003, 2006. https://www.urbandictionary.com/define.php?term=trustafarian. Accessed 14 Apr 2018.

CHAPTER 4

The Gendered Dynamics of the Recruitment of Screenwriters

It's quite a slow burn, I think. Those conversations can start and you might not be doing something with someone for three years. But you keep talking or you keep kind of nosing around stuff together. (Jo, employer)

Even after securing that elusive first job, continuing in employment is a challenge for screenwriters; building a career and particularly earning enough to live on is an incredibly precarious, unpredictable, and nebulous process. In film labour markets, very few opportunities are publicly advertised and there are hardly any recruitment firms working in the area of film jobs beyond secretarial and administrative work, or some technical production roles. The norm is to find employment through socialized processes such as networking, meetings, pitching ideas, and selling yourself alongside your product:

…you don't get sent for a job interview or anything, you just get sent to meet somebody. And if you spark with that director or producer, they will think about you and try to get you work later on, so if you fuck up those meetings, you're probably not going to get work. (Tessa, screenwriter)

Nick backed up the idea that agreeableness might be as, or more important, than experience when he spoke about a writer that he regularly employed:

He's only got one produced feature credit, and he's the loveliest guy on earth…

© The Author(s) 2018   87
N. Wreyford, *Gender Inequality in Screenwriting Work*,
https://doi.org/10.1007/978-3-319-95732-6_4

The insecurity and anxiety produced by the unpredictable nature of project-based employment and the lack of a regular income means that workers often feel that they need to be in a continuous process of looking for work (Randle and Culkin 2009).

Employing screenwriters on a project-by-project basis allows employers to only pay for part of a screenwriter's time, and puts the onus on the screenwriter to ensure they secure enough work to make a living wage, either as a screenwriter or by combining this with other forms of employment (such as teaching, script reading, or other forms of writing). It also releases the employers from the burden of having to provide benefits, such as sick pay, holiday pay, or maternity pay as the 'risks and responsibilities are to be borne by the individual' (Gill and Pratt 2008, p. 3). It further allows employers to elicit free work from screenwriters, as they must prove themselves worthy to continue to the next (paid) stage in their contract. David Hesmondhalgh (2007, p. 6) acknowledges:

> Paradoxically, this freedom – which is in the end, a limited and provisional one – can then act as a form of control by maintaining the desirability of often scarce and poorly-paid jobs.

It is much more likely that the reason creative workers are given the 'freedom' of freelance employment is the uncertainty of the success of any creative product, and the high cost of production and product development in relation to the reproduction costs. It is no coincidence that the Hollywood Studios have kept hold of film distribution, whilst scaling back and outsourcing development and production (Christopherson 2009). In the UK film industry, many of the potential employers of screenwriters, such as film producers, have working lives that are also project-based and precarious. In fact, many of the producers may consider themselves to be freelance workers, even though they are the driving force in originating the projects, pulling the team together, and financing a new venture through various private and public entities.

> Single entrepreneurs or contracted freelancers, typically working in solitary 'virtual' or 'network' environments, may have little recourse to the plexus of support offered by managers, colleagues, the union or the occupational therapists. (Banks 2007, p. 58)

Is it even reasonable to expect that they could be in a position to offer security and stability to the screenwriters they employ?

Most of a screenwriter's work is done during a pre-pre-production phase, referred to by film workers as 'development'. This is the part of the filmmaking processes that happens prior to financing and pre-production. The primary tasks in this period are identifying and evaluating possible film projects, identifying and evaluating writers to work on them, and then the process of writing and rewriting the screenplay. All of this is undertaken to get the project to a point where it is considered to be attractive by other personnel whose involvement is critical for the film to get made: directors, actors, and financiers. Those who manage development work are most usually producers, who are predominantly self-employed, and development executives, who are sometimes employed by those producers with the available finances. Development executives can be employed either full- or part-time and are usually on an annually renewable contract but often with few benefits or job security. Alternatively, and sometimes in addition, a freelance script editor can be contracted to work with the screenwriter, and frequently, 'readers' will be paid a very small fee to assess screenplays, and sometimes novels and other source material. Finally, of course, writers are employed on a project-by-project basis, sometimes only for a couple of drafts before being replaced, making it a very precarious position:

> Yeah I spent my whole time working on [Film Title] thinking I was about to get sacked! (Natasha, screenwriter)

For screenwriters, there is likely to be considerable unpaid work required—writing entire screenplays that can be used as samples of their style and ability, or promoted to producers as original ideas to be optioned and to then pay the writer to revise (at the risk of then being replaced by another writer). Even after several commissions and even produced films, a screenwriter will usually be expected at minimum to write a short document for free at the start of the project: an outline of the story, or a 'treatment' which fleshes out some of the details of the story and characters, and gives more of a sense of the tone and style:

> ...you usually have to go and do a lot of work, you know, unpaid work to even get a kind of initial commission. (Usma, screenwriter)

Very rarely are any of these individuals employed through a process of answering a job advertisement and successfully passing through an interview and formal assessment. If this happens, it is usually in a government-financed organization or a broadcaster: those who are accountable by legislation to provide equal opportunities (although in practice this is not as straightforward as it sounds, as will become clear). As already discussed, Pierre Bourdieu noted in his hugely influential work *Distinction* (1984, p. 151) that recruitment in the 'new professions' associated with cultural production 'is generally done by co-option, that is, on the basis of 'connections' and affinities of habitus, rather than formal qualifications'. Candace Jones (1996) uses the phrase 'being socialized into the industry culture' to describe the process by which the film industry creates rules and behaviours which mark someone out as belonging.

Only by finding an entry-level position and observing and assimilating the cultural norms from within is it possible to become accepted as part of the industry and therefore find ways to gain further employment. However that, as I demonstrated in the previous chapter, is in itself subject to judgements of the right 'fit' by those already 'in' the labour force. Nevertheless, administrative staff will often take on extra curricula reading work in order to advance their careers. Readers can progress to freelance script editors if they earn the trust of the company for whom they assess material. Script editors and readers are often also working to become screenwriters, as discussed in Chap. 2. Very occasionally, readers will progress to become a contracted in-house development executive or decided to try their hand at producing. Kate was one of my participants who described this route into her current position:

> I came into the industry as a reader and read for about two years for various companies and then got a job working for a producer who was setting up his own production company within a TV company, and for ten years, through firstly that company, in a sort of story editor role, and then a head of development role and then started producing films for him. (Kate, employer)

The problem with this process is that it tends to favour those who are most like the people already employed. Newcomers must 'fit in' and prove that they have the right sensibility and taste, can be trusted, and are not going to require a lot of time and attention of very busy employers to train them up but instead can pick up the acceptable ways of performing and carrying out the tasks by themselves. In the process of doing this, anyone joining the UK film industry is likely to have to soak up its dominant discourses, for example, about what audiences want to watch, what sales agents look for in a new film, and how best to identify good stories and talented people. This learning is done by observing and talking and getting feedback from those already in employment. Mark Banks (2007) argues that for cultural firms and organizations, reproducing very similar products in the hope of replicating their success is an obvious strategy to deal with the unpredictable nature of the cultural market. Who better to reproduce the same old thing, than the same old people, or at least someone very like them?

Screenwriters do not have access to entry-level positions in the UK film industry. To write a feature-length screenplay requires the same skills and processes whether you are a multi-award award-winner or a first-timer. Only the fee is likely to be different and perhaps more time needed for those at the beginning of a potential career. Previous experience writing for theatre, television, or radio was common amongst my screenwriter participants, suggesting that these can provide a route into screenwriting work and may be more accessible to newcomers. But Ian describes a common practice of production companies: '...we don't look at any unsolicited material at all.' This implies, by omission, that the opposite is true: most screenplays are *solicited* by employers—from agents or directly from the writer through personal or professional connections. As a budding film screenwriter, you must find a way to access these channels if you want to be considered for work. One employer talked of getting an idea from a screenwriter 'in a very casual conversation' (Laura, employer). Another talked of one particular film as 'a concept that the director and I had come up with as being an interesting project' (Pete, employer). Gillian said the writer 'has to be someone I've heard of or know or has written something I've heard of'. Others gave the distinct impression that finding writers through agents was *not* a preferred method:

I've never done the rounds of agents because actually all they do is send you the old crap that nobody wants (Pippa, employer)

I think they're all the same [laughs] in terms of they're all going to believe their clients are great. And I don't think they're very discerning, really. (Gillian, employer)

Right. How writers find work is through their agent. Their agent will – or certainly should – be talking to the production companies and the broadcasters. And they will be keeping their ear to the ground to find out what projects have been greenlit and what opportunities there are for writers to be employed on those projects. That's what an agent should do. What has become more necessary is that writers go out and find that stuff out for themselves. (Esther, screenwriter)

This leaves personal connections and recommendations as the primary way that screenwriters can find work. However, increasingly, there is evidence that reliance on personal networks and informal employment practices has different outcomes for men and women (Grugulis and Stoyanova 2012). Hiring on short-term contracts in a context of ambiguity, risk, and uncertainty necessitates reliance on social networks and informal subjective criteria with outcomes that reinforce the status quo (Bielby and Bielby 1999). In this chapter, I examine the subjective methods of assessment to which screenwriters are exposed and unpack how industry-wide discourses work to uphold gender inequalities. I will demonstrate that these discourses have become legitimized as 'best practice' by both screenwriters and their potential employers and highlight the function of the discourses, which go beyond talk to tangibly limit opportunities for women in the UK film labour market.

PROJECT-BASED WORK AND SOCIALIZED RECRUITMENT PRACTICES

So there's a lot of kind of...um...being a social lubricant let's say. (Frank, employer)

Creative Skillset's (2010) report on the status of women in the creative industries in the UK found that representation was highest in sectors with larger employers in which more stable, permanent employment models are common, such as terrestrial television (48 per cent), broadcast radio (47 per cent), cinema exhibition (43 per cent), and book publishing (61 per cent). It's not hard to see why permanent employment might be more attractive for women workers because of the increased opportunity for maternity pay and leave, and the possibility of negotiating reduced hours to accommodate caring for others.[1] By contrast, motherhood has been shown to have a detrimental effect on networking for work. Karen Campbell (1988) demonstrates how 'women with young children have more restricted network range, and lower network composition', but finds no correlating disparity for men who start a family. In the next chapter, I will offer a more detailed analysis of the effects of motherhood on women creative workers, but here, it is important to note that since mothers are still required to allocate more time to domestic responsibilities than fathers, or men and women without children (Hochschild and Machung 1989; Renzulli et al. 2000), they also have less time for other activities. However, motherhood does not provide the complete explanation and indeed can be used as an oversimplified excuse as we have already seen (Gill 2014). For example, Denise Bielby and James Baron (1984, p. 38) have demonstrated that 'autonomous employers operating small firms need no explicit rationale for excluding female workers; they can unilaterally exercise their preference for an all-male network.' So how can we account for such discriminatory practices?

Structural factors, which suggest how the opportunities available to an individual may be limited by their social position and background, are the favoured explanation in studies of gender and networking (Ibarra 1992; McGuire 2000). Since networking 'is primarily a social activity' (Cromie and Birley 1992, p. 242), it is therefore likely to be highly influenced by the status and social position of the person doing the networking. This argument is most persuasive when considering the limited numbers of women and black, Asian, and minority ethnic (BAME) individuals in the more senior, decision-making roles. Screenwriters are most frequently commissioned (employed) by producers and financiers, the majority of whom are men (73 per cent of producers and 82 per cent of executive producers British films produced in 2015 were men (Cobb et al. 2016)). However, employers were keen to press upon me their desire to find good screenplays and screenwriters, whatever their background or identity:

> For me I crave the day I read a script and it blows me away. I've never had it yet. (Colin, employer)

> We are so craving for good stories for something they can go and make so if it's written by a man or woman I don't think they care less. I really do. (Eloise, employer)

> The good thing about being a writer, I think, particularly here, is you don't need to be accredited, I mean if there's just a fabulous script, you're in. No-one cares who wrote it. (Pete, employer)

This certainly seems to substantiate the structural argument. If producers are so open and desperate to find a good screenplay, then maybe it is simply a case of how to get a diverse range of screenwriters' work in front of them? On the other hand, it is wise to consider what work is done by this discourse of 'craving' and 'not caring'. Just like the discourse of the special creative, 'magic' individual discussed in Chap. 2, the idea of the illusive perfect script appearing out of nowhere conceals the subjective judgements by which ideas are deemed worthwhile and the necessary process of collaboration also discussed in Chap. 2, which produces the real creative gems.

Most academic research on finding employment using personal networks in the film labour markets has tended to focus on the physical production phase of the industries (Blair 2001; Blair et al. 2001, Christopherson 2009). Some of the observations and conclusions of this work are not easily translated to roles outside the production community. For instance, Helen Blair's (2000) formulation of the 'semi-permanent work group' (SPWG)—a team of individuals who move between jobs as a unit with only the most senior member responsible for procuring work—applies to film production departments, but similar protective enclaves are not available for screenwriters. They may be able to build on past success and secure a subsequent contract with a producer that they have worked with, a practice that Susan Rogers (2007) confirms is prevalent in the UK film industry, but this is not the same as a SPWG since the producer is likely to be working with several other writers on different projects at the same time and the screenwriter will usually need more than one employer in any given year. Ian Macdonald (2010, abstract) argues that the development process is instead better understood as a Screen Idea Work Group (SIWG), 'a flexible constructed group organized around the development and production of a screen idea'. Whilst this notion has some usefulness in allowing an examination of 'the changing flux of power relationships...and the actual negotiation process involved in the working of that SIWG' (Ibid., p. 49), it doesn't entirely reflect the reality of the film labour market, where economic and social capital are very strong indicators of where power is located and upheld. Although Macdonald concedes that there is some hierarchy in the way that decisions are made and enforced, his argument that anyone can contribute with equal validity to the discussion of the SIWG, including friends, financiers, script readers, and development executives, masks the reality of strongly hierarchical employment structures and a distribution of cultural capital in line with that hierarchy, which means some opinions are definitely perceived as being more equal than others.

Therefore, in order to understand more precisely the wider mechanisms of informal recruitment and its ramifications for key creative workers such as screenwriters, I found it necessary to turn to the research on networking for work in other industries, including those where personnel are recruited in a more formal manner through job advertisements and by Human Resource departments. As I will demonstrate, the usefulness of this literature to understanding inequalities in the film industry is clear, since even within formal employment structures, it has been shown that informal networks play a powerful role in upholding gender inequality (McGuire 2002). Gail McGuire's interviewees—over a thousand financial services employees—confirm that, even in large firms with human resource departments, informal networks are the place where the real power and opportunities are. Some are even disparaging of those who rely on the formal processes. As one interviewee reported: 'He said that vice presidents routinely exchanged such favors and that only "losers" went to human resources (i.e. used a formal procedure) to try to obtain promotions' (McGuire 2002, p. 318). McGuire's subjects also suffered from a gendered inequality of opportunity. What McGuire's research doesn't provide is an understanding of exactly *how* informal recruitment works to ensure different outcomes for women.

In her study of new media workers, Ros Gill (2002) reports that some of her interviewees found networking to be 'a form of gendered exclusion – the activities of an "old boys" network'. She cites one woman as longing for a return to a more formal and transparent job market and refers to what Lady Howe, chair of the Hansard Society Commission on 'Women at the Top', called Hansard's Law: 'The clubbier the culture, the less likely women are to make the top' (Franks 1999, p. 52). In my research, the employers were keen to disavow—unprompted—that such mechanisms exist in the film industry. The most frequent way they did this was by referring to the very visible women in senior positions in the three largest, publicly funded film financing entities—the British Broadcasting Corporation (BBC), Film Four, and the BFI.

> There was a time, not so long ago when it was pointed out to me that major areas of film finance in the UK were being run by women. (Rob, employer)

> I think a lot of the gatekeepers are women and let less women in, I really think so. (Colin, employer)

> Interestingly enough the three biggest roles in the British film industry were held by women not that long ago. (Eloise, employer)

Leaving aside for a moment that these positions are currently held by two men and one woman and therefore the time period when I was conducting my interviews may have been unusual, there is indeed evidence that these women may have played a part in the support of women creative workers (Steele 2013). However, they all reported to senior men, and none was in a position to fully finance a film, which means of course that their influence as women championing women would be limited. Indeed their potential private finance partners are most frequently men:

I notice that distributors are very male. They're all male. (Gillian, employer)

I mean, to be fair, all three of the financiers were men. (Jo, employer)

...but if you look at the business side of things if you look at the distributors, it's certainly very, very male dominated. (Eloise, employer)

...a lot of our time, all of us, is spent dealing with men. And men, in the end are running most of these organizations, however strong the women's voices may be within them. (Yvonne, employer)

In my current research for Calling the Shots (Cobb et al. 2016), I found that women accounted for just 18 per cent of executive producers on British qualifying films in production in 2015. Only 1 per cent of executive producers were women of colour. Furthermore, only 16 per cent of the films had more women executive producers than men, and an enormous 61 per cent that had no women executive producers at all. Moreover, even when women hold senior positions, Gail McGuire's (2002) research reveals that women receive less instrumental help from their network members, whereas BAME men were only discriminated against due to structural disadvantage, that is, when they obtained positions with more status, they received the same amount of help from their networks as white men do. More recent research (Fang 2015) revealed that even when women have the same background and education, the same access to seniority, and spent the same amount of time networking, the biased way that they are perceived meant that they receive far less chances to advance than the men doing identical levels of networking.

Looking specifically at screenwriters in the United States, Denise and William Bielby's use of quantitative data built up over many years puts them in a very powerful position to look at the career progression of women. They conclude that women are 'encountering an impenetrable glass ceiling' (Bielby and Bielby 1996, p. 256). Most strikingly, they have been able to track the data for earnings to determine whether there is a trend towards the breaking down of gender barriers—what they call the model of declining disadvantage, or whether women continue to be discriminated against and never make up the gap in their earnings compared to their male peers (the continuous disadvantage model). Or worse still, that successful employment has more impact for men than for women and the gender gap actually increases as both gain experience (the cumulative disadvantage model). It is disappointingly predictable that they find the worst case scenario is true: cumulative disadvantage is apparent in the data and there is no evidence of declining disadvantage that might have indicated that the situation for women was improving.

So women screenwriters suffer disadvantages at every stage in the employment process, and informal, networked, and clubby recruitment process serve men better. Having been a part of these processes in the UK film industry for many years, I found it really difficult to understand how this happened in practice. Everyone I knew was very nice, open and polite, seemingly egalitarian, and apparently focused on finding the best work, as my participants articulated above.

> Nobody is sexist, how could you be? (Nicola, employer)

Yet, anyone who has experienced these processes also knows that whilst they are amicable and often enjoyable on the surface, they are also fraught with the likelihood of disagreements about the value of people and projects, and finding a match with someone is very rare:

> …you're sort of going through thinking 'oh did I say the right thing? Did I pitch the right thing?' you know 'maybe they didn't like what I pitched, but they liked that'. All that sort of emotional energy that you expend, but often that's part of work I suppose because you're analysing 'did I pitch my idea in the right way?' because so much of it is that kind of thing were you suggest the wrong, it could be anything, just a stray word that made their face fall. (Usma, screenwriter)

> …I really hate going out and doing a general meeting. It's my least favourite thing in the world to do so I avoid it. I did a few of them when I was starting out, because otherwise my agent would have been cross with me I think. But I made it very clear, not in the meetings I hope, but with my agent that I really didn't like doing them. (Rachel, screenwriter)

There's an agent who sent me a script once and I told the agent I wasn't terribly taken with the script, and she took it very personally, thought I was challenging all of her taste. (Frank, employer)

Were women finding it harder than men to make productive creative connections at these meetings? Either way, I set out to understand exactly how these gendered biases and exclusions were apparently going on right under my nose. The rest of this chapter will seek to unpack exactly how UK film labour market practices and discourses limit opportunities for women screenwriters, even in an apparently egalitarian creative industry such as UK film production and finance, where overt sexism is rarely deemed acceptable behaviour.

Understanding the Gendered Outcomes of Informal Recruitment Practices

I think I probably don't get as many meetings as the male writers I know who seem to get meetings all the time (Usma, screenwriter)

A dominant discourse shared by employers and screenwriters and used to account for the unpredictability of career opportunities is the idea of the film industry as a meritocracy and the notion that 'talent will out'. This phrase refers to the commonly held belief that if you have any talent or ability, you will inevitably be recognized by the film industry and a successful career will follow, and that those that have had success have been chosen based on merit alone:

… there's a side of me that also feels very irritated by people who say there should be more women, there should be 50/50, because for me it has to be ultimately based on merit. (Eloise, employer)

This was also often related to the view that the selection of projects and screenwriters is based on 'what the market wants'—that is, what sells:

I don't think there will ever be a really self-conscious 'oh we really, really need to be favouring' – you know, I don't think we'll get to a point, because there's a commercial imperative, so I don't think there will ever be a place of active, positive discrimination. (Nick, employer)

However, some of the screenwriters did express opinions that suggested they did not believe good work was always recognized:

... there is no point in railing against the people that make these decisions because a lot of people don't – wouldn't – know a good screenplay from a bar of soap to be totally honest. (Catherine, screenwriter)

As I have demonstrated, this discourse of meritocracy allows the speaker to justify not taking action to redress inequalities—as can be seen in the quotes earlier from Nick and Eloise.

Another repeated discourse attributed to apparently neutral market forces was the desire for 'experienced' writers, with a demonstrable track record:

I would rather pay more money to Simon Beaufoy to write a screenplay, or Frank Cottrell Boyce or Abi Morgan, people we have relationships with but who are at the top of their game. I'd rather pay more money to those people because I think it's got a better chance of getting made, than what you might call a second tier writer, who simply isn't going to get there. (Ian, employer)

Increasingly, the smaller you are as an independent, the bigger the writer that you have to net (Laura, employer)

Everyone involved, the studio, the financiers, the cast are looking for that level of comfort that an experienced writer will bring to the table. (Nick, employer)

This preference supports arguments that cumulative disadvantage may be the reason for continued gender inequality in the film industry (for example, Faulkner and Anderson 1987). With women not being employed in key roles in sufficient numbers, they have less experience and credits when the next opportunity comes along. However, the recent report from the Writer's Guild of Great Britain (Kreager and Follows 2018) found that after having their first film made, men screenwriters were 39 per cent more likely to have a second feature made than a woman screenwriter. In addition, cumulative disadvantage does not explain why employers talked about the contradictory and apparently endless search for 'new talent', or 'the next big thing':

...that sort of slight wrestling match between those bigger names who I'd ideally like to get to but they're always invariably unavailable for a really long time, and discoveries that you might find. (Vanessa, employer)

Discovering talent is kind of a sexy part of the industry. (Jo, employer)

Somehow, this search for the new keeps turning up writers who fit the existing mould of white, middle- or upper-class men. In order to account for this, I have identified how two key discourses of 'risk reduction' and 'trust' in the talk of employers of screenwriters can function to present exclusionary practices as benign, and even as a 'logical' and 'rational' response to the high risk of making an expensive creative product. In this way, discrimination and inequality are upheld by mechanisms that are accepted as good business practice, leaving little room for any requirement to improve the industry's equal opportunity record.

Creative work takes place in a context of high risk, where the financial cost of the product must be paid out while profit is still uncertain (McKinlay and Smith 2009). Each product is a unique, speculative endeavour in which the usual supply/demand dynamic is reversed and there is huge uncertainty about whether anyone will actually buy the product (see Hesmondhalgh 2007, for a full discussion on how cultural industry companies respond to the perceived difficulties of making a profit). My interviewees repeatedly described a common solution that film producers can utilize, in order to attempt to attract investors to the risky prospect of a new film: employing key creative personnel who are known in the industry and have a track record. However, the difficulty in assessing an individual's contribution to the success of past projects (Bielby 2009) creates two distinct recruitment practices that were frequently referenced by my research participants.

The first of these methods is to identify screenwriters who are trusted by recognized authorities, most commonly either individuals with recourse to significant film finance or producers with prominent success:

I heard this person that everybody respects loves this new writer, so it can only mean that they're great. (Eloise, employer)

We've got good relationships with Working Title[2] so we talk to them, ask their advice, who they think is good. (Colin, employer)

The other practice repeatedly referred to by the research participants is a reliance on people they already know. This clearly resonates with research carried out by Susan Rogers (2007), which found that 50 per cent of writers of British films had a previous working relationship and 42 per cent had a personal relationship with the producer, director, or production company responsible for their hiring. This most commonly occurs when screenwriters who have been identified by the previous method are unavailable or unattainable, but is also significantly observable in the discussions of those employers who fall into the previous category of recognized authorities, for example:

> But you know a lot of our work comes from relationships that exist. (Yvonne, employer)

> In the first instance – there will be a handful and it really only is a handful of you know, really tried and tested writers that we've generally got pre-existing relationships with, have worked with before and have probably produced films with, you know, people that we know, people that we trust. They will make their way onto the list in pole position and then we will comb through the lists and try and find someone who might have written in that genre before, might have some experience, might be of an age where it would make sense and then we'll look at TV writers, sort of new and interesting voices and so we'll put some sort of new or leftfield ideas on – and then we'll generally just go to [Man Screenwriter] [laughs] or [Man Screenwriter]. (Nick, employer)

Identifying these two related discourses reveals that screenwriters need to be in a personal or professional relationship with one of the key financiers or successful production companies to stand the best chance of being hired in the film industry. The employers who spoke to me showed little if any embarrassment about the reliance of the industry on 'who you know', which suggests the practice is both accepted and legitimized, and indicates that—in this world—contacts are extremely important:

> It's a small, incestuous world. (Vanessa, employer)

> It's a guy I've known for a long time. (Eloise, employer)

> I think we've been a little bit reliant on people finding us or being recommended, and us going to a fairly small pool of usual suspects. (Jo, employer)

This practice of sticking with people you know well is even proposed as a productive way to manage a potentially vast pool of interested candidates by small companies with limited resources. This is not a new concept, nor one particular to the film industry:

> The problem facing the employer is not to get in touch with the largest number of potential applicants; rather it is to find a few applicants promising enough to be worth the investment of thorough investigation. (Rees 1966)

Attributing responsibility to risk-averse financiers who want a writer with a track record, and the subjective nature of creativity and creative relationships, it is easy for employers to believe they are 'gender blind'. However, academic research in other fields has already called this assumption into question—most notably the 'blind' auditions which opened up symphony orchestras to women musicians (Goldin and Rouse 2000). So it's possible to say with confidence that the evaluation of creativity is not always as objective as it may appear to be to those doing the evaluation. Recently, there has been a wider acceptance of this notion in both film and wider culture, with talk of 'implicit bias' and organizations such as the British Film Institute (BFI) and the BBC requiring personnel to undertake unconscious bias training (Singh 2014). Whether this proves to be sufficient to influence equality of opportunity has yet to be proven.

Meanwhile, how can screenwriters form these key relationships with one of a small number of influential people? More specifically, for the purposes of this chapter, how does this reliance on the friendship and favour of selected individuals become gendered? From my research, I have identified some key areas, although they are as problematic as they are helpful to wannabe screenwriters.

Trust and Homophily

So he approached my business partner. They were next door neighbours. This is how it happens. (Jay, employer)

When asked what made for a good relationship with a screenwriter, the most frequent answer I was given by the employers I interviewed was 'trust'. Trust was mentioned 96 times in my conversations, and by 24 participants, for example:

Natalie: What do you think makes for a good relationship with a screenwriter?
Kate: I think for me it's about trust.
Vicky: I think trust. I think you always know when you've got, when you're working with a writer that trusts and likes you.
Rob: There's total trust, okay?
Jo: Trust, trust, trust, trust, trust.

This was something the experienced screenwriters also appeared to be aware of:

> I think they need security because it's a terrifying thing to hire somebody really young on a wing and a prayer. (Jo, screenwriter)

> I think honesty and trust are absolutely crucial (Catherine, screenwriter)

However, the employers do not demonstrate a desire to embrace the vulnerability and risk that is associated with trust as a distinct concept (Mayer et al. 1995) as indeed it is precisely these difficulties that they hope to overcome by finding a screenwriter whom they feel they can trust. The concept of trust in their discourses is closer to the notions with which it is commonly conflated: cooperation, confidence, and predictability (Ibid.). Confidence and predictability fostered through familiarity were apparent in the participants' understanding of trust:

> You've got to be able to trust that person. (Natasha, screenwriter)

> … we kind of knew each other very well and we'd spent a lot of time together developing the project so she trusted me. (Jo, employer)

Indeed, those employers who didn't specifically mention trust in regard to working relationships drew on closely aligned notions of respect, honesty, collaboration, openness, and loyalty. However, women as well as people of working class or BAME groups are not given equal access to employment in the UK film and television industries precisely because they are not trusted by the industry establishment who are still most frequently white, middle- and upper-class men (see Grugulis and Stoyanova 2012). Rosabeth Kanter's ground-breaking study of gender at work, *Men and Women of the Corporation* (1977, p. 49), argues that in 'conditions of uncertainty', people fall back on social similarity as a basis for trust. More recently, Lauren Rivera's (2011) study of elite employers in America similarly found that employers seek criteria in prospective employees that mirror their own history.

Every film is a unique product and must be marketed to potential audiences as such. Veteran screenwriter William Goldman (1983) famously said of the film industry that 'Nobody knows anything', referring to the impossibility of predicting the success of creative work. There is a great deal of uncertainty about which films will find an audience sufficient to make a profit, and most films never do. At the point of screenplay commission, this uncertainty is at its greatest. The conditions prevail for those involved to want to work with others who are most like them, who are more likely to share cultural references and to pull together around decisions.

> Making a film is really hard, and so if you set out on the journey with some-body who you just don't quite get on with … (Vanessa, employer)

> It's an instinctual thing when you talk to them, you've got that connection to them, and you feel like when you're discussing a project it can progress in the right way. (Colin, employer)

A reliance on homophily provides the employers with the desired conditions to trust those that they are employing, but a lack of awareness of its contribution to their recruitment processes masks the way such subjectivity upholds the inequality of gender, race, and class in key creative positions.

As I discussed in Chap. 2, homophily is the extent to which two individuals in a network are similar and can be understood as the tendency for people to want to associate with those they feel they are most like. Interpersonal similarity increases ease of communication, improves predictability of behaviour, and fosters relationships of trust and reciprocity (Ibarra 1993). People's networks have a strong tendency to contain others who are similar along multiple dimensions, including gender, age, ethnicity, and sexuality (Blau 1994). This supports the evidence that networking is an activity that excludes (Christopherson 2009; Grugulis and Stoyanova 2012). Burt (2002) argues that 'network closure facilitates sanctions that make it less risky for people in the network to trust one another'. As we have seen earlier, the film industry relies on such small networks and such vague and shifting entrance points that it is often necessary to have a relative working in the industry in order to kick-start your career.

Women need additional advocacy to foster trust in potential employers (Ibid., Rivera 2011). Herminia Ibarra (1992) demonstrates that women are less likely to be friends with those who can help their careers, primarily because of the lack of women in senior and influential roles. Networking for work is a relatively unconscious act where job information is often passed on through social process rather than purposefully designed occasions (Blair 2009; Granovetter, 1995). Many of the research participants talked about the mutual backgrounds, long-term relationships, and shared social circles of those they work with:

… sometimes you meet a writer socially between drafts. (Frank, employer)

[Man Producer] and [Man Screenwriter] are very good friends. (Vanessa, employer)

[Good screenwriters are] I guess the kind of people you want to sit in a pub with for six hours. (Kate, employer)

My sample, which was artificially weighted to create a gender balance not reflected in the reality of the film industry, contained discussions of homophily between women as well as men, for example:

… we don't have a similar background or anything but the fact that we both have a female sensibility (Jo, employer)

But with men continuing to far outnumber women as producers, executive producers, and directors of films (Cobb et al. 2016), the film labour market is likely to be much more biased. Indeed, the prevalence of women employing women in my sample suggests that those who are working are finding a large percentage of opportunities through other women and perhaps are not so trusted by men:

I've only worked with one male director. (Natasha, screenwriter)

All three of my feature films were directed by women. All three produced by women. (Catherine, screenwriter)

My research supports Denise Bielby's (2009, p. 239) claim that in the film industry, 'high levels of risk and uncertainty' turn stereotyping and discrimination 'into everyday business practices'. This chapter is an attempt to challenge the symbolic violence (Bourdieu and Wacquant 1992) of discourses of 'meritocracy' so prevalent and embedded in the creative industries that they are accepted and seen as legitimate even by those who benefit least from them. By studying the recruitment and working lives of feature film screenwriters, it is possible to identify mechanisms that work to uphold gender and other inequalities, even when those processes are not conscious or deliberate by those taking part. The results potentially have wider application in other creative professions, and indeed in other labour markets, where more formal recruitment systems have been repeatedly shown to operate as facades for parallel and powerful informal recruitment practices that are the key to the best and most lucrative jobs (Granovetter 1995).

I have shown that where conditions of high risk and uncertainty prevail, individuals use risk reduction strategies in their recruitment processes such as a reliance on the opinions of trusted or powerful individuals. Those individuals in turn reduce their own perceived risk by working with screenwriters who are known to them either professionally or personally. When an individual's credits or experience cannot be relied upon, the employers turn to homophily to facilitate trust. In an industry where social and educational capital have more weight than formal qualifications and there is no one set route to 'getting in', recruiters use homophily and shared habitus to enable them to feel confident in their choices. Objective, or even subjective, evaluations of work are claimed by my participants, but they also indicate that recommendation, either personally or in the form of multiple commissions, is frequently used as security, even for new writers. While white, middle- to upper-class men still dominate decision-making positions in the film industry, this in turn upholds the status quo and these powerful men are able to draw on the established discourses discussed here to present exclusionary practices as logical, understandable, and indeed, good business practice. One of the questions raised by my findings is why we still see others of a different gender, ethnicity, class, age, sexuality, or indeed physical ability as so different that we find it difficult to trust them. This is something I will return to in the final chapters. Before that I consider how motherhood is discursively positioned amongst my research participants and analyse the potential costs of maternal assumption to women seeking a screenwriting career.

NOTES

1. Less than 10 per cent of all jobs advertised with flexible working conditions pay over £20,000 full-time equivalent. The best paid part-time jobs are negotiated by individuals in full-time positions (Timewise 2017: Key conclusions).
2. Working Title is the company behind such successful films as 'Les Miserables', 'Notting Hill', 'Four Weddings and a Funeral', and 'Frost v Nixon'. See http://www.imdb.com/company/co0057311/ for a full list of their credits.

REFERENCES

Banks, Mark. 2007. *The politics of cultural work*. Hampshire: Palgrave Macmillan.
Bielby, Denise D. 2009. Gender inequality in culture industries: Women and men writers in film and television. *Sociologie du travail* 51 (2): 237–252.
Bielby, William T., and James N. Baron. 1984. A woman's place is with other women: Sex segregation within organizations. In *Sex segregation in the workplace: Trends, explanations, remedies*, ed. Barbara F. Reskin, 27–55. Washington, DC: National Academy Press.
Bielby, Denise D., and William T. Bielby. 1996. Women and men in film: Gender inequality among writers in a culture industry. *Gender & Society* 10 (3): 248–270.
Bielby, William T., and Denise D. Bielby. 1999. Organizational mediation of project-based labor markets: Talent agencies and the careers of screenwriters. *American Sociological Review* 64: 64–85.
Blair, Helen. 2000. Active networking: The role of networks and hierarchy in the operation of the labour market in the British film industry. *Management Research News* 23: 20–21.
———. 2001. 'You're only as good as your last job': The labour process and labour market in the British film industry. *Work, Employment and Society* 15 (1): 149–169.
———. 2009. Active networking: Action, social structure and the process of networking. In *Creative labour: Working in the creative industries*, ed. Alan McKinley and Chris Smith, 116–134. Hampshire: Palgrave Macmillan.
Blair, Helen, Susan Grey, and Keith Randle. 2001. Working in film–employment in a project based industry. *Personnel Review* 30 (2): 170–185.
Blau, Peter M. 1994. *Structural contexts of opportunities*. Chicago: University of Chicago Press.
Bourdieu, Pierre. 1984. *Distinction: A social critique of the judgement of taste*. Cambridge, MA: Harvard University Press.
Bourdieu, Pierre, and Loïc Wacquant. 1992. *An invitation to reflexive sociology*. Chicago: University of Chicago Press.
Burt, Ronald S. 2002. The social capital of structural holes. In *The new economic sociology: Developments in an emerging field*, ed. Mauro F. Guillén, Randall Collins, Paula England, and Marshall Meyer eds, 148–190. New York: Russell Sage Foundation.
Campbell, Karen E. 1988. Gender differences in job-related networks. *Work and Occupations* 15 (2): 179–200.
Christopherson, Susan. 2009. Working in the creative economy: Risk, adaptation, and the persistence of exclusionary networks. In *Creative labour: Working in the creative industries*, ed. Alan McKinlay and Chris Smith, 72–90. Hampshire: Palgrave Macmillan.
Cobb, Shelley, Linda Ruth Williams and Natalie Wreyford. 2016. Calling the Shots: Women working in key roles on UK films in production during 2015.

https://www.southampton.ac.uk/cswf/project/number_tracking.page. Accessed 26 Mar 2018.

Creative Skillset. 2010. Women in the creative media industries. http://www.ewa-women.com/uploads/files/surveyskillset.pdf. Accessed 14 Apr 2018.

Cromie, Stan, and Sue Birley. 1992. Networking by female business owners in Northern Ireland. *Journal of Business Venturing* 7 (3): 237–251.

Fang, Lily. 2015. Your Rolodex matters, but by how much depends on your gender. Knowledge Instead. https://knowledge.insead.edu/career/your-rolodex-matters-but-by-how-much-depends-on-your-gender-3862. Accessed 14 Apr 2018.

Faulkner, Robert R., and Andy B. Anderson. 1987. Short-term projects and emergent careers: Evidence from Hollywood. *American Journal of Sociology* 92 (4): 879–909.

Franks, Suzanne. 1999. *Having none of it: Women, men and the future of work.* London: Granta.

Gill, Rosalind. 2002. Cool, creative and egalitarian? Exploring gender in project-based new media work in Europe. *Information, Communication & Society* 5 (1): 70–89.

———. 2014. Unspeakable inequalities: Post feminism, entrepreneurial subjectivity, and the repudiation of sexism among cultural workers. *Social Politics: International Studies in Gender, State & Society* 21 (4): 509–528.

Gill, Rosalind, and Andy Pratt. 2008. In the social factory? Immaterial labour, precariousness and cultural work. *Theory, Culture & Society* 25 (7–8): 1–30.

Goldin, Claudia, and Cecilia Rouse. 2000. Orchestrating impartiality: The impact of "blind" auditions on female musicians. *American Economic Review* 90 (4): 715–741.

Goldman, William. 1983. *Adventures in the screen trade.* New York: Grand Central Publishing.

Granovetter, Mark. 1995. *Getting a job: A study of contacts and careers.* Chicago: University of Chicago Press.

Grugulis, Irena, and Dimitrinka Stoyanova. 2012. Social capital and networks in film and TV: Jobs for the boys? *Organization Studies* 33 (10): 1311–1331.

Hesmondhalgh, David. 2007. *The cultural industries.* Los Angeles: SAGE.

Hochschild, Arlie, and Anne Machung. 1989. *The second shift: Working families and the revolution at home.* New York: Penguin.

Ibarra, Herminia. 1992. Homophily and differential returns: Sex differences in network structure and access in an advertising firm. *Administrative Science Quarterly* 37: 422–447.

———. 1993. Personal networks of women and minorities in management: A conceptual framework. *Academy of Management Review* 18 (1): 56–87.

Jones, Candace. 1996. Careers in project networks: The case of the film industry. In *The boundaryless career: A new employment principle for a new organizational era*, ed. Michael B. Arthur and Denise M. Rousseau, 58–75. New York: Oxford University Press.

Kanter, Rosabeth Moss. 1977. *Men and women of the corporation.* New York: Basic Books.

Kreager, Alexis, and Stephen Follows. 2018. Gender inequality and screenwriters. A study of the impact of gender on equality of opportunity for screenwriters and key creatives in the UK film and television industries. *The Writers Guild of Great Britain.* https://writersguild.org.uk/wp-content/uploads/2018/05/Gender-Inequality-and-Screenwriters.pdf. Accessed 13 June 2018.

Macdonald, Ian W. 2010. So it's not surprising I'm neurotic the screenwriter and the screen idea work group. *Journal of Screenwriting* 1 (1): 45–58.

Mayer, Roger C., James H. Davis, and F. David Schoorman. 1995. An integrative model of organizational trust. *Academy of Management Review* 20 (3): 709–734.

McGuire, Gail M. 2000. Gender, race, ethnicity, and networks: The factors affecting the status of employees' network members. *Work and Occupations* 27 (4): 501–524.

———. 2002. Gender, race, and the shadow structure: A study of informal networks and inequality in a work organization. *Gender & Society* 16 (3): 303–322.

McKinlay, Alan, and Chris Smith, eds. 2009. *Creative labour: Working in the creative industries.* Hampshire: Palgrave Macmillan.

Randle, Keith, and Nigel Culkin. 2009. Getting in and getting on in Hollywood: freelance careers in an uncertain industry. In *Creative Labour*, ed. Alan McKinlay, 93–115. London: Palgrave.

Rees, Albert. 1966. Information networks in labor markets. *The American Economic Review* 56 (1/2): 559–566.

Renzulli, Linda A., Howard Aldrich, and James Moody. 2000. Family matters: Gender, networks, and entrepreneurial outcomes. *Social Forces* 79 (2): 523–546.

Rivera, Lauren A. 2011. Ivies, extracurriculars, and exclusion: Elite employers' use of educational credentials. *Research in Social Stratification and Mobility* 29 (1): 71–90.

Rogers, Susan. 2007. British Films: who writes British films and how they are recruited. UK Film Council. http://www.bfi.org.uk/sites/bfi.org.uk/files/downloads/uk-film-council-writing-british-films-who-writes-british-films-and-how-they-are-recruited.pdf. Accessed 26 Mar 2018.

Singh, Anita. 2014. BBC staff take 'unconscious bias' course to encourage more diverse recruitment. *The Telegraph.* https://www.telegraph.co.uk/culture/tvandradio/bbc/10794205/BBC-staff-take-unconscious-bias-course-to-encourage-more-diverse-recruitment.html. Accessed 14 Apr 2018.

Steele, David. 2013. Succes de plume? Female Screenwriters and Directors of UK Films, 2010–2012. http://www.bfi.org.uk/sites/bfi.org.uk/files/downloads/bfi-report-on-female-writers-and-directors-of-uk-films-2013-11.pdf. Accessed 17 Apr 2018.

Timewise. 2017. Timewise Flexible Jobs Index 2017. https://timewise.co.uk/what-we-do/research/flexible-jobs-index-2017/. Accessed 14 Apr 2018.

CHAPTER 5

The Impact of Motherhood on Screenwriters

So for me, the baby is now, the baby will be six weeks on Thursday so actually it was my biggest fear was coming out of the hospital I was like 'How
am I going to work? How am I going to work?' It was horrible. (Tessa,
screenwriter)

There is 'one factor that above all leads to women's inequality in the
labour market – becoming mothers' (Commission for Equalities and
Human Rights 2007, p. 66). It's difficult to talk about women and work
without talking about childcare. The same is not true of a discussion of
men and work, and this is still one of the most obvious difficulties to be
managed by working women, even those who choose not to have children. In the UK film industry, only 14 per cent of women have children
compared to 40 per cent of men (Creative Skillset 2009, p. 9). In the
population as a whole, 74.1 per cent of women with dependent children
under 19 are in employment (Penfold and Foxton 2015). Policymakers,
and indeed mothers themselves, often talk about the desirability of flexible
labour to accommodate family responsibilities (See, for example, Cranfield
and Working Families 2008; Creative Skillset 2010; Timewise 2015). As I
have discussed, creative work has been shown to offer an exemplary case
study for flexible labour markets. However, although there is a growing
body of research interrogating the continued absence of women in creative professions, there is little of the academic literature that critically
examines the reasons for gendered outcomes in relation to motherhood.

© The Author(s) 2018   111
N. Wreyford, *Gender Inequality in Screenwriting Work*,
https://doi.org/10.1007/978-3-319-95732-6_5

One of the main reasons for this oversight is the lack of women with children who are actually working in the creative industries, which makes it difficult to capture the data about them. Whilst I do not wish to suggest that motherhood is the only, or even primary reason for continued gender inequality in creative work (see Gill 2014), in this chapter, I hope to problematize the idea that flexible working offers a solution to the difficulties of balancing children and work. This argument has potential application outside the creative professions, and highlights the necessity of a wider recognition of society's need for a supply of people as well as products. My research underlines the need for real-life solutions that are in line with feminist concerns about unrecognized maternal labour: solutions which challenge the perception of a man's life cycle as the norm in the world of work and bring into the workplace a greater understanding and accommodation of the demands and responsibilities of parenting.

In the second half of this chapter, I explore some of the key features of flexible creative labour and analyse how my participants' talk exposes the difficulties presented when combining these aspects of working life with caring responsibilities. I assess the costs of freelance, project-based work, informality in recruitment and work cultures, and the so-called creative freedom of escaping a 'nine-to-five' office environment. Before I come to that, however, I first examine how parental responsibilities are understood as gendered in the way that workers in the UK film industry discuss women and family life. I identify key discourses that are frequently drawn upon to establish this inequality as incontestable, such as women as natural nurturers of children, and show how they work to position women as less than ideal for screenwriting work.

The view of women as inevitable mothers contributes to an unfavourable perception of them in the work place. The potential of women to have children, and the associated disruption to their career, can lead to *all* women being perceived as less worthy of investment—of time, of career advice, of promotion, and even of pay (Fitt and Newton 1981; Groysberg 2008). Key writing on gender, work, and organizations has drawn attention to how women are positioned as less-than-ideal workers (Acker 1990; Franks 1999; Kelan 2009). While gendered assumptions prevail, it is difficult for women to overcome 'the stigma of motherhood' (Wajcman 1998, p. 46). In my interviews, motherhood was cited as one way to understand the lack of women in screenwriting and other professions:

I just can't see what it is, apart from childcare. (Rachel, screenwriter)

I think because women have babies that's a big part of it. (Fiona, screenwriter)

The only explanation that makes even a little bit of sense to me and if you're happy for me to suggest that women as primary carers of children make up a statistically significant portion of the people you're talking about. (Will, screenwriter)

Ros Gill (2014) contends that motherhood has become the acceptable way to talk about the lack of women in creative industries, and this certainly seemed to be confirmed by my research. In this chapter, I explore how film industry discourses about women position them as less-than-ideal workers because of their potential to have children, and how this is naturalized and accepted by those who work in the UK industry. I highlight the penalties of this maternal assumption for women wanting a screenwriting career, and show how women have difficulties taking up the subject position of committed, creative worker:

'The question of who brings up the kids has a material effect on all women's careers.' – Beeban Kidron, director, *Bridget Jones: The Edge of Reason*. (Cochrane 2010)

It was common amongst my participants to present motherhood as a natural instinct for women. In a key discourse, women were repeatedly positioned as both *wanting* children and *choosing* to devote their time to 'nurturing' them:

...possibly it's traditional to see the female partner of the relationship as the one that does the nurturing, while the man does the hunter-gathering and female screenwriters can buy into that as much as anyone else. (Frank, employer)

Women are better nurturers. They are hard-wired to look after their offspring. (Lance, screenwriter)

A lot, it happens a lot. You know, they might want to be a film producer but then they fall in love and that's all gone. They just decide they want to have children so they give it up. And men don't have to make those choices. (Pippa, employer)

> I've asked this question of people 'why are there so few female directors?' the answer to that might even strike a chord with you 'they get married and have families and it's more than a full time job'. (Rob, employer)

Despite feminist attempts to question the homogeny of the category of 'woman' (most notably (Butler 1990)), it is still very difficult for anyone presenting themselves as a woman to avoid the assumption that they will at some point become a mother, and will subsequently devote a substantial part of their time to looking after that child or children.

By framing motherhood as a natural instinct of all women, any adverse effects on a woman's career as a consequence of having children is understood as being part of her individual choice and therefore not something to be addressed more widely by the film community. The idea that women might be treated differently simply because of their potential ability to have children was not frequently discussed in my interviews. However, Yvonne spoke of her desire to support other women to have children and how it was a concern not always shared by those she was working with:

> That's easy if you're a woman to help other women. [Allow them to] Take time off, help them feel protected, welcome them back in at the rate they want to come back in. And make them feel it's completely normal to feel exhausted and screwed up about it for a long time until they're settled into it for what they want. I love that. That's easy. What's harder is getting the rest of the world who are co-financing your films to actually engage with that. (Yvonne, employer)

There is wider evidence to support the notion that women might be treated differently in the workplace simply because of their potential to have children. In Margaret Wetherell, Hilda Stiven, and Jonathan Potter's ground-breaking investigation of discourses of final year university students around gender and employment opportunities, one of the young men suggested:

> I suppose you can always see how an employer's mind will work, if he has a choice between two identically qualified and identically, identical personalities, and one is male and one is female, you can sympathize with him for perhaps wondering if the female is not going to get married and have children and then there's always the risk that she may not come back after, she may well do, a lot of women do, but uh I don't know he may well decide that the risk is not worth taking. (Wetherell et al. 1987, p. 62)

In their study, eight of the ten women students thought that juggling a career and children would be a problem for them, while all of the men students hadn't considered it a problem. Although this particular study is now 30 years old, the quotation above clearly echoes some of the comments about women, marriage, and children in my interviews. In addition, more recent reports suggest that women are still viewed as being more responsible than men for the care of children. In a 2014 survey of Harvard Business School Graduates (Ely et al. 2014), for example, three-quarters of the men expected that their partners would do most of the childcare, and indeed, many more of them reported this as a reality, as well as around 50 per cent of them expecting that their careers would take precedence over their partner's. In a rare example of candour, one salesman in Boris Groysberg's article on 'star' women who work on Wall Street confessed:

> Say there are two analysts, John and Joanne – equally smart, equally good analysts, both in their late twenties/early thirties, both spend 14 hours a day at work. The day is only 24 hours long, so I have to allocate my time intelligently…Who is most likely to stay at the firm? Based on my experience, I have to say John. Joanne is going to get married…she might decide to have children…Is this not rational? It's just the way the business is. (2008, p. 78)

Screenwriter Corrine explained to me that she had not wanted to take the time to have children for fear of getting 'out of the loop' and being seen as a 'one-film wonder'. Emma also mentioned a fellow screenwriter who had made a choice about children:

> I read one interview with her recently where she basically did not, decided not to have a second child in order to maintain her screenwriting career. It's in black and white. (Emma, screenwriter)

When considering what is accomplished by discourses connecting women with childcare, Janet Smithson and Elizabeth Stokoe (2005) have argued that:

> It is in the on-going construction of social categories (such as 'professional worker', 'breadwinner', 'woman') and the activities and characteristics people link to them (like 'working all hours', 'caring', 'looking after children') that is central to the perpetuation of gendered assumptions and practices. (pp. 152–153)

In addition, they explain, the more established a categorization and link, the more natural it appears and therefore the more invisible the construction. The capacity for biological motherhood has become intrinsically linked with a corresponding predisposition to nurture and care for others that is widely accepted as an essential part of being a woman. This was clearly demonstrated in my interviews with the UK film industry workers:

> God, we're generalizing and it's so embarrassing, but women tend to be quite good at nurturing. (Eloise, employer)

> Is there a nurturing aspect to this development side and women can feel drawn to that? Nursing a baby through production. (Jack, screenwriter)

> I'm sure you've got the statistics, people go 'oh there's lots of female producers. They're nurturing. Producing is a nurturing thing.' (Laura, employer)

Conversely, men were firmly positioned as not being responsible for childcare:

> With a man he's not looking after kids, he's not suddenly going to ring you up, can't deliver because somebody's ill, some kid's ill, you know? (Vicky, employer)

> I've spoken to male writers who, as I say, are definitely very good at saying 'the wife and kids have to not bother me for the three weeks I'm working'. (Frank, employer)

Certainly there was little discussion of men having to compromise as a result of having children. Many were even explicit in suggesting that looking after children wasn't a problem that men faced:

> ...men tend not to take as much share of bringing up the children. That is a sort of shackle on, generally, across the whole of it women just generally have a bit less time. (Pete, employer)

> That's the reason I'd love to be a man because actually I'd love to marry a woman who'd have kids for me and I could have that but I could go to work. (Pippa, employer)

The associated disruption to a woman's career was generally talked about as something to be expected and accepted, closing down possible discussions of whether this was fair, necessary, or indeed alterable:

> ...obviously women's life is different to men's life because, well not all of them, but a substantial amount of them are going to become mothers and there's no question that that has a huge impact on your career and what you can do and what you can't do. (Eloise, employer)

> I'm not saying women aren't committed but we've got all this other stuff going on and as you get older you do have children. (Emily, screenwriter)

Some women screenwriters had a rationale for their responsibilities for childcare that was framed as practical, with no recourse or acknowledgment of the role of gender norms in creating these different life narratives:

> I feel like because I'm the person who manages to work from home, that I should be the one who does the juggling (Emma, screenwriter)

> I think the fact that we've got children is the reason why I've allowed myself to be in a position where my husband is supporting me. (Fiona, screenwriter)

The impact of being taken out of the workforce for several years, or having to make compromises in your career was disarticulated by a discourse that actually worked to suggest that women could simply start or return to a screenwriting career once their children had grown up:

> Well I started writing probably when he was ten. (Catherine, screenwriter)

> ...once they reached the age when they could go to school by themselves and come back by themselves I thought 'fantastic! I'm going to have so much more time, I'm going to be so much more productive' (Rachel, screenwriter)

> Some female writers don't really start emerging until their kids have got to a certain age – you've got Jane Goldman who is somebody who has sort of waited for the kids to grow up before really throwing herself into the work (Frank, employer)

This discourse fails to take account of mothers who need to earn money during the earlier years of their children's lives and suggests a degree of unacknowledged privilege for successful screenwriters, reinforcing the class advantage discussed in earlier chapters. Jane Goldman, in particular, the screenwriter of *Kick-Ass* (Vaughan 2010), *X-Men First Class* (Ibid., 2011), and *The Woman in Black* (Watkins 2012), amongst others, is exceptional in many ways. She is married to Jonathan Ross, a successful television personality who reviews films and interviews film directors and actors for a living. It is therefore possible to assume that she had some advantages when it came to getting introductions into the film world, and that she was also not reliant on earning an income whilst establishing her screenwriting career. Using Jane Goldman as an example of what is possible for women screenwriters fails to acknowledge that most women with children do not have her social or economic capital.

There were two men screenwriters that I talked to that did have some significant childcare responsibilities. Tony, in particular, found it very difficult to carry on working whilst being a caregiver:

Tony: I was [first child]'s primary carer and I was writing then, and it was very hard, totally hard.
Natalie: How were the hours broken down? When did you write?
Tony: [silence]
Natalie: Did you feel like you weren't getting enough time?
Tony: I wasn't getting enough time. And if it happened again, you know, the way I write now, before when I was younger it was an hour here, an hour there, you can get away with that. Now, it's whole days, into the evening, so how that's going to work out, I've no idea. That's why you've got to be paid properly.
Natalie: So have you not been in that situation since having [second child]?
Tony: No.

Robert found it less of a struggle since his child was of school age by the time he took over as her primary carer, but relied on help from his family:

My daughter's uncle lives around the corner so he tends to stay here then and do the childcare while I'm away.

The implication is that many parents who have responsibility for childcare can struggle to find adequate time to complete their work, especially when the children are small. Like all wage labour in a capitalist system, creative work relies on someone else to take care of domestic chores and responsibilities. However, my research supports the idea that men may not suffer from the same assumptions by potential employers as to their commitment or priorities, or have to juggle work and childcare as frequently as women. As Mark Banks and Kate Milestone (2011, p. 75) convincingly demonstrate, men and women have become 'more intensively ascribed with essentialized gender characteristics and the language of biological necessity', in order to justify the continued division of labour along gendered lines as not only necessary but desirable by individuals.

Whilst it may be a feminist ideal to break down gendered assumptions and problematize the idea of difference based on biological and essentialist notions, the reality for most women is that their potential to become mothers will be likely to affect assumptions made about them, and the reality of becoming a mother will have a significant effect on their career and earning potential. This is not the case for the vast majority of men who become fathers. Many of my participants, men and women, had explored ways to combine childcare responsibilities with the demands of work, with varying degrees of success, but all of them are actually working in the UK film industry. What of those whose voices are not captured because they have not been successful in finding a way to make it work? Might they account for some of the missing percentage of women screenwriters? In the second half of this chapter, I will explore in more detail the features of screenwriting work that make it particularly difficult for those with caring responsibilities. Before that, however, I want to look at how these gendered assumptions, so resonant of feminist critiques of the enduring breadwinner model of work, might make it more difficult for women to position themselves as the ideal screenwriter.

DEMONSTRATING COMMITMENT: THE IDEAL SCREENWRITER

As I discussed in detail in Chap. 2, a common way that UK film workers identify suitable candidates for screenwriting work was through indications of their commitment to writing.

> They don't actually want you to have a life. (Screenwriter, Creative Skillset 2008, p. 8)

This was evidenced through the ways that they demonstrated that writing took precedence over all other parts of their lives. By talking about working long and unsociable hours, screenwriters are able to position themselves as creatively driven in a way that is understood as stemming from natural talent. This discourse of the driven and committed creative individual has the effect of excluding anyone with other responsibilities or demands on their time. It is therefore very difficult for women with children to present themselves as ideal screenwriters.

Although men may have children, and some of them may be struggling to find time to work, the dominant perception that women have an instinct to nurture, as discussed in the previous section, is *perceived as being at odds* with a commitment to a creative profession. Screenwriters are frequently discussed in my interviews as needing to put themselves and their work ahead of family life:

> I know a writer that locks himself in his room and has nothing to do with his wife and children for the three weeks he wants to focus on something. He seems to be very good at cutting himself off that way. (Frank, employer)

> I think they can then use that as an excuse to say 'I really need my independence to be a writer, because I can't cope with this' whereas women don't tend to do that. Women don't normally walk away from their kids and say – well there have been examples – but on the whole they would try to work around the kids, whereas I think men are more likely to say 'you don't understand I'm a genius and my whole future's being buggered up by having to take little John to football.' (Freddie, screenwriter)

As can be seen by these examples, the two discourses of the need for solitude to be creative and women as more natural nurturers of children than men are very much tied together in UK film workers' talk.[1] Stephanie Taylor (2011) has shown how women struggle to position themselves as exemplary creative workers due to the conventional requirement for women to be other-oriented. In my examples, the use of this gendered assumption is that the speakers can argue that it is an apparently natural association rather than an unfairly gendered division of labour, which in turn exempts them from acknowledging the sexism in their talk, and of recognizing that something needs to change.

Some of my women participants described differences they observed between their own attitudes and those of their men partners when it comes to juggling work and family responsibilities, although notably, these real women are also working, unlike the women imagined by Frank and Freddie earlier:

> I do think there's quite a difference watching my husband. I will go to work, go to a meeting and there'll still be in the back of my head 'I need to get home by five because really I need to make sure the nanny can get home on time and the kids need their tea and I need to get them to do their home-work.' And that's all going on in the background and I don't think men – I think there are probably a few men who do that – but most of them don't. (Emily, screenwriter)

> Yes of course, it's that whole guilt thing you have about leaving your kids and you're the one who's emotionally committed to them but of course the man is too. My husband just went away for four months to (city) to make this TV show and he was miserable, he hated it, but he did go. If I'd been offered it I would never take it in a second. But he goes away all the time for his work. (Nicola, employer)

These differences in concern for the children and related responsibilities are due to the socialized expectations of men and women as breadwinners and caregivers, respectively, rather than due to any intrinsic disposition (Banks and Milestone 2011; Taylor 2011). Both Emily and Nicola seemed to be aware of this but still found it difficult to escape the roles expected of them:

> I find separating home and work quite difficult. I do have childcare luckily and a husband who will step in when needed but I think it's also a mental thing. I do find it hard to separate myself from my kids' social calendar. I'm still organizing play dates for them while I'm trying to juggle everything. And I think there still is that expectation on women to be perfect at every-thing. I think it's a social construct now that we have to be great mothers but it's still there. We have to bake the cakes, we have to organize play dates, practice the violin, do everything so well, oh and yeah there's this thing called a job and you have to be brilliant at that as well. And it's exhausting. You eventually think I can't be bothered and it's usually the job that goes because the kids can't. (Emily, screenwriter)

> You know I've got an amazing husband but I do everything to do with the kids, I'm organizing all of their lives at the same time as doing my job, at the same time as – and he's a brilliant dad, but why doesn't he know when their half terms is? We all get the same emails. I had a big row with him the other

day he said 'when's half term'? I said 'I wrote it in my diary why didn't you write it in your diary?' And I think it's just a massive gender thing and it's the way society is and it comes up in every industry. (Nicola, employer)

In these examples, there is a discourse of women as the default parent, the person responsible for staying on top of the many and varied demands of family life and for whom 'the scope and volume of managing this many lives and details comes with a surprisingly huge emotional and mental exhaustion that is unique to the default parent' (Blazoned 2014). It is difficult for women to escape the role of having primary responsibility for children and family life, even when they are employed. There is practical and emotional work for women to do as they take on the burden of ensuring their children's activities live up to the child's and society's expectations, remembering commitments and continuing to smile as they juggle everything. On the other hand, Hannah, whose work had meant her spending some time away from her child, described how 'you do end up feeling a bit guilty', something none of the men I interviewed admitted to feeling. It seems that for many mothers, they are never completely off-duty.

This discourse indicates the continuance of invisible women's labour that can disadvantage women in the workplace. Indeed, even in the course of this study, I found it difficult to articulate the many responsibilities that I experienced which arose from being the primary carer for my children. To talk about chores and childcare hardly seems to scratch the surface, as illustrated by Nicola and Emily earlier. I felt this keenly in my own life whilst trying to complete my research. The inability to ever be free of thinking, planning, remembering, and carrying out the associated responsibilities, from booking dentist appointments to buying presents for children's parties, and the affective labour involved in smiling at the school gates, and patiently putting aside your own work to help with homework or just give a consoling cuddle has not been sufficiently documented and requires further investigation outside the scope of this book.

In most professions, it is a challenge to balance the needs of the workplace with the needs of children and this burden still falls most frequently on the shoulders of women. Even when an employer has an Equal Opportunities Policy, much of the work done by it is often to try to help women fit into jobs and professions constructed around a man's life cycle (Liff and Cameron 1997; Smithson and Stokoe 2005; Wajcman 1998).

Measures such as part-time, flexible hours, and maternity pay attempt to accommodate the need for women to bear and raise children but also clearly put women in the position of feeling their needs don't match those of the employer. Workers doing less than full-time hours are seen as less desirable and less worthy of pay and promotion. According to Women Like Us, an award-winning organization that helps women find work that fits with their new needs after having children, part-time work is overwhelmingly associated with low pay. Only 3 per cent of vacancies in London are for part-time roles paying over £20,000 full-time equivalent (Stewart et al. 2012, p. 6). Judy Wajcman argues when organizations write their Equal Opportunities Policy 'by leaving full-time work as the dominant option ... [they] construct part-time work not merely as different but also as inferior' (Wajcman 1998, p. 27). Just like they were in my interviews on screenwriting labour, part-time hours are seen as a sign that the worker isn't fully committed to the job. In a post-Fordist labour market, employers appear to have become even more paranoid about their ability to get their money's worth from employees:

> ...new employment relations still require the performance of a breadwinner mentality. This mentality is characterized by an individualized worker who can focus on work full-time. (Kelan 2009, p. 1172)

Some screenwriters do take on other work to support their career, but this is more difficult for women who have caring responsibilities:

> And therefore they are not really at liberty to say 'I've got a MacJob for half a week so I can write the rest of the time'. You know, they're doing other things, important things. (Pete, employer)

In fact, very few workers, inside and outside the UK film industry are able to get away with just 'full-time' hours—with work frequently bleeding into the evenings, the early mornings, and the weekends, particularly with the nature of mobile technology and international relations across different time zones. Work on film productions is often acknowledged as involving excessive hours:

> I thought I'd be able to go back ... and I'd kind of do a nine to five day. And then they weren't able to keep the job within those hours. (Production Manager, Creative Skillset 2008, p. 11)

However, although screenwriting work is not as constrained by location or time frame, my screenwriters often described working in a similar extreme manner:

> No, no regular hours, even on the job I'm doing, as we know I'm supposed to have regular hours and then it all goes crazy. (Usma, screenwriter)

> ...if my deadline is looming and I can maybe do three all-nighters in the couple of weeks preceding. I've done that loads of time. So how many hours is that? 24 hours in some days possibly? It's not, with breaks obviously for food or tea or whatever but you are nevertheless working 18, 19-hour days. (Catherine, screenwriter)

> There were late night phone calls, there were trips out to Germany, there were trips up to London, there were suppers missed, and so on and so on (Will, screenwriter)

Jobs, and workers, are seen as gender-neutral concepts although in reality Joan Acker has shown that 'both the concept of "a job" and real workers are deeply gendered and "bodied"' (Acker 1990, p. 150). She argues that the abstract worker is expected to have 'no sexuality, no emotions and does not procreate' (Ibid., p. 151), which helps to reproduce the idea that work is gender neutral but in reality:

> Women's bodies – female sexuality, their ability to procreate and their pregnancy, breast-feeding, and childcare, menstruation and mythic "emotionality" – are suspect, stigmatized and used as grounds for control and exclusion. (Ibid., p. 152)

At the same time, men 'need not be involved in, or affected by, equality measures' (Liff and Cameron 1997, p. 36). Judy Wajcman (1998 p. 11) convincingly demonstrates that managerial jobs 'position women as the problem and accept men's life experience as the norm'. My research demonstrates that this argument is equally applicable to freelance creative work. Wajcman also observed the benefit that men receive in the workplace when they get married, and especially when they have children. There is an associated assumption that their wives will stay at home with the children, which means that these men are perceived as being freed from other domestic responsibilities that might burden the single man— such as shopping for groceries, keeping the house clean, and waiting in for deliveries and repairs. With someone else to take responsibility for these chores and more, men are perceived as being freed up to focus on work, thereby presenting as a more committed employee. Career women with children, however, can face the opposite assumption that they are bringing less to their jobs once they are married or have children—even when they remain full time. The belief (and in many cases like my participants, the reality) that women will be doing a 'second shift' (Hochschild and Machung 1989) of work and domestic responsibilities means that they are often perceived as not fully committed to their career, more likely to be running out of the door to pick up children from childcare and to stay at home when children are ill.

> The social construction of 'jobs' already has within it the assumption that workers will be men and that these men will have wives to take care of their daily needs. (Wajcman 1998, p. 39)

One woman film producer who is yet to have children of her own is quoted in the Creative Skillset and UK Film Council Report *Balancing Children and Work in the Audio Visual Industries* (2008) and freely admits:

> I'd rather use a guy who has got no responsibilities and is available all the time…Completely no tolerance policy for me I'm afraid because it directly impacts on my business. (p. 8)

Although these assumptions fail to acknowledge that not all women are mothers, or that not all mothers are in heterosexual relationships and so do not necessarily have a man to 'look after' or are the only ones doing the childcare, what is clear is that women are still struggling with additional responsibilities in greater numbers than men, and that men are less likely to suffer adverse perception from employers.

In my sample, all except two of the men screenwriters had children who lived with them. Four of the women screenwriters didn't have children and three more had children, but they were grown up. Wajcman claims that in order to succeed, women are required to become more like men. The reality for many women is that in order to succeed in many professions, they may find that they need to forgo having children. Some of the women discussed with me how they had made decisions about when and whether to have children in direct relation to their careers, including one participant who spoke sadly about postponing children at a critical point in her career and then discovering that she had left it too late and was no longer able to conceive. One younger woman screenwriter expressed concern about how it might affect her future career:

> I've also spoken to (friends who are writers) who have said 'you won't write anything for the first five years of your child's life because you just won't do it'. You can't get round it, it just becomes too absorbing.... And I wouldn't want to lose that sort of part of myself because that's who I am. (Natasha, screenwriter)

As I outlined in the previous section, only two of my men screenwriter participants had significant responsibilities for childcare, and one of those was a single father with a child of school age. It was far more common for the women screenwriters to discuss how they navigated the demands of childcare.

> I used to have very set hours because when my kids were smaller I used to take them to school and then come home and write frantically until the time when I had to go and pick them up in the afternoon. Um -then when they reached the age when they could go to school by themselves and come back by themselves I thought 'fantastic!' (Rachel, screenwriter)

> When I was bringing him up and I was needing to do childcare, my career was so kind of scrappy that I was actually quite easy to fit in with childcare and in some ways it made, having the discipline of taking him to school and bringing him back, you know, I knew I had to work within those hours so that actually worked out. But no, I wasn't busy enough, I wasn't commissioned enough. (Usma, screenwriter)

> I feel like because I'm the person who manages to work from home, that I should be the one who does the juggling. (Emma, screenwriter)

In direct contrast, the majority of the men screenwriters who had children had a partner who was doing the childcare, and it was clear that this directly enabled them to work:

> I'm very grateful that I can jump on a train and go to a meeting with a director or pitch to a producer or even go to visit the set of a movie that's being made a lot more readily than my wife could in our current arrangement. (Will, screenwriter)

Natalie: Do you get tired of working evenings and weekends when you've got a family?

Jack: Yes it's tiring and deeply stressful because the wife is thinking 'when is this going to bear fruit? When is this going to pay off?' because I'm either working at it in family time or I'm distracted or bad-tempered or anxious or you know. So yeah it takes a toll.

It can be argued that most men (and some women) are required to sacrifice aspects of their personal life, and time spent with their children and families, in order to bear the burden of being the breadwinner and rise up the career ladder.

Creative work, as we have seen, is exemplified by characteristics that potentially offer an opportunity to work around other commitments—for example, working without direct supervision, outside of an office, choosing your own hours, and indeed having gaps between projects. It has therefore been assumed that this is more compatible with childcare responsibilities:

> I would have thought it was easier to be a screenwriter in the industry than a director because that totally takes over your life. If you're a writer you have more control about when you do it and your own schedule, so I don't understand it. (Rob, employer)

> Funnily enough writing is one of the few jobs you can do and be at home with your baby, once you've got over the idea 'I don't even know my name'. (Esther, screenwriter)

In the next section I will attempt to demonstrate the ways in which this ideal not only falls short of reality, but indeed, in an echo of Ros Gill's observations on the continuance of gendered inequality in the creative industries (Gill 2002), it is these very traits of flexibility and informality that make it particularly difficult for those with childcare responsibilities.

THE COST OF CREATIVE LABOUR

> I've got mates who left it and left it and left it and haven't got children. (Catherine, screenwriter)

In this section, I unpack some of the characteristics of apparently 'flexible' creative work to examine how they might disadvantage mothers in particular. Academic accounts have argued that the celebrated features of working in the new cultural industries, such as informality and flexibility, 'are the very mechanisms through which inequality is reproduced' (Gill 2002, p. 86). Creative labour research highlights the general preponderance of certain characteristics, such as long hours and 'bulimic' (Pratt 2000) patterns of working, poor pay, leisure and socializing as work, profound experiences of insecurity and anxiety about finding work, and has also noted the continuance of inequalities along the lines of age, gender, ethnicity, and class. However, consideration of motherhood as a cause of gender inequalities has been given scant attention in the academic literature, let alone how it intersects with other axes of inequality such as race and class.

In UK creative industry accounts, there is some awareness of the difficulties of juggling work and childcare responsibilities (Sinclair et al. 2006, Creative Skillset 2008, 2010), but these are not subject to any critical examination of the gendered assumptions behind these struggles. A report commissioned by the Sundance Institute and Women In Film LA (Smith et al. 2013) interviewed 51 women filmmakers and executives and 19.6 per cent spontaneously mentioned families and childcare as hampering women's careers. The fact that this percentage isn't higher most likely reflects the fact that many of these women will have had to forgo or postpone having children in order to succeed and therefore childcare isn't an issue.

The characteristics of creative labour, as exemplified by screenwriting, cause inequality of opportunity for those with childcare responsibilities, whom I have shown to be predominantly women. Film work is the epitome of flexible work as individuals and small or micro businesses come together for short periods of time on temporary projects and are seemingly free to work when and where they choose. However, it is only because women continue to take responsibility for childcare and the home that men are able to take up these new flexible positions in the creative economy (Adkins 1999). By examining in detail three key aspects of creative work that seemingly offer choice and control to the individual—freelance employment, informality, and working outside an office—we can see how this works in practice. By drawing on existing literature and bringing it into dialogue with film industry accounts from my own research, I demonstrate how these characteristics actually create as many obstacles as opportunities for mothers.

MOTHERHOOD AND MANAGING FREELANCE, PROJECT-BASED WORK

Screenwriters are employed on a project-by-project basis, carry out the majority of the work on their own and are reasonably free, outside of financial considerations, as to where they do that work and when. Surely, this is a profession that is more compatible with looking after children? As Denise Bielby (2009) asks:

> Writing for film and television does not require long-term commitment to a single corporate employer. The work can be done in any setting during hours of the writers own choosing. Shouldn't Hollywood prove the exception to the glass ceiling faced by women in most professions? (p. 247)

Many of my *employer* participants echoed this view of the flexibility of the screenwriting profession:

Gillian: Sure, they might be doing a few other things, like picking up their children [laughs], or doing other readings.
Natalie: So you think they'd have time to do that?
Gillian: Yeah, of course.

Yep, if you've got children at nursery you can write from ten to two or whatever it is. (Pete, employer)

Writing is the perfect career for a woman who has children, because you can do it from home. (Pippa, employer)

My sample—and indeed the film industry as a whole—is made up of a majority of women who don't have children and of course men. This constituency might not be aware of the precise difficulties of balancing work and childcare. Indeed, like successful men screenwriters, successful women screenwriters often have someone else who does the childcare for them. Leading UK screenwriter, Abi Morgan,[2] interviewed for *The Telegraph* (Farndale 2011), describes herself as 'a relatively independent woman who has been able to combine a career with raising a family', but whilst 'the children are around', she also says, 'I have a wonderfully supportive husband [Jacob Krichesfsta]. He's an actor so is often at home.'
My women screenwriting participants had help from various sources, but like Morgan, partners featured prominently:

My husband's cut down on his hours because he's, so he can do more kind of childcare and stuff. (Tessa, screenwriter)

We have a nanny, and my mum. And my husband! ...he works four days so he takes one of the days when I'm not here. (Emily, screenwriter)

...my boyfriend is an actor so his work is similarly flexible. So I sort of feel like, if we did have a child, which we're hoping to do in the next not so many years, that we could kind of work it out. (Natasha, screenwriter)

It is harder to capture the data from those who might disagree with this view of the compatibility of screenwriting with parenting. These screenwriters may indeed have left or never entered the industry for this reason.

Look at all the execs that have left our industry around the time they had children. Why aren't they writing? (Laura, employer)

Laura recognized that she had only managed to balance her own unpredictable freelance career with having a family 'because my partner has a steady job' and wondered what happens when 'there's a man and he's trying to do it and not getting any development money what does he do? If he's trying to support a family?' It seems that for women, flexible working means taking on extra responsibilities, which men are not required to do when they are working in the same way. Women are expected to do the childcare, whatever else they might be doing. However, having children does not seem to prevent men from pursuing a screenwriting career in the same way that it does for women. Interestingly, Laura went on to use class to understand this problem: 'So then you get into class and the whole thing about film producers being trustafarian.' A man screenwriter with children is viewed as needing an additional source of income to support his career while his partner looks after the children. The idea that the man could take on the childcare as do women screenwriters is not even entertained by Laura.

There were examples in my interviews of how care work might not be very compatible with screenwriting:

...they're worried their career will completely stall. (Catherine, screenwriter)

...five thirty to seven in the morning might be at the moment the best I'm going to get (Emma, screenwriter)

Um...at the moment because [child] doesn't really sleep, my brain isn't working that well so I can work till about nine, nine-thirty and then I stop. (Fiona, screenwriter)

Screenwriters interviewed for the UK Film Council's scoping study on women screenwriters articulate strikingly similar concerns:

The difference between your personal choices and your career is a really key one. Women who have kids have time out and time out can be quite fatal. You don't have a guaranteed slot waiting for you to come back into like people in employment do. There is a constant fear of 'if I drop out for a while, will I ever get back in?' (Screenwriter)

You can't suddenly say to the producer, 'From now on I just want to work two days a week.' (Screenwriter)

You need to be in that world. You can't just do it for one hour. So maybe that would be hard for a woman with kids. You need to be able to have at least four hours a day. (Screenwriter)

It's fine if your wife's at home putting the kids to bed, but what are you supposed to do if you are the wife? (Screenwriter) (all quoted in Sinclair et al. 2006, p. 59)

Not all the screenwriters felt the same way:

I think the work environment's wonderful because it's entirely at my own choosing. I get up in the morning and I go to work and then my children come home and I'm here. (Ibid.)

However, the arrangement described in this example only becomes possible once all children are of school age, which could be over six years for a woman who has two children, two years apart. Up until that point, other forms of childcare are needed.

In *Having None of It,* Susan Franks (1999) examines the conflicts between working and childcare responsibilities for women, arguing that flexible, freelance work like that of screenwriting can be difficult to combine with family life. She gives the example of home workers in the clothing manufacture trade who 'are subject to sudden deadlines where they must drop everything and work' just like screenwriters. 'Reconciling this with regular childcare and children's routines can be difficult' (p. 90). Most formal childcare such as nurseries, nannies, and child minders are not available on a supply-and-demand basis.

> That was the big freelance thing in particular about the possibility of the ad hoc, and also long-term childcare about not knowing the hours and not knowing when, or wanting half a day sometimes, and how do you do that, unless you reach the point of having a full-time nanny but not necessarily having the full-time income to support it. (Freelance Worker, Creative Skillset 2008, p. 7)

One screenwriter, who doesn't live in the UK, was considering taking exceptional measures to find childcare:

> ...it sounds awful but there are so many illegals here who love cash jobs, so it's easy to get a Spanish, like, nanny or something who will help you out and like, for a day's work you're going to pay like £50 which is unheard of. (Tessa, screenwriter)

Another based in the UK had managed to find some flexible childcare that accommodated her unpredictable hours, but acknowledged the rarity of this:

> I'm actually really lucky with the child-minder I've had that I arranged a basic with her of two days a week and she is flexible on the other days, so I've always been able to add days. But a lot of child-minders that I went to visit when I was choosing, one said 'I've got these two days available 'cos everything else is full' and that wouldn't have worked for me at all. (Fiona, screenwriter)

The precarity of her situation is passed onto the childminder, who is required to accommodate a varying income. Fiona also acknowledged that she could only cope with the fluctuations herself because she was married to someone who can support her, although this was something she struggled to reconcile with her own identity as a modern, working woman:

> I think before we had children, he was encouraging me to leave my job and become an independent producer and do all the things I wanted to do but I couldn't really get my head round the idea of him supporting me. As soon as we had a child I thought, 'well you've got to anyway because I've got to take these nine months', so now's a good time to let me do that and you just

suddenly understand that all his money is all ours and but it takes a little, it's hard to work that out. (Fiona, screenwriter)

Other screenwriters relied on informal childcare from friends and relatives:

Natalie: And who looks after your daughter when you work?
Hannah: Either my partner, or friends now. It's always been family or friends we've never had any professional help, not with housework or childcare, so it's always been, yeah.

I didn't have family supporting me but I had a really strong network of mates who did. And we sort of got through it. We sort of did. But I do remember thinking 'this is madness. This is a kind of absolute madness'. (Catherine, screenwriter)

If you have preschool-age children, waiting lists for professional services can be long, often up to a year, and fees must be paid for every week, whether the parents are working or not. Clearly, this is difficult if your work is project-based and not permanent. Mark Banks and Katie Milestone point out that 'for employers, flexibility means that workers must give preference only to business priorities and duly contort themselves' (2011, p. 82), leaving little control for the individual worker over when and where they choose to execute their roles. In fact, a comparison of the data from the 2010 Creative Media Workforce Survey shows that in cinema exhibition, all the workers are permanent employees and 43 per cent of them are women. In the facilities sector, where 7750 of the 18,600 jobs are freelance, only 26 per cent of the workers are women (p. 9). Of course these figures don't tell us the nature of these jobs, or what level of seniority or responsibility the women are at, but it is interesting to compare with the fact that all film screenwriters are freelance and only around 20 per cent of them are women (Cobb et al. 2016).

Many of my women participants who have children described difficulties connected to their ability to work. Many were afraid to take any time off due to the precarious nature of project-based work. Tessa described how she felt that she couldn't take a break after having a baby:

I was really scared because I've spent such a long time trying to get momentum to my writing career. And you know I went through periods of really horrible, scary, dreadful poverty. (Tessa, screenwriter)

Fiona describes the particular challenges of creative work and being a young mother:

> With producing it's answering an email here, making a quick call, do this, you can dip in and out of it. With writing, you have got to be in the flow of it. So I'd say in the first six months of my baby's life I didn't write at all. (Fiona, screenwriter)

Hannah, who is a director as well as a screenwriter, described how she kept working through her child's earliest moments and seemed to go to some length to justify it:

> My first feature I was eight months pregnant when I shot it, I breastfed through the edit, having done that, you know, having had a caesarean in between I just thought it was only going to get easier so I couldn't ever find any excuse not to, you know, I couldn't use her as an excuse anyway because it's what I wanted to do and I know she's proud of me and I'm passionate about my work and I just think that's as valuable as anything. (Hannah, screenwriter)

Some women appeared to put themselves through punishing schedules in order to be able to write and have children:

> Emma: I like a regular writing schedule and to be honest what I'm doing at the moment is I think my regular writing schedule might be an hour or an hour and a half from five thirty to seven for four days a week just to, because it will add up.
> Natalie: In the morning you mean?
> Emma: Five thirty to seven in the morning might be at the moment the best I'm going to get.

> I have friends who have children and basically what they have done – their children are much bigger, older now, but what they did in the early days was they would work in the night and then when baby was sleeping in the day they would sleep too. (Esther, screenwriter)

> ...after the kids are in bed at eight after a long day of looking after them, then as soon as they're in bed I turn on the computer. (Fiona, screenwriter)

With working lives like this, is it any wonder, therefore, that women may sometimes not be able to prove themselves as committed as men?

I meet so many women who say 'I want to write an action movie', or 'I want to write a thriller' or 'I want to write this stuff' and I think actually there maybe is a factor, is that I also meet lots of male writers who also say that stuff and if no-one pays them to write it they go off and write it on spec and the female writers three years later they say 'I really want to write a thriller' and you're like 'why haven't you just written one to show you can do it, actually?' (Kate, producer)

These additional responsibilities faced by mothers are made invisible by the naturalization of motherhood, the expectation of total round-the-clock commitment by passionately devoted creative workers and the requirement that women put other's needs before their own 'without protest' (Taylor 2011, p. 13). In the next section, I will examine why finding creative work presents particular challenges for those with children to take care of.

MOTHERHOOD AND INFORMAL RECRUITMENT

[S]elfishness is required and a lack of encumbrance in other parts of your life is required. (Will, screenwriter)

As I have examined the outcomes of informal processes of procuring work in some detail already, in this section, I will simply turn to the specific problems that arise from childcare responsibilities. As I have shown, most individuals working in the film industry are in a continuous process of searching for work, and that process is mainly an informal one done through socializing and making contacts 'on the job'. Clearly, in networking, opportunity is significant, and workers who are the primary carer for young children may not be available for networking events, which often take place outside work hours (Croft 2001; Nixon 2003).

...the writing is actually a very small part of the job, you've got to get out there and sell yourself and that's very difficult to do as most of is it social and in the evenings, and then you've got to pay babysitters, or your husband's got to be at home and he's not home by the time all the events start which is always six o'clock. Why? And it's like really simple things like if they held the event at 8 o'clock – you could go. Put the kids to bed and nip out. So very simple things like that could help. I think you'd see a rise in women at these events if they weren't at six o'clock. (Emily, screenwriter)

Yeah I try to imagine how it should be, like round each others houses until two in the morning, drinking whiskey, smoking cigarettes and arguing over lines and plots and things like that...I actually go to bed around nine or ten. 10pm is late now! (Tessa, screenwriter)

[Good screenwriters are] I guess the kind of people who you want to sit in a pub with for six hours. (Kate, employer)

Karen Campbell (1988) demonstrated that women's networks are restricted when they have young children. There was no correlating disparity for men who start a family. The informal nature of work and recruitment in the UK film industry might seem at first to create a more accommodating environment, but that can be short-lived:

I remember the point when I stopped being able to take [child] to meetings, because he didn't just sit on my lap quietly. (Fiona, screenwriter)

...if you're at home, gonna get married, have kids, that's going to remove you from the world so it's going to be hard to stay focused on this (Jay, employer)

...obviously I'm breastfeeding so it doesn't always work out but I'm just kind of working a couple of hours a day at the moment. (Tessa, screenwriter)

One of my interviewees discussed the difficulty that informal networked recruitment practices can create for mothers who lose their jobs:

Suddenly I was there with no job and income and a child and I couldn't afford childcare – and you sit there waiting for responses and then you find yourself out of the loop, you're not aware of what they're commissioning. (Laura, employer)

A study by Jennifer Starr and Marcia Yudkin at the Wellesley Center for Women (1996) showed that single women entrepreneurs and all men entrepreneurs have a different ability to allocate their time to business activities rather than domestic responsibilities than married women. It is also noteworthy that research shows that women receive less instrumental help from their network members, regardless of the status of themselves or those in their network. Gail McGuire's (2002) suggestion is that women may be perceived as being less worthy of help as they are statistically less likely to be successful than men. It seems likely that the effects of motherhood on a woman's career may be contributing to this:

...career women are well aware that taking up these [maternity] leave entitlements serves to confirm men's view that women as a sex are not suited to managerial work. (Wajcman 1998, p. 26)

However, it is very difficult for individuals to challenge these difficulties or structural inequalities in informal employment processes where there is often no recourse to equal opportunities policies and Human Resources departments, let alone complaints and tribunals.

> We don't even have an HR department. You know, just the way that film companies are managed and run it's all very entrepreneurial, then it kind of grows and it's all a bit ad hoc, lot's of proper, we don't have benefits. So I think that just exacerbates the whole thing. (Gillian, employer)

Indeed, individuals may err on the side of caution, given that informal working cultures shape their own rules of what is considered normative and reasonable, regardless of legality or contractual breaches. (Thomson 2011). Job seekers cannot afford to disadvantage themselves by appearing to require special treatment, particularly in a profession where ability is identified at least partly by the overt appearance of excessive commitment:

> You can pick up people are just not quite committed for some reason. Which could be anything. It could be too busy, could be family stuff, could be other stuff going on in their life, you don't know. I think you can pick up their ambivalence a bit. (Gillian, employer)

A professional and devoted attitude was understood by both the screenwriters and their employers as an attribute of the ideal screenwriting candidate as can clearly be identified in their talk:

> ...from a producer's standpoint you want writers who are punctual, who answer their emails, who do their work quickly. (Patrick, screenwriter)

> ...they're looking for someone they trust to deliver. (Ed, screenwriter)

> ...on a professional level for me there's an element of pragmatism I'm looking for which is about getting the job done and getting the film made (Frank, employer)

> ...you know it's someone who is very willing to collaborate, isn't defensive and is very willing to rewrite and rewrite and rewrite and finds energy to do that. (Laura, employer)

Once again within this discourse, there is an implied suggestion that the ideal screenwriter is free of other commitments, and the use of notions such as 'trust' and being 'willing' again suggest that women may be judged as less suitable simply by their physical ability to possibly, one day, procreate.

MOTHERHOOD AND CREATIVE FREEDOM

Women have children and um, I think that probably brings them to their senses, takes them, yes, just makes it too difficult to try. (Freddie, screenwriter)

In this final section, I want to touch briefly on how working outside a formal nine-to-five corporate environment might differently impact men and women pursuing a creative career. Screenwriters aren't required to work in an office or keep particular set hours. Indeed, they are expected to be working on more than one project at once, as that gives them more cultural capital, which the employers can use to reassure themselves that they've chosen a good writer and to sell the project to other partners. This means that they have the potential flexibility to juggle other responsibilities away from the eyes of their employer who isn't sure when they are working and often doesn't really care:

As long as someone delivers it doesn't matter what they do. (Nick, employer)

No, I couldn't care less. It makes no difference to me whatsoever. They could spend 10 minutes. They could spend 10 weeks. (Paul, employer)

However, it can also lead to an increased difficulty in carving time out for writing work, especially for those who are still trying to establish their career. Far from being viewed as a benefit, working from home was perceived as an obstacle to work for some of the women in my research. As shown earlier, Emma felt that since she was based at home, she ought to 'be the one who does the juggling'. Similarly, Emily attributed her difficulty separating home and work to the fact that she works at home:

You know, I'm there when they come home from school, even though I have an office at the end of the garden, they'll still come and see me when they get home because I'm there. (Emily, screenwriter)

Fiona described the complex dynamics of trying to work with small children:

> At the moment I can only work when [first child] goes to nursery three days a week and I can only work when [second child] is asleep. I take her to meetings and I can do phone calls and things, but if she's awake I wouldn't sit and stare at my computer. (Fiona, screenwriter)

Emma, who writes from 5:30 to 7:00 every morning, claimed that she needed this regular schedule, otherwise 'anything else will take over. You know, projects you're working on for other people, family stuff.' Only when the whole household was asleep was she able to prioritize her writing. Fiona also tried to make sense of the fact that being a mother meant not being able to work directly with the director who was rewriting her screenplay:

> I just can't do anything for the next six months – it's the equivalent of me and he sitting down together and doing the work and I can't – he's in [a different country] and I've got a baby. So, I'm happy to let him do it but I think if I wasn't a producer I'd be finding that really hard. (Fiona, screenwriter)

The men screenwriters with young children didn't express the same concerns. Jack proudly told me that he picked the children up from school on Fridays, even though he was often 'working at it in family time'. Will enjoyed being able to have lunch at home with his wife and children, presumably before returning to his desk. Frank described 'male writers who, as I say, are definitely very good at saying 'the wife and kids have not to bother me for the three weeks I'm working'', whereas Nicola, an employer who has children herself, understood the challenges faced by women screenwriters:

> As a screenwriter you're working from home so 'why can't you pick them up from school?' and 'how come you can't go to this play date?' and I imagine that is quite difficult and screenwriters don't earn a lot of money and if their husbands are earning more money they'll be like with the screenwriting 'should I give it up and look after the kids?' or 'should I do it in the evening?' and if you look after kids you're so tired and the idea that you can then sit down and write after you put the kids down at 8.30, it's so exhausting. (Nicola, employer)

As I have described, even in households where both parents are working, women still find themselves doing the majority of domestic chores. Therefore, chores, like childcare, could be challenging for women who work from home to escape responsibility. Of those who talked about other domestic chores, four of the women I spoke to said that they did 95 per cent or all of the chores, whereas the men were more likely to claim that they were shared ('She might tell you different!' (Ed, screenwriter)). By contrast, many of the women who are working as screenwriters also commonly claimed to be markedly undomesticated and exist without worrying about chores too much:

I live in chaos most of the time (Catherine, screenwriter)

Neither of us are particularly house proud so we probably do the minimum. (Usma, screenwriter)

I'm not very domesticated. (Hannah, screenwriter)

We live in quite a messy house. (Fiona, screenwriter)

This discourse of non-domesticity potentially suggests that doing chores is not terribly compatible with a screenwriting career, although the benefits of this incompatibility were noted by Catherine, who lives alone: 'when I'm on a deadline and then my house is astonishingly tidy because I would rather tidy than sit down and you know, do it.'

The very serious consequence of such gendered approaches to creativity and family life is that for women writers, 'the institution of marriage and family often conflicted with their career path as writers' (Pohlman 1996, p. 21), echoing Stephanie Taylor's (2011) work on artists. Livia Pohlman studied the effect that having children had on 20 contemporary novelists, and her research has notable echoes of my own. Of the nine men writers she interviewed, seven had families by the time they were 30. Their wives provided practical support in terms of childcare and household labour—these men weren't required to see flexible, creative work as a means to juggle these responsibilities, despite the fact that eight of the nine men worked from home. A base of stability allowed them to focus on creative work and eight of the nine had a private den or office in which to work. Conversely, out of the 11 women novelists interviewed, 9 expressed concern that having a family would decrease their productivity and 4 did not have children, 2 of these having made the decision not to have children in order to focus on their career. The women writers with children complained of a loss of freedom, concentration, and time to be creative. They suffered sleep deprivation and a feeling of isolation. In stark contrast to the men writers' experience, the women writers describe their partners' attitudes in terms of tolerance rather than outright support. Most tellingly, perhaps, with Virginia Woolf's voice ringing loudly in our ears, only one of the seven mothers had 'a room of their own' in which to work. Both my screenwriter participants and the women in Livia Pohlman's study find the demands of domesticity, particularly childcare, to be at odds with their writing ambitions, and frequently describe losing valuable time and space to their other 'responsibilities'.

In 1938, Cyril Connolly famously wrote, '...there is no more sombre enemy of good art than the pram in the hall' (Connolly 1938, pp. 109–110). More recently, novelist Maggie O'Farrell challenged this assumption and those anxious to convince her that 'Every baby costs you a book, you know!' (O'Farrell 2003). It's not inconceivable for a woman to have children and a lucrative creative career, but just like women in senior management who have children, they are not in the majority. How motherhood affects creative careers is a difficult problem to research, since first-hand accounts of those working in creative professions like film and novel writing are limited to those who have ostensibly 'made it' and therefore do not allow a framework that can account for those women who are not present, and the reasons for this. Rachel Thomson (2011, p. 16) argues that 'for many the 'motherhood penalty' is a shock faced in relative isolation' and so presents difficulties for those trying to recognize or resolve the issue. Motherhood therefore risks becoming a hidden, forgotten cause of inequalities in the creative industries and indeed in the wider workforce. Maggie O'Farrell's ability to find successful mothers for her article who manage to continue writing, and even flourish after having children calls to mind feminist questioning of the universal commonality within the category of 'woman' (Butler 1990), but fails to take into account the ways that class, degrees of previous success, and indeed age may play a part in who succeeds in juggling these responsibilities and who is lost. The reality for most working women, as I have demonstrated, is that they continue to risk disadvantage in at least three distinct ways linked to motherhood. They will likely be perceived as potential mothers, whether they want children or not, and therefore viewed as less committed and less worthy of investment; they may very well need to make a choice between having children or having a career, unlike most men; and if they do have children, they will most certainly be expected to make personal and professional sacrifices that fathers are not routinely required to make.

In the UK, motherhood and having children is still regarded as a personal choice with little regard to the necessity of a continuing supply of taxpayers to support the needs of an—increasingly—ageing population. Keeping work and family separate ignores this consideration and ensures anyone with childcare responsibilities will have difficulties maintaining the perception that they are the ideal worker for a job—committed and always available. Whilst this clearly has the most impact on women who still bear the burden of most of the childcare in the UK, let us not forget that it also impacts significantly on children and fathers, who are unlikely to see each other as much as they might like. However, whilst this might be deeply felt by individual men, there are few campaigns about men's right to parental leave, and even what there is focuses on women being able to share the responsibilities. Even changes to the law have not resulted in many men seeming keen to join women in balancing work and family life, with only 2 per cent of couples taking up the UK's newly introduced shared parental leave (Gore 2018). In fact, grand*mothers* (not grandfathers) are twice as likely to look after children during the day than their own fathers (Burrows 2013).

The real cost of motherhood risks becoming the forgotten or sidelined aspect of gender inequality in the work place. Whilst women are viewed as naturally nurturing and as prioritizing this over their own creative fulfilment by choice, men are allowed to flourish creatively without compromise when they become parents. This in turn enables a reinforcement of the idea that to be creative, you must be totally committed at the expense of other aspects of life, and anyone unable to demonstrate this single-minded commitment may be viewed as a less-than-ideal candidate for creative work such as screenwriting. In my conversation with him, Patrick attributed his big break to being able to give up his 'day job' and devote himself full time to screenwriting. He describes a producer telling him:

> He said 'look, it's ok, it's good, but you should be doing this full time.' He said 'you're either in or you're out with this game.' (Patrick, screenwriter)

As long as this remains the expectation of employers, and as long as women are positioned as the more natural caregivers of young children, motherhood will continue to present significant obstacles for women seeking careers in screenwriting.

NOTES

1. As a side note, I came across this discourse repeatedly in academia whilst writing this book. As a mother, I can confirm that there are many parallels between the difficulties of film work and the difficulties of academic work. If you are reading this book, I can also confirm that whilst extremely challenging, it is sometimes possible to write and mother over an extended period of time.
2. Abi Morgan is a successful British screenwriter working across television and film. A list of her screen credits can be found at: https://www.imdb.com/name/nm0604448/

REFERENCES

Acker, Joan. 1990. Hierarchies, jobs, bodies: A theory of gendered organizations. *Gender and Society* 4 (2): 139–158.

Adkins, Lisa. 1999. Community and economy: A retraditionalization of gender? *Theory, Culture & Society* 16 (1): 119–139.

Banks, Mark, and Kate Milestone. 2011. Individualization, gender and cultural work. *Gender, Work & Organization* 18: 73–89.

Bielby, Denise D. 2009. Gender inequality in culture industries: Women and men writers in film and television. *Sociologie du travail* 51 (2): 237–252.

Blazoned, Meredith. 2014. The default parent. *Huffington Post*. https://www.huffingtonpost.com/m-blazoned/the-default-parent_b_6031128.html. Accessed 18 Apr 2018.

Burrows, Gideon. 2013. Childcare – Why don't men pull their weight? *The Guardian*. https://www.theguardian.com/lifeandstyle/2013/jul/05/childcare-men-pull-weight. Accessed 19 Apr 2018.

Butler, Judith. 1990. *Gender trouble: Feminism and the subversion of identity.* New York: Routledge.

Campbell, Karen E. 1988. Gender differences in job-related networks. *Work and Occupations* 15 (2): 179–200.

Cobb, Shelley, Linda Ruth Williams and Natalie Wreyford. 2016. Calling the shots: Women working in key roles on UK films in production during 2015. https://www.southampton.ac.uk/cswf/project/number_tracking.page. Accessed 26 Mar 2018.

Cochrane, Kira. 2010. Why are there so few female film-makers? *Guardian*. https://www.theguardian.com/film/2010/jan/31/female-film-makers. Accessed 18 Apr 2018.

Commission for Equalities and Human Rights. 2007. Fairness and freedom: The final report of the equalities review. *The Equalities Review*. http://webarchive.nationalarchives.gov.uk/20100806180051/http://archive.cabinetoffice.gov.uk/equalitiesreview/upload/assets/www.theequalitiesreview.org.uk/equality_review.pdf. Accessed 18 May 2018.

Connolly, Cyril. 1938. *The enemies of promise.* Chicago: University of Chicago Press. Revised Edition (2008).

Cranfield University and Working Families. 2008. Flexible working and performance: Summary of research. https://www.workingfamilies.org.uk/wp-content/uploads/2014/09/Flexible-Working-Performance-2008.pdf. Accessed 18 Apr 2018.

Creative Skillset. 2008. Balancing children and work in the audio visual industries. https://creativeskillset.org/assets/0000/6250/Balancing_Children_and_Work_in_the_Audio_Visual_Industries_2008.pdf. Accessed 19 Apr 2008.

———. 2009. Film sector – Labour market intelligence digest. http://creativeskillset.org/assets/0000/6007/Film_Labour_Market_Intelligence_Digest_2009.pdf. Accessed 17 Apr 2018.

———. 2010. Women in the creative media industries. http://www.ewawomen.com/uploads/files/surveyskillset.pdf. Accessed 14 Apr 2018.

Croft, Martin. 2001. Perfect pitch. *Marketing Week.* https://www.marketingweek.com/2001/03/29/perfect-pitch-2/. Accessed 19 Apr 2018.

Ely, Robin J., Pamela Stone, and Colleen Ammerman. 2014. Rethink what you "know" about high-achieving women. *Harvard Business Review* 92 (12): 100–109.

Farndale, Nigel. 2011. Abi Morgan interview. *The Telegraph.* https://www.telegraph.co.uk/culture/8623286/Abi-Morgan-interview.html. Accessed 19 Apr 2018.

Fitt, Lawton Wehle, and Derek A. Newton. 1981. When the mentor is a man and the protégé a woman. *Harvard Business Review* 59 (2): 56.

Franks, Suzanne. 1999. *Having none of it: Women, men and the future of work.* London: Granta.

Gill, Rosalind. 2002. Cool, creative and egalitarian? Exploring gender in project-based new media work in Europe. *Information, Communication & Society* 5 (1): 70–89.

———. 2014. Unspeakable inequalities: Post feminism, entrepreneurial subjectivity, and the repudiation of sexism among cultural workers. *Social Politics: International Studies in Gender, State & Society* 21 (4): 509–528.

Gore, Will. 2018. No wonder fathers aren't taking up parenting leave. Looking after a baby full-time is much harder than a job. *The Independent.* https://www.independent.co.uk/voices/parental-leave-fathers-dads-not-taking-it-up-harder-than-work-a8206821.html. Accessed 19 Apr 2018.

Groysberg, Boris. 2008. How star women build portable skills. *Harvard Business Review* 86 (2): 74.

Hochschild, Arlie, and Anne Machung. 1989. *The second shift: Working families and the revolution at home.* New York: Penguin.

Kelan, Elisabeth. 2009. *Performing gender at work.* Hampshire: Palgrave Macmillan.

Kidron, Beeban. 2004. Director Bridget Jones: The Edge of Reason. Screenwriters: Helen Fielding (novel), Andrew Davies, Helen Fielding, Richard Curtis and Adam Brooks. Universal Pictures.

Liff, Sonia, and Ivy Cameron. 1997. Changing equality cultures to move beyond 'women's problems'. *Gender, Work & Organization* 4 (1): 35–46.

McGuire, Gail M. 2002. Gender, race, and the shadow structure: A study of informal networks and inequality in a work organization. *Gender & Society* 16 (3): 303–322.

Nixon, Sean. 2003. *Advertising cultures: Gender, commerce, creativity.* London: Sage.

O'Farrell, Maggie. 2003. Is the pram in the hallway the enemy of good art? *The Guardian.* https://www.theguardian.com/world/2003/mar/17/gender.uk. Accessed 19 Apr 2018.

Penfold, Matthew, and Fred Foxton. 2015. Participation rates in the UK – 2014 – 2. Women. Office for National Statistics. http://webarchive.nationalarchives. gov.uk/20160106100617/http://www.ons.gov.uk/ons/dcp171766_398888.pdf. Accessed 18 Apr 2018.

Pohlman, Livia. 1996. Creativity, gender and the family: A study of creative writers. *The Journal of Creative Behavior* 30 (1): 1–24.

Pratt, Andy C. 2000. New media, the new economy and new spaces. *Geoforum* 31 (4): 425–436.

Sinclair, Alice, Emma Pollard, and Helen Wolfe. 2006. *Scoping study into the lack of women screenwriters in the UK.* A report presented to the UK Film Council. UK Film Council. http://www.bfi.org.uk/sites/bfi.org.uk/files/downloads/uk-film-council-women-screenwriters-scoping-study.pdf. Accessed 26 Mar 2018.

Smith, L.S., Katherine Pieper, and Marc Choueiti. 2013. Exploring the barriers and opportunities for independent women filmmakers. Sundance Institute and Women in Film Los Angeles Women Filmmakers Initiative.

Smithson, Janet, and Elizabeth H. Stokoe. 2005. Discourses of work–life balance: Negotiating 'genderblind' terms in organizations. *Gender, Work & Organization* 12 (2): 147–168.

Starr, Jennifer, and Marcia Yudkin. 1996. *Women entrepreneurs: A review of current research.* Vol. 15. Special report. Wellesley: Wellesley College. Center for Research on Women.

Stewart, Emma, David Curtis, Paul Gallagher, Lorraine Lanceley, and Richard Buck. 2012. *Building a sustainable quality part-time recruitment market.* Joseph Rowntree Foundation. https://timewise.co.uk/wp-content/uploads/2014/05/JRF_Findings_Summary.pdf. Accessed 19 Apr 2018.

Taylor, Stephanie. 2011. Negotiating oppositions and uncertainties: Gendered conflicts in creative identity work. *Feminism & Psychology* 21 (3): 354–371.

Thomson, R. 2011. Making motherhood work. *Studies in the Maternal* 3 (2): 1–19. https://doi.org/10.16995/sim.67.

Timewise. 2015. Business case for flexible working. https://timewise.co.uk/insights/business-case-for-flexible-working/. Accessed 18 Apr 2018.

Vaughan, Matthew. 2010. Director, Kick-Ass. Screenwriters: Jane Goldman, Matthew Vaughn. Lionsgate.

———. 2011. Director, X-Men: First Class. Screenwriters: Ashley Miller, Zack Stentz, Jane Goldman, Matthew Vaughn, Sheldon Turner, Bryan Singer. 20th Century Fox.

Wajcman, Judy. 1998. *Managing like a man: Women and men incorporate management*. Cambridge: Polity Press.

Watkins, James. 2012. Director, The Woman in Black. Screenwriters: Susan Hill (novel), Jane Goldman. Sony Pictures.

Wetherell, Margaret, Hilda Stiven, and Jonathan Potter. 1987. Unequal egalitarianism: A preliminary study of discourses concerning gender and employment opportunities. *British Journal of Social Psychology* 26 (1): 59–71.

CHAPTER 6

Being Outnumbered

So for me, the biggest difficulty being a screenwriter is my gender and my race. (Esther, screenwriter)

In the previous chapters, I have explored some of the ways in which embodied capital has an impact on the employment prospects for screenwriters in the UK film industry. Chapter 2 demonstrated that homophily is a key mechanism through which screenwriters are able to establish the respect and trust necessary to secure employment. Chapters 3 and 4 provided evidence of how social similarity facilitates advantage within the film industry's informal recruitment practices. In Chap. 5, I discussed how women are discursively positioned as having different priorities and predispositions from men. Pierre Bourdieu's theories offer a way to link all these contexts of screenwriting work to better understand continued inequality of opportunity. For Bourdieu (1977), an individual's social, economic, and cultural capital, along with their dispositions, taste, preferences, and interests, can be understood as socially constituted capacities that operate at a subconscious level and are embodied in a person in a way that makes them appear natural. Whilst Bourdieu's work focuses predominantly on class difference, this chapter and the next will follow feminist arguments that his ideas are extremely useful for analysing gender. In particular, his concept of the habitus enables an understanding of both how an individual's interests and skills are socially constructed and how (as a result) men and women experience the world differently. People are

© The Author(s) 2018
N. Wreyford, *Gender Inequality in Screenwriting Work*,
https://doi.org/10.1007/978-3-319-95732-6_6

socialized to act in certain ways and their resulting habitus can delimit an individual's potential for action within a field.

The rest of this book draws together all the strands and examines the way Bourdieu's thinking can be usefully applied to understand how gendered inequalities in screenwriting work happen in practice. In this chapter, I explore how habitus makes success more difficult for women screenwriters as they may not be perceived by potential employers to have the right 'feel for the game' (Bourdieu 1990, p. 6)—or indeed may themselves not feel that they fit in to the environments where processes of filmmaking occur as easily as men do. In Chap. 7, I consider how taste is constructed as part of the gendered socialization process and how this leads to discernable consequences for women seeking to make a living in creative professions such as screenwriting. I show how Bourdieu's concepts are useful not only for understanding why there are fewer women screenwriters than men screenwriters, but also why the situation is changing so little despite increasingly widespread acknowledgement of continued inequality.

Although the commonality of the experience of women has rightly been called into question by feminist thinkers (Butler 1990), the difficulty in escaping a gendered identity still means that individuals can experience life as in a multitude of gendered ways. For example, even though many schools now allow girls to wear trousers as an alternative to skirts as part of their uniform, the cut and additional embellishments on trousers sold as for girls (such as flowers on zip pulls or embroidery) will ensure the garments can be differentiated from those labelled for boys (with combat-wear style pockets and often sturdier fabrics). In addition, the wearing of skirts by boys does not yet appear to have reached the same level of acceptability. School shoe suppliers have finally bowed to consumer pressure to stop advertising boys' shoes as hard-wearing and that of girls as pretty, but the removal of gendered labels in stores has yet to undo the binary social programming of parents and children. It is still only a brave child who breaches the proscribed gender norms and risks the policing and ridicule of their peers—and possibly adults. Laura illustrated to me the difficulty of stepping outside expected gendered roles and professions:

> I would welcome more female directors although I worry that some of the women I meet who are super successful feel slightly not true to their own nature, or, it's like they're aping a way of behaviour, perhaps because they think that's the only way it will work. (Laura, employer)

Kate's failure to articulate her understanding of gender differences may reflect the variety of women's experience, but it is also a sign that the way men and women may come to experience the world differently can be subtle and inscribed into everyday actions and interactions in a way that makes it difficult to observe and talk about:

Natalie: Do you think it makes any difference whether you're a man or a woman as a screenwriter?

Kate: Yes. Um – I think it sort of makes a difference in everything in the world [laughs]. I can't sort of define what the difference is.

Pierre Bourdieu's focus on the minutiae of the social world as a site for analysis is helpful in making some of these experiences visible. Bourdieu has rightly received much criticism for his lack of consideration of gender. It has been suggested that he positions sexuality and gender (and race) as secondary to class (Lovell 2000), and that he appropriated the work of French feminist thinkers without acknowledging or citing them (Bilge 2006). However, feminist scholars have begun to recognize the usefulness of Bourdieu's thinking for understanding gender inequality and have sought to extend and build on his theories through a feminist lens. A good—and duly critical—example of the possibilities can be found in *Feminism After Bourdieu*, edited by Lisa Adkins and Beverley Skeggs (2004), which brings together a collection of critical feminist thinking which is 'deploying, recasting, criticizing and extending the abundant theoretical resources his sociology offers' (Bilge 2006). To demonstrate the usefulness of Bourdieu's work to an understanding of gender, I draw in this chapter on Toril Moi's article: *Appropriating Bourdieu: Feminist theory and Pierre Bourdieu's sociology of culture* (1991). Coming from a background in both literature and philosophy, much of Moi's work has explored the interplay of the embodied social, cultural, and psychological aspects of gender with women's writing.

In the article, Moi outlines a way to use a conception of the gender habitus to demonstrate how symbolic violence is used to suppress the very discourse of the experience of women. This is particularly useful in theorizing why women's voices may not be considered as worthwhile as men's and why women screenwriters, and their stories, are not seen on our screens as often:

The right to speak, legitimacy, is invested in those agents recognized by the field as powerful possessors of capital. Such individuals become spokespersons

for the doxa[1] and struggle to relegate challengers to their positions as het-
erodox, as lacking in capital, as individuals whom one cannot credit with the
right to speak. (Ibid., p. 1022)

Gender is understood as socially constructed, something that has to be
learned but is not a fixed set of rules and indeed changes according to
where and *when* you are. In the UK, women no longer have to get their
husband's permission to take out a bank loan, but still may find their but-
tons do up the opposite way to those on their brother's clothes and their
shorts are much shorter and tighter; women may need to keep their knees
together on public transport whilst enduring their neighbour's manspreading.[2] Bourdieu's theory of preferences and skills as socially constructed,
and then naturalized in an individual's habitus, is a useful concept for
shedding light on how both men and women accept gender differences as
natural and unquestionable, even when they are unfair.

The habitus internalizes the structure in which it grows up. Individuals
acquire a sense of 'belonging' or 'otherness' in certain situations that
influences their ability to act entirely freely in their choices. Steph Lawler
(2004) has argued that what gives habitus its power is that the individual
is judged by others not for what they do or have, but for who they apparently are, making it much harder to overcome the perceptions and assumptions of others. I examined how these gendered assumptions and
behaviours inscribed in an individual's habitus can contribute to different
outcomes in the screenwriting labour market. Beginning by looking more
closely at how my participants talked about belonging (or otherwise), I
will show how women are more likely to be both perceived as, and feel
like, outsiders. I will then look more closely at how habitus may impact on
opportunity by examining the importance and the mechanisms of the
screenwriter/director relationship as discussed by my participants.

TAKING PART

People that knew more than me, were more experienced, that were practically always male and didn't seem to care for me very much. And there were
moments when I thought: this isn't the game for me; this isn't the environment for me. (Hannah, screenwriter)

In this extract from our conversation, Hannah articulates how, on
attempting to establish a career in the film industry, she was aware of feeling

different to those already working there. She foregrounds gender as a noticeable point of difference, and links it to the idea that she lacks experience and did not feel welcomed. Bourdieu's concept of the habitus, which he has described as 'a feel for the game' (1990, p. 6) is echoed in her concern that 'this isn't the game for me'. Hannah previously had a long and successful career as a writer in a different medium. Her feelings of being out of place are not about her inexperience as a writer, but about this new 'environment' and feeling like an outsider in it. She isn't alone.

> [I]f you're like a twenty year old all you hear are men's names, and all the big screenwriters and all the big directors. So you just think 'wow, I'm going to go into this industry and it's all guys. Am I ready for that?' (Emily, screenwriter)

'Girls' screenwriter and showrunner[3] Lena Dunham echoes this in an interview:

> I think people don't always recognize that if a young woman is looking at the landscape of Hollywood, what they see are almost only challenges, and so they might say 'that's not where I want to go. I want to go where there's a space for me' (Simmons 2014)

Feeling out of place or unwelcome is not always in response to overt exclusion. As Terry Lovell (2000) argues:

> In modern/postmodern society there are few remaining 'games' ('social fields of practice') fully reserved for men, from which women are formally excluded, although many in which we are not exactly welcomed or taken seriously as players. (p. 12)

Lovell criticizes Bourdieu's theories as being overly structural with little room for individual agency. However, as can be understood from Lovell's own example of Rosa Parks freely choosing to sit in the 'white' section of the bus, the possibility of social transformation is accompanied by significant difficulties for any individual that undertakes it. Individual resistance rarely leads directly to systemic change without the involvement of a larger community. This can help explain why individual women having successful film careers have not changed the overall numbers or attitudes.

Keith Randle, Cynthia Forson, and Moira Calveley (2015) have convincingly demonstrated that habitus is used in the socialization process of

UK film and television labour markets. An individual's habitus is both a marker of already belonging and a product of having internalized the rule of the field. As I have shown, employers looking for assurance in their choice of screenwriter fall back on homophily as recognized through the habitus. Even for individuals who *do* find a way into filmmaking work, making contacts and getting paid, 'details such as who one's friends are, dress codes or accent can all be examined for sociological clues' (Ibid., p. 6). As a consequence, women and those of a working class or black, Asian, and minority ethnic (BAME) social group can find that their access to the most lucrative networks and opportunities is limited (Grugulis and Stoyanova 2012), and their careers are consequently restricted. Film industry outsiders are identified by their habitus:

> They were not the 'right' gender or race, and they did not have the right accents, hairstyles, clothes or backgrounds to join the best networks. Being kept outside these social groups excluded them from jobs. (Ibid., p. 1326)

Creative work is contingent on subjective and situated judgements about what constitutes artistic merit and whose ideas are worth funding and promoting. As earlier chapters have shown, access to creative work is unequally distributed along lines of gender, race, and class, and the recognition of merit and ability is often marked by an individual's position on these axes. Bourdieu's theoretical analysis of the details of social life allows an approach that considers these factors as indicators of power and position.

An awareness of being different or not fitting in due to gender, race, class, dress, social habits, and interests was noticeable in the talk of those of my participants whose backgrounds were *not* typical of the film industry. For example:

> [Y]ou go into a room full of dark-suited men. It could be as hard as that. It could be sort of we've got a choice between this guy – you know people also pick people that they want to have dinner with, you know? And I think maybe a male writer might have more of an air of somebody they can hang out with, go and smoke a pipe with or whatever it is. (Vicky, employer)

> [H]aving a shy writer who doesn't talk at all is perceived as being a problem. Whereas some garrulous, funny, that's really helpful, or entertaining, whatever, that's really helpful, you know. So you get taken out to dinner by the studio and you're witty and entertaining and what have you. (Freddie, screenwriter)

I think it's just a human instinct to work with people that you're comfortable with and you're used to having around and when a young, Indian woman comes in and says 'I'm a film producer', they haven't seen a young, Indian woman producer before. (Pippa, employer)

This awareness is particularly pertinent when viewed alongside a commonly found discourse in the talk of film workers that endorsed the advantages of working with creative partners who share your sensibilities. There were even implications that when this commonality is absent, the film project can suffer:

The projects I've had that haven't worked, I look back on them and there are parts of the problem would be, you know, among other things, your relationship with the producer just isn't right and you're not seeing eye to eye on the project, you're talking at cross purposes, etc., etc. so it just helps, knowing, just knowing that you're on the same page and your references are the same references, that you like the same films, that the vision of project, you've both got the same thing in mind for it, etc., etc., You don't *have* to be friends with them but I find that the two go hand in hand. (Patrick, screenwriter)

Natalie: What makes for a good working relationship?
Paul: Shared sensibility. For starters. I think.

This key to a good working relationship was often expressed as an ability to comfortably spend time together. In this way, the reliance on a shared habitus is disguised and the speakers avoid potentially offensive references to differences of appearance, gender, or background:

[T]he relationship feels better if you're comfortable being in a room together. (Frank, employer)

The Line Producer on [Film] gave me a piece of advice, which I think is genius, which is 'don't ever make a film with people that you wouldn't choose to go on holiday with'. (Frankie, screenwriter)

I guess it's a lot about communication and personality, you know, making a film is really hard, and so if you set out on that journey with somebody who you just don't quite get on with, or who is difficult to deal with, then it can make it so much more painful. (Vanessa, employer)

Indeed the word 'relationship' appears to have a particular discursive function in many of my interviews:

> I form relationships with people and we stick together, not in the way, not in the great way that maybe Paul Laverty[4] and Ken Loach[5] have done, or, you know because that's a fantastic relationship, I don't have a relationship with a director like that and I wish I did, but I do have very, very strong and enduring relationships with producers. (Catherine, screenwriter)

> It's just so much harder if you don't have that relationship with private school producers. (Emma, screenwriter)

> It's two things isn't it? It's the relationship and their idea. (Gillian, employer)

In an informal labour market, having contacts or knowing names is not sufficient to secure work. By using the term 'relationship', my research participants are suggesting something deeper and more meaningful that is sustained over time. In a network culture, multiplex ties—that is, being friends with the person who can potentially employ you—give greater results but are more frequently experienced by men (Ibarra 1992), since men are more frequently found in senior positions with a responsibility for hiring, and homophily is so important in recruitment processes, as I have already shown. Using the word 'relationship' can potentially allow the speaker to convey a sense of being close to their connections and additionally conveying themselves as having the right social capital and habitus.

Many employers described the recognition of shared sensibilities and interests that lead to good work as being instinctive, a kind of subconscious connection:

> I think when you're, it's an instinctual thing when you talk to them, you've got that connection to them, and you feel like when you're discussing a project it can progress in the right way. (Colin, employer)

> [Y]ou just have a connection. (Gillian, employer)

> There were various things that we just connected on and kind of understood each other. (Jo, employer)

There were also references to 'chemistry', in a use normally associated with romantic relationships but similarly viewed as instinctual and corporeal as opposed to a conscious intellectual judgement:

[S]o I think for me I try to see if that chemistry works (Jay, employer)

I think a lot of it is just chemistry, you know, you meet someone you feel like you're on the same page, you get on with them. (Pippa, employer)

This naturalizes and individualizes a selection process which favours others with similar backgrounds, and shows how an understanding of the habitus could draw attention to potentially unconscious processes of discrimination, more popularly referred to as 'unconscious bias' or 'implicit bias' (Banaji and Greenwald 2013).

However, in my research, this need for social similarity was not limited to the people involved in the process but also extended to *the creative work itself*. In this extended extract from my conversation with Nick, he describes how the success of HBO's television series *Girls* (Dunham 2012) had sparked a desire at his production company to work with a young woman screenwriter in the UK:

> We get a directive from [head of company] saying, 'Okay, we need to be writing, we need to be working with hot young female writers, writing truthful, honest stories about what it means to be a modern woman'. Well, you know, no shit Sherlock, but those sort of writers, you know – male or female – who can write something urgent and Zeitgeist-y don't grow on trees, but we'll have a look. So we did actively throw the net out to find that female writer in the UK, and we talked about ideas and worlds for stories and, heard some interesting pitches and had some interesting discussions. Ultimately, nothing that came through the door was quite right for – you know there's a difference between [head of company] saying something like that and putting his money where his mouth is. You know 'that's just going to be a story about peace-loving hipsters and periods'. Well, what d'you bloody want? (Nick, employer)

In this description of his search to fulfil the request of his superiors, Nick clearly highlights the difficulty of going out to 'discover' a new, young screenwriter who is writing stories that can connect with a young audience. The anecdote is a good example of the way that film workers consider that there are special individuals out in the world who are waiting to be discovered by them, as described in Chap. 2. However, the final reaction, and in particular the reference to menstruation by Nick's boss (or at least in Nick's interpretation of his boss' reaction), indicates a gendered judgement of the women screenwriters' story ideas. Menstruation is something that both can be viewed as a natural part of being a woman but is socially positioned as a shameful bodily function that should be kept hidden—although it is clearly not possible for those women who have or do menstruate to physically 'hide' from it. It is men who do not want to see the reality of it. The suggestion is clear: Nick's employer—who is a man—found the women's story ideas *distasteful*.

I will explore the importance of differences in taste in more detail in the next chapter. What is important here—in the context of habitus and employment opportunities—is the way this example shows how difficult it can be for an individual to understand the importance or appeal of an experience which is not familiar to them, and how this can work to disadvantage women when so many senior positions are held by men. Indeed, this suggests to me that the reason that so many stories apparently made for and by women are romances (Smith and Cook 2008) may have more to do with this being a point of intersection of women's experience in a heterosexual man's lifespan. These are the stories that a man in a commissioning or financing role can understand. Dating, love, and romantic relationships, then, are not in fact what *women* are interested in, but the only moments that *heterosexual men* are interested in women. Although many of my participants considered relationships and romance to be the topics that women are most interested in writing and watching, if there really was a space for women to explore their particular concerns and experiences, would it not include many more films about motherhood, for example, the menopause, or indeed menstruation?

Similarly, BAME writers in my study bemoaned the assumption that they must always write about crime, poverty, and urban housing estates, perceiving that these are the only times when white people are interested in BAME stories and doesn't in fact reflect their own experience and interests:

> I think for BAME talent the perception is that we've only got one story to tell, that is 'drugs and guns and council estates'. And I know very little about council estates or drugs or guns so the difficulty BAME writers have is changing the perception of what they can do and changing the perception of yes there is a working class and those stories absolutely should be told, but what we'd like to see is a much wider palate of life. (Esther, screenwriter)

> One of the most interesting and alarming conversations I had in the last few years was with [white head of public funding body] – she had read a few things

of mine but was kind of confused, she couldn't understand, I think, why I wasn't doing socially-worthy, social realism stories about immigrants. Why I was doing genre, why I had written a romantic comedy and the thing I was pitching was a psychological horror. It was almost like, you know, why are you doing this? (Usma, screenwriter)

There is a strong suggestion that commissioners may find it hard to recognize the value of stories that do not reflect their own view of the world. Whilst it might be tempting to attribute this to perceptions about who wants to write what, I believe my research suggests this ignores a significant problem in film work: the commissioners and financiers find it hard to see the value of stories told from a perspective that they don't share. Women and BAME writers are othered and not allowed to tell the same kinds of stories as white men. Hannah described facing such a lack of understanding in her work, which seems strongly rooted in a lack of shared habitus:

Suddenly we were having those kind of debates about how the characters would behave and I have to say that really shocked me – I was kind of 'what do you mean you don't understand her?' 'Yes, but I don't get that', 'Well, yes, you're not a woman, so maybe that's all right if you don't get it.' (Hannah, screenwriter)

As suggested by this quotation from Hannah, this lack of comprehension of lived experience also extends to the types of roles women are allowed to embody *on screen*. Some of my women participants talked about struggles they had while developing their screenplay projects with men collaborators. They spoke of conflicting ideas about the truthfulness and believability of women characters:

[O]nce we get onto the female roles and I'm going 'no, no, no, she wouldn't say that!' and they're going 'why not, but that's my fantasy woman?' and I'm saying 'but that's really disgusting and I'm not going to put it in my script!' (Emily, screenwriter)

I've actually been, I worked with a writer/director on a film and we got shortlisted for a fund, and this was quite interesting, she'd written this female lead woman who was a fighter, you know she was spunky, she was the kind of girl, she had it all. She was good looking, she was confident, and I'm interested in you! And all the male readers of that script passed on it. Every male reader said: 'I hate this'. 'I hate this woman'. 'I don't want to see her made'. And it was quite a shock to my system because I'm like 'God, I LOVE her', what a great character! She's someone I could never be, and a lot of women are going to identify with her. I mean this woman was like a lot of male characters, a lot of guys, so you know she was spunky, she's got something to say and she's got attitude. And it was quite interesting I think all her, I think one of her mentors was a male writer/director and he said 'I hate this character' and she immediately, as the writer, froze and was totally devastated. (Vicky, employer)

In this last extract, it is clear that Vicky, a woman producer, shared an interest in and appreciation of her woman screenwriter's character. However, even men working in one of the lowest paid positions, as script readers, feel able to express subjective gendered opinions as valid criticisms that might influence the future of the project and the confidence of the screenwriter. One woman screenwriter even described being asked by a man director to remove the women characters and turn the lead into a man:

> He wanted me to take away every female character in the script. He wanted to turn [male character] into one of the biggest characters in the script. And I turned round and I was like: No. I'm not doing any of these changes. Everyone loves the script. I've won like a fucking award for this script. I'm not doing it. (Tessa, screenwriter)

She said that she was subsequently removed as the screenwriter on her own story for refusing to make the changes. In this way, the commissioning and script approval/acquisition process edits out certain types of stories, characters and is likely to have an effect on the careers of those who write them, as it did for Tessa.

Some women screenwriters expressed criticisms of certain men screenwriters' portrayal of women characters, perhaps for similar reasons. Gender seen through the eyes of another does not always seem to match up to lived experience.

> And there [are] some male writers who continually put out these hackneyed ideas of women. Writers like David Hare, who create women who are incredibly sexy and high up in politics – right? And she can run in heels. Well done her. And very sexually available. You know there's just, it's not real. This woman doesn't have a dishwasher to empty, I don't believe in her. (Natasha, screenwriter)

It's very interesting because everyone lauded him at first because he could write such amazing female characters and he was always writing about females on the verge of their sexual awakening or something. And I read his stuff and I was like 'this is kind of gross'. One, I don't relate to it at all, about like, weird stuff like, you know, girls talking about their nipples looking like raspberries or whatever and I was like 'I don't relate to that. I don't think it's very accurate'. And I think the people who were going on about how he's writing so well about teenage girls are actually men. (Tessa, screenwriter)

I think in most of the stuff that I will – I don't mean this pejoratively but what I call 'the boy's programmes' – I think that women aren't often very well drawn in those and they are functional and sometimes they are what another friend of mine calls 'a cipher in a dress'. (Esther, screenwriter)

All of these examples are discussing subjective judgements of character and illustrate how the value or merit of different components of film scripts changes depending on who is assessing them. The gendered dimensions of this process are difficult to ignore:

[I]t's also one of the frustrating things when you go in and you're sitting in a room with a really interesting woman exec who obviously on a personal level wants to nurture and encourage you but you know the minute she goes out of the room she's got to pitch you and your project to people who just don't care. (Usma, screenwriter)

The women screenwriters clearly feel that they can provide a more authentic depiction of women's experiences, but these examples also indicate that it is difficult for them to convince men employers of this. The screenwriter's power is likely to decrease as the film progresses from development to production:

Writers are the bottom of the rung, sadly. They start off at the top of the rung, then by the time the film's made, they're at the bottom [laughs]. You know most of them say 'I won't even get a ticket to the premiere'. (Vicky, employer)

The creative control of a film will at some point be transferred to the director, who usually assumes authorship or at least is viewed as having the ultimate 'vision' for the final piece. In the second half of this chapter,

I examine the role of the director in the development process and the power they have in selecting which films get made—and which screenplays are left on the shelf. I will demonstrate how this problematizes the desire for shared habitus in creative collaborations, or at least indicates the necessity of increased diversity in decision-making roles.

THE DIRECTOR'S CHOICE

[Y]ou just know watching half of them 'that's got to be written by a man' you just know it is and it's just something completely instinctive that, I dunno, either it gets on your nerves, or alienates you or you just don't get it, you wonder what's funny about that? And you know a woman wouldn't have written it. And maybe that's a generalization but you feel it and often it turns out to be true. So I think there are differences in subject matter, interests and maybe even taste. (Hannah, screenwriter)

The film workers that I spoke to described the director as critical to securing the necessary finance to get a screenplay made into a film:

[T]he director's going to get the film made – film is the director's medium, the person who drives it forward. (Ian, employer)

This country is absolutely director driven, it's not writer driven. – That's going to be the first question 'Who's the director?' (Jay, employer)

I find it very difficult to green light a film without a director I'm excited by. (Yvonne, employer)

Attracting a director and being able to work with them was seen as an important part of a screenwriter's job:

[B]ecause a film is a director's medium in inverted commas, you've got to get in with your director and you've got to give him a script that he really wants to do and that he feels passionate about. (Patrick, screenwriter)

Well the writer and the director they've just got to gel. They've got to understand each other's language and desires and have the same vision. (Emma, screenwriter)

This last quotation from Emma suggests that similarity of habitus might play a role in facilitating this crucial relationship and note that Patrick doesn't hesitate to use masculine pronouns for his imagined director. Others echoed Emma's thoughts about commonalities being important when collaborating with others on a film:

> [T]here was an affinity in terms of the tone they were going for and the vibe they were going for. (Eloise, employer)

> I guess it's just easier if you're a guy dressed the same as all the other guys that come in. You've got two ticks before they've even read your work. (Vicky, employer)

For the women I interviewed, this could often lead to positive opportunities and experiences with other women:

> One instance where the development process was fantastic, utterly fantastic and again, interestingly enough I was working with a group entirely with women (Catherine, screenwriter)

> I have a woman who is my sort of script editor if you like – and my first assistant director is a woman and we three girls, we are so safe with each other, we are so secure with each other, and it's so creative and we laugh and we diminish the tension a lot of the time. (Hannah, screenwriter)

However, given the lack of women in all key creative and decision-making roles in the UK film industry, the opportunities for this shared habitus are likely to be limited, as we have already seen in regard to hiring practices. For a screenwriter, it seems social similarity to the director might once again be an important factor in the success of their creative product. More than this, as I have described earlier, a screenwriter's habitus may also influence their subject matter and style of writing.

Directors are unlikely to have the time to make more than one film a year. They therefore make very careful decisions about which projects to undertake.

> I think the director they look at it and think 'am I going to immerse myself in this for the next year? This is going to be my life. Do I want it to be my life? Do I want to talk about it for days?' (Jay, employer)

There was a clearly identifiable discourse in my interviews of the director needing to feel an instinctive personal and emotional connection to the screenplay:

Directing you have to go with your gut. You have to trust your gut. That is the thing that you have to fall back on. (Frankie, screenwriter)

I think they're looking for really good stories that they believe, I guess (Jo, employer)

I think it's something that connects with them personally. Because you have to spend two years of your life making it so you have to love it. So I think each director is totally unique so who knows why they're drawn to the material because some people can be drawn to a script that's not that good but they can see something in it. (Nicola, employer)

Interestingly, Nicola's comment suggests that the screenplay's *merit* may have less to do with whether it is selected by a director. It is more important that something within the idea or story that connects personally with the director. This suggests that once again, the habitus, as the embodiment of an individual's background, preferences, likes, and dislikes, plays a key role in which projects are selected by directors and, as a consequence, are able to move forward towards production.

This is of course problematic because of the domination of wealthy white men in directing roles (Cobb et al. 2018; Lauzen 2018). The role was clearly positioned in my interviews as gendered.

[T]he director is usually male. (Laura, employer)

There's a real prejudice that film directing's a man's job as well. You know, it's like a soldier is a man's job. Being a film director is a man's job. (Colin, employer)

I can sort of understand why there aren't so many women directors (Paul, employer)

No one ever gets called a male director (Natasha, screenwriter)

In my interviews, there are several instances of participants using male pronouns when talking about directors (see Patrick given earlier, for example), and in contrast, there is not one instance where a participant used a female pronoun when talking about directors in general. There was, however, an awareness of women directors not getting work:

If you look at short films being made there are lots of female directors and I think there's a huge problem in female directors moving from shorts to features. (Kate, employer)

I've seen lots of great women-directed shorts. I don't know why they're not getting funded. (Colin, employer)

There's so few women directors (Frankie, screenwriter)

Crucially, a gendered dimension to a director's selection of projects was made apparent in my interviews:

I think what he loved about it was the father and son story and the truth of the difficulties of that and the awkwardness because you know the mum has left. (Vanessa, employer)

It would make sense, wouldn't it – if most directors are men, they respond to – loosely – male themed stories. (Paul, employer)

This goes some way to explaining why the percentage of women screen-writers in development is about 25 per cent (Sinclair et al. 2006), but it drops to 16 per cent for films that actually get made (Kreager and Follows 2018). It is clear that women screenwriters are less likely than men to have their project selected to go forward into production and that the predominance of men directors may be significant in this. Many of the women screenwriters that I spoke to had limited experience with men directors:

So if that gets made it means that all my films will have been made by women. (Catherine, screenwriter)

I've worked with three female directors (Emily, screenwriter)

I've only worked with one male director. (Natasha, screenwriter)

When they did work with men, they often expressed disappointment at the outcomes:

I did this Screen International thing. I think the only female director was [director] and I liked her and she was doing other things at the time and she's still working with the same writer that she worked with at the film school or whatever…and I remember saying to my agent 'hook me up with [director] because I'd love to work with another female…a lot of guys I've worked with are a bit wishy-washy about stuff where as [director] was much more like 'I knew from the moment I started the script that I wanted it to be this kind of image. (Tessa, screenwriter)

Tessa's sense of creative connection to the director she met is described in individual terms but could possibly also reflect a shared understanding through gendered habitus. Usma described her experiences with directors in a way that seems very gendered, but seemed keen to downplay any role that gender might have played:

Yes, well this particular director I really enjoyed working with but then she, I'm not sure if it was because she was a woman. I think we just sort of clicked as people. I've not had a particularly rewarding time working with any of the male directors I've worked with. No, I mean, I wouldn't say that, you know, generally, maybe with a couple of exceptions, I wouldn't say I had a great time. But I think it's probably par for the course. I wouldn't think it's particularly tricky because I was a woman and they were men. (Usma, screenwriter)

Compare this with some of the men screenwriters' views on collaboration with directors:

Personally I quite like developing scripts with the director from early on, if not from the beginning, you know, having the director involved as soon as possible, because I just think then you're creating something together and you're both pulling in the same direction again (Robert, screenwriter)

[G]enerally I love working with directors because you're talking to the people who are going to make your films so it's always very exciting. (Patrick, screenwriter)

In addition, there was a notable comment from one of the more experienced screenwriters, Rachel, who talked about her many screenplays that are as of yet unproduced:

I mean it frustrates me because I have so many projects that are written and people like and are good and so on and you go, you know, 'if you could just all get on and make them' (laughs). People would go 'wow! You're so productive!' You know I've done what feels like four years work in the last two and none of it is actually visible to anybody else so that is frustrating and in the end I think it would in the end if it goes on for long enough make you worried. (Rachel, screenwriter)

Like Usma, Rachel doesn't directly attribute this to her gender, but the discourse of the gendered nature of directors' project selection that I have highlighted suggests that it may indeed be a key factor. Indeed, Catherine had experienced something similar:

I then made two feature films back to back, and that was in 2006. So seven years later, since that, I have been commissioned constantly. And I haven't had another film made, but I was counting it up the other day I probably had twenty-one commissions, I think probably, twenty-one actual commissions in that time. (Catherine, screenwriter)

Feminist thinkers have successfully deconstructed the notion of gender as essential. Bourdieu, however, is able to offer a way to understand gender as both constructed and at the same time a very real and lived experience. Most of those with the power to select screenplays for production are rich, white men, and they are more frequently drawn to projects that they feel a personal connection to, which are most likely to be written by and featuring, other rich, white men, limiting what makes it to the big screen. Even the men I spoke to had experiences of this which were frustrating:

I'm always conscious of the fact that directing is a rich boy's game...the ones who pick and choose they're privileged men, and consequently they have quite a sheltered life-view and they're quite inexperienced and they're not really interested in much, which makes it even more frustrating that they're imposing their taste on the rest of us. (Ed, screenwriter)

As is becoming increasingly apparent, taste is a concept that emerged from the analysis of my interviews as very key in film workers' discussions about collaboration and employment opportunities. Pierre Bourdieu (1984) has shown in great detail how taste is socially constructed according to socio-economic groupings. In the last of my chapters, before I draw some overall conclusions, I examine the way that apparently 'female' taste is viewed in the UK film industry with discernable consequences for women seeking to make a living in professional creative screenwriting.

NOTES

1. For Bourdieu, 'doxa' is the term used to denote what is taken for granted in any particular society (Bourdieu 1977).
2. 'Manspreading' is a contemporary term to describe the practice of sitting in public with your legs wide apart, often covering more than your allocated seat space. The practice is considered to be predominantly something that men do, often at the inconvenience of women.
3. In the US television industry, but increasingly in the UK too, a showrunner is the creator of a television show who acts as both lead writer and executive producer.
4. Paul Laverty is a British screenwriter who has worked with director Ken Loach on the majority of Loach's fictional feature films including Cannes Film Festival Palme d'Or winners "The Wind that Shakes the Barley" (2006) and "I, Daniel Blake" (2016), which also won the BAFTA for Best Film.
5. Ken Loach is a British film director who has worked with screenwriter Paul Laverty on the majority of his fictional feature films including Cannes Film Festival Palme d'Or winners "The Wind that Shakes the Barley" (2006) and "I, Daniel Blake" (2016), which also won the BAFTA for Best Film..

REFERENCES

Adkins, Lisa, and Beverley Skeggs, eds. 2004. *Feminism after Bourdieu.* Oxford: Blackwell.

Banaji, Mahzarin R., and Anthony G. Greenwald. 2013. *Blindspot: Hidden biases of good people.* New York: Delacorte Press.

Bilge, Sirma. 2006. In *Feminism after Bourdieu,* ed. Lisa Adkins and Bev Skeggs. *Canadian Journal of Sociology Online.* https://www.researchgate.net/profile/Lisa_Adkins/publication/27224492_Feminism_After_Bourdieu/links/543751b00cf2dc341db4d591.pdf. Accessed 19 Apr 2018.

Bourdieu, Pierre. 1977. *Outline of a theory of practice.* Vol. 16. Cambridge, UK: Cambridge University Press.

———. 1984. *Distinction: A social critique of the judgement of taste.* Cambridge, MA: Harvard University Press.

———. 1990. *In other words: Essays towards a reflexive sociology.* California: Stanford University Press.

Butler, Judith. 1990. *Gender trouble: Feminism and the subversion of identity.* New York: Routledge.

Cobb, Shelley, Linda Ruth Williams, and Natalie Wreyford. 2018. Calling the shots: Women directors and cinematographers on British Films since 2003. https://s25407.pcdn.co/wp-content/uploads/2018/02/Calling-the-Shots-

Report-Feb-2018-Women-directors-and-cinematographers.pdf. Accessed 26 Mar 2018.

Dunham, Lena. 2012. Creator and Director: Girls. Home Box Office.

Grugulis, Irena, and Dimitrinka Stoyanova. 2012. Social capital and networks in film and TV: Jobs for the boys? *Organization Studies* 33 (10): 1311–1331.

Ibarra, Herminia. 1992. Homophily and differential returns: Sex differences in network structure and access in an advertising firm. *Administrative Science Quarterly* 37: 422–447.

Kreager, Alexis, and Stephen Follows. 2018. Gender inequality and screenwriters. A study of the impact of gender on equality of opportunity for screenwriters and key creatives in the UK film and television industries. *The Writers Guild of Great Britain*. https://writersguild.org.uk/wp-content/uploads/2018/05/Gender-Inequality-and-Screenwriters.pdf. Accessed 13 June 2018.

Lauzen, Martha M. 2018. The celluloid ceiling: Behind-the-scenes employment of women on the top 100, 250, and 500 films of 2017. San Diego State University. https://womenintvfilm.sdsu.edu/wp-content/uploads/2018/01/2017_Celluloid_Ceiling_Report.pdf. Accessed 26 Mar 2018.

Lawler, Steph. 2004. Rules of engagement: Habitus, power and resistance. *The Sociological Review* 52 (s2): 110–128.

Lovell, Terry. 2000. Thinking feminism with and against Bourdieu. *Feminist Theory* 1 (1): 11–32.

Moi, Toril. 1991. Appropriating Bourdieu: Feminist theory and Pierre Bourdieu's sociology of culture. *New Literary History* 22 (4): 1017–1049.

Randle, Keith, Cynthia Forson, and Moira Calveley. 2015. Towards a Bourdieusian analysis of the social composition of the UK film and television workforce. *Work, Employment and Society* 29 (4): 590–606.

Simmons, Bill. 2014. Lena Dunham on the 'Girls' Backlash, lack of female show-runners, and getting fired. *Grantland*. http://grantland.com/features/lena-dunham-on-the-girls-backlash-lack-of-female-showrunners-and-getting-fired/. Accessed 19 Apr 2018.

Sinclair, Alice, Emma Pollard, and Helen Wolfe. 2006. *Scoping study into the lack of women screenwriters in the UK*. A report presented to the UK Film Council. UK Film Council. http://www.bfi.org.uk/sites/bfi.org.uk/files/downloads/uk-film-council-women-screenwriters-scoping-study.pdf. Accessed 26 Mar 2018.

Smith, Stacy L., and Chrystal Allene Cook. 2008. Gender stereotypes: An analysis of popular films and TV. Annenberg School for Communication and the Geena Davis Institute on Gender in Media. https://seejane.org/wpcontent/uploads/GDIGM_Gender_Stereotypes.pdf. Accessed 20 Aug 2018.

CHAPTER 7

Gendering Taste

I think wherever you come from is going to inform your writing, and your gender is a massive difference, or a massive specific in your life. (Kate, employer)

This chapter considers gendered hierarchies of taste in the talk of UK film workers and demonstrates that this is a key site for understanding the lack of opportunities for women screenwriters. It is underpinned by the work of Pierre Bourdieu, in particular *Distinction: A Social Critique of the Judgment of Taste* (1984), in which he offers a critique of how distinctions of taste are reinforced in daily life, in terms of a dominant and dominated aesthetics. I argue that those who work in the UK film industry consider women's tastes inferior, of less value, and even *dis*tasteful. I analyse how this contributes to the upholding of gender inequality in professional screenwriting work. Women are still frequently perceived as a special interest group by the film industry (Christopherson 2009). They are ghettoized as consumers and practitioners in genres concerned primarily with human relationships and the pursuit of romantic heterosexual love as the root to happiness (Smith and Cook 2008), an opinion that I came across repeatedly in my interviews, for example:

[T]his period adaptation that we've got, there's a long list of female writers because it's that sensibility, it's a romantic story, I sound like such a cliché saying it out loud but I think it's true that a woman writing stories about a woman and she has an affair with someone and then she goes back to her

© The Author(s) 2018
N. Wreyford, *Gender Inequality in Screenwriting Work*,
https://doi.org/10.1007/978-3-319-95732-6_7

husband. There are men that could write that and write it brilliantly but you sort of think maybe a woman can write it slightly better? (Nicola, employer)

These stories are marketed to women audiences, and provide the majority of employment opportunities for women screenwriters (Bielby and Bielby 2002). Although in the early days of Hollywood women made up the majority of screenwriters and scenario writers, by the 1940s, women had begun to be increasingly restricted to writing 'women's pictures' or were brought in to write parts for successful actresses (Francke 1994).

One of the most persistent debates around women screenwriters is whether women write differently from men, have different preoccupations, styles, and points of view, and whether women as viewers have different interests, needs, and tastes to men (see, for example, Francke 1994; McCreadie 2006; Seger 2003). Marsha McCreadie interviewed many women screenwriters who felt typecast by their gender—for example, here is Lisa Loomer, screenwriter of *Girl, Interrupted* (Mangold 1999):

> The only difficulty I experience is that I get offered a lot of 'women's' projects – coming-of-age stories, romances. Don't get me wrong. I have nothing against 'women's stories' – I'd like to see more of them. I just don't like to be typecast as a writer. (McCreadie 2006, p. 15)

However, Linda Seger claims that 'Women's films change the focus, often emphasizing the character's emotions, behaviour and psychology above the character's actions' (2003, p. 118)—something many men screenwriters might take issue with as well as women writers. However, Seger also demonstrates that women have successfully written 'male' action films and argues that denying there is such a thing as a 'woman's voice' may simply contribute to the devaluing of women's interests and stories. Taste, as inscribed in the habitus, offers a way to theorize the contradiction that Seger's arguments illustrate so succinctly.

I'd like to use an example from a successful film by a woman writer/director to try to introduce this idea. In Nora Ephron's 1993 film, *Sleepless in Seattle*, the character Suzy, played by Rita Wilson, describes the climax of another film—*An Affair to Remember* (McCarey 1957). Suzy's increasingly emotional description of the film is accompanied by the men characters in the scene rolling their eyes. The film's protagonist, Sam Baldwin, played by Wilson's real-life husband Tom Hanks, famously concludes her performance by declaring: 'That's a chick's movie'. The term 'chick's movie' or 'chick flick', suggests that some films are aimed towards, and enjoyed by, women viewers. These films are usually emotional and about love and relationships, whether comedic or dramatic—a theme also seen in publishing's similarly termed 'chick lit' label. Sam then goes on to parody Suzy's emotional description whilst talking about *The Dirty Dozen* (Aldrich 1967), a film about a mass assassination mission of German officers in World War II. *The Dirty Dozen* is being held up as a contrast to *An Affair to Remember*: an example of a 'guy's film', full of action and conflict and heroics—that is, completely different in content and tone.

Sam's little boy, Jonah, played by Ross Malinger, is depicted as not being able to comprehend Suzy's behaviour, but later on in the film, his young girlfriend instinctively has the same tearful, emotional reaction to the film as Suzy. Ephron has said Suzy's scene 'had cutting room floor written all over it', because it serves no purpose in the film in terms of moving the plot forward (American Film Institute Archives 2002). She also called it her favourite scene in the same interview. So if it's not part of the plot, the scene is serving a different purpose. It offers viewers a way to understand contrasting tastes in film viewing choices. Ephron acknowledged that with *Sleepless in Seattle*, she was 'trying to have our cake and eat it, too' (Frascella 2012) by trying to be 'smart, sophisticated and funny' about romantic films as well as wanting to be one of those films at the same time. She admits that *An Affair to Remember* left her 'awash in salt' when she first saw it and would likely have the same effect if she watched it now. However, in an echo of the Rita Wilson scene, Ephron says to Lawrence Frascella, the *man* interviewing her, that 'maybe you wouldn't be crying.'

Despite her cynical, feminist sensibility, Ephron seems to be suggesting that preferences for certain types of films emerge according to one's gender. This becomes a commercial consideration for the film industry because of the distaste that boys and men come to have for anything identifying as 'female' taste. Linda Obst, who produced *Sleepless in Seattle*, explains:

> Girls will go to a guy movie if it's good, but guys will not go to a movie if it appears to cater to girls.... In other words, if a movie is supposed to be for everyone – and that's always the goal these days – you target it toward men. (Barnes 2013)

This Brooks Barnes' *New York Times* article from which Obst's quote is taken, is about pitching a movie idea to 'industry insiders' to get feedback on the idea's viability. Obst's remarks as a successful producer demonstrate how men's concerns and interests dominate the filmmaking process from the very beginning. It also goes a long way to explaining film's apparent obsession with young men as the prime cinemagoers, even though they are no longer the biggest section of the audience (Sinclair et al. 2006). It's not the size of the group that makes them so key to film financiers, but it's their unwillingness to compromise and watch a film that isn't centred on 'a guy'.

As discussed in the previous chapter, what makes Bourdieu so useful for a feminist analysis of real-world injustices, is that he moves beyond the arguments of construction and performance and 'does not lose sight of the fact that if women are socially constructed as women, that means that they are women' (Moi 1991, p. 1034). Gender is one of the first identity labels that babies are assigned, before they even have a name as this will most likely be predicated on the decisive binary announcement 'It's a boy/it's a girl!' as they arrive into the world, or even many weeks earlier as part of antenatal screening programmes. From this point, it is impossible for this new human to avoid the socializing process of gender, in many cases increasingly even against the parent's wishes. Certainly, it is not hard these days to find social media campaigns run by parents objecting to the narrow roles subscribed to their children through clothing, toys, books, colours, adverts, television, and even bedding and tableware. The 'Let Toys Be Toys' campaign group (http://lettoysbetoys.org.uk/) grew out of a thread on parenting site 'Mumsnet' (https://www.mumsnet.com/), which brought together parents frustrated by the increase in marketing and promotion to children that pushed narrow gendered stereotypes. They have successfully campaigned to have gendered signs removed from toy stores, children's clothing websites, book covers, and more. However, the reality for most parents is that their children remain policed by advertisers, the media, the world around them, their peers, and other adults, picking up clues and controls on what they are 'supposed' to be interested in, and more importantly, what they must avoid for fear of judgement and ridicule.

Unusually, it is boys who have more to fear in this process. It is still far more acceptable for a girl to play football or own a train set than it is for a boy to take ballet lesson or own dolls. Unfortunately, this is not because we have at last found an arena where girls dominate. The disappointing incentive for this disparity is that:

> Permitting, let alone encouraging, boys to be more girly is scary. We want our boys to keep being like boys because masculinity is still where the power lies. And we want our girls to be more like boys for the same reason. (Strauss 2018)

Not letting boys associate with anything that's been socially assigned to girls is an indication of how little girls and women are valued. Boys who steer away from the assigned masculine interests and pursuits risk losing their social status (Ibid.). From this, it is not difficult to see why Toril Moi (1991) argues that gender actually has much in common with Bourdieu's concept of class: it is perceived as natural and self-evident, it is socially and historically reproduced, embodied, and renders an individual open to judgement. She argues that the habitus is at least partly constructed by a socialized process of inscribing gender onto the individual:

> [T]o produce gender habitus requires an extremely elaborate social process of education and inscription of social power relations on the body, so even such basic activities as teaching children how to move, dress and eat are thoroughly political. (p. 1030)

Bourdieu's theory of taste as socially constructed and then naturalized in an individual's habitus, is particularly relevant to understanding why girls might steer away from STEM[1] careers (O'Mara 2014), or why they might choose to write with a pink pen (Furness 2012). The habitus internalizes the structure in which it grows up. Individuals do not act entirely freely in their choices.

In film labour markets, men and women certainly appear to be regarded as very different. Patterns of employment often follow gender stereotypes, a segregation which has been shown to uphold inequality (Hesmondhalgh and Baker 2015). Hair and Make Up departments, for example, are domi-nated by women, whilst jobs that use technical machinery such as camera operators and cinematographers are still workforces predominantly made up of men (Cobb et al. 2018). In this chapter, I consider how gender is constructed as part of an individual's habitus, with manifest consequences in the world of work. For example, in extension to the example earlier, the labour women in general are expected to undertake on their own physical appearance (see Elias et al. (2017) for a thorough exploration of this issue) may make them more disposed than men to a career in film and television Hair and Make Up departments, and also gives them the appropriate habitus and superior capital to be recognized as skilled in that particular field. This may indicate that women have a fair chance of employment in film and other creative careers, but hierarchies of reward and recognition within creative professions often mean women are found in roles that have less status. So that, whilst it is possible to claim that women make up half the film workforce (Creative Skillset 2012, p. 33), in reality, they are still scarce in senior and key creative roles such as CEOs (4 per cent) and directors (see above), whilst they have a higher representation in cleaning (63 per cent), HR (73 per cent), and administration (80 per cent).

Bourdieu (1984) proposed that the dominant powers of a society define aesthetics, and by means of that definition, it is social class that tends to determine a person's interests, tastes, and likes and dislikes. Using everyday examples such as food and music, he demonstrated that preferences were shared among socio-economic groupings. This variance in aesthetic tastes reinforces inequalities by making 'difference' appear natural and apparently legitimating social differences. In particular, it is important for the dominant class to make a 'distinction' between their own tastes and those of the lower classes, in order to mark themselves as 'better':

> In matters of taste, more than anywhere else, all determination is negation, and tastes are perhaps first and foremost distastes, disgust provoked by horror or visceral intolerance ('sick-making') of the tastes of others. (Ibid., p. 49)

There is an active process of othering, which Bourdieu tracked along class lines. Indeed, he even observed how a legitimated piece of art can be devalued by becoming popularized. A good example of this is the British Broadcasting Corporation's (BBC) use of Luciano Pavarotti singing *Nessun dorma*, the final aria of Puccini's opera *Turandot* (1926) for its 1990 World Cup football coverage theme tune (see Bailey 2015). Writing in the *Guardian*, Mark Oliver (2007) referred to the usage as 'ridiculed for its mass, housewife CD buying popularity', implying that wide exposure and availability had devalued the particular performance and indeed the aria itself because it could now be appreciated and 'owned' by less distinguished people (in a way that is clearly also gendered here in his use of 'housewife').

This essentializing and polarizing of taste and aesthetics was described in my interviews, but in relation to gender:

[I]t's definitely 'oh there's a woman in the room'. And they'll say that. 'Gillian what do you think?' you know, as if like, but then other times slightly sort of a different species, 'oh you don't like action, this isn't for you anyway'. 'You're not really the audience'. (Gillian, employer)

I had every rom-com known to man, *27 Dresses*[2], *Bride Wars*[3]; it all came to my door. (Hannah, screenwriter)

It was very clear that women are not supposed to do genre, they're not supposed to action, or thrillers, maybe we can do comedy but a certain kind of comedy but really what we're supposed to do is drama and if we can do gritty, heartfelt drama that's good. (Usma, screenwriter)

Bourdieu does touch upon gender in relation to taste and food in *Distinction*, but he seems to have less awareness or insight into this as a socially constructed difference as he does in his that analysis of taste and class. For example, he reports that:

Meat, the nourishing food par excellence, strong and strong-making, giving vigour, blood, and health, is the dish for the men, who take a second helping, whereas women are satisfied with a small portion. It is not that they are stinting themselves, they really don't want what others might need, especially the men, the natural meat-eaters. (1984, p. 190)

Bourdieu seems to link men with signs of dominance, for example, 'par excellence', 'strong', 'vigour', but rather than view this through the same social lens he views class, he perceives the differences he describes in women and men as 'natural' and calls them 'strictly biological differences' (Ibid.). Indeed, Bourdieu seems only interested in women when they can further illustrate his claims about class and taste, showing an incredible lack of insight on occasion, for example, suggesting that upper-class women know 'the intrinsic, natural beauty of their bodies' (p. 204) and don't suffer from the same body issues of women from lower classes. I argue that feminist scholars should not allow Bourdieu's own shortcomings—and perhaps ironically, his own inability as a man to recognize the lived experience of women—to prevent us from thinking about gender *with* Bourdieu's concepts, as Toril Moi (1991) has done. I have introduced Moi's thinking on Bourdieu in previous chapters, so here, I will just reiterate, and add to, some of the key points.

Moi describes the usefulness of seeing gender in terms of the dominant and the dominated just as Bourdieu describes class. She understands the dominators as those in possession of significant capital in the field, which enables them to set the rules and speak with legitimacy, whilst silencing and excluding those that they dominate. Most importantly for my research, she shows how an understanding of taste as part of a gendered habitus can help to explain why men's success in the field of screenwriting is experienced as merited, rather than a simple recognition of dominant tastes:

> Legitimacy (or distinction) is only truly achieved when it is no longer possible to tell whether dominance has been achieved as a result of distinction or whether in fact the dominant agent simply appears to be distinguished because he (more rarely she) is dominant. (Moi 1991, p. 1023)

Moi pinpoints the value of Bourdieu's concepts of habitus, capital, and distinction, and how they function within a given field to both enable suppression of one section of society by another, and to disguise the processes by which this happens. Although subordinate social classes may appear to have equally strong views about what constitutes good taste, merit, or value, there is an imbalance of power:

> The working-class 'aesthetic' is a dominated aesthetic, which is constantly obliged to define itself in terms of the dominant aesthetics. (Bourdieu 1984, p. 41)

This observation echoes feminist criticisms of women as the 'other' (de Beauvoir 1949) and post-structuralist attentions to the notion of 'female' as defined by what is 'not male' (Butler 1990; Irigaray 1985) and highlights the similarity between the dynamics.

Feminists have long highlighted how men's lives, work, and concerns have been deemed more interesting and valuable than women's (Friedan 1963). In post-feminist cultures (Gill 2007b), men don't often consider themselves intrinsically more interesting, but through history, education, and culture, white, upper-class men's tastes, concerns, preoccupations, and preferences are positioned as superior, and of greater worth and merit. Creative women of all classes, backgrounds, and ethnicities have been marginalized by the educational and cultural establishment. Making these hidden naturalized hierarchies visible offers a way to potentially challenge their dominance:

Bourdieu's highlighting of [the] ultimately arbitrary character of social distinctions (so that, for example, what counts as 'tasteful' is an effect, not of
intrinsic properties, but of social relations) gives us a way to challenge the
taken-for-granted ('the doxic' in Bourdieu's terms). (Lawler 2004, p. 113)

Bourdieu recognized that taste is not simply an expression of individuality,
nor is it a harmless preference for one thing over another:

Aesthetic intolerance can be terribly violent. Aversion to different life-styles
is perhaps one of the strongest barriers between the classes. (Bourdieu 1984,
p. 56)

Indeed, it is one of the most effective ways that those with power are able
to hold onto their power. 'Good' taste is displayed through symbolic violence as a natural quality of an individual, making it appear innate and
objective rather than learnt and highly subjective. This is particularly clear
in the creative industries, where, as I will demonstrate, 'taste' is one of the
principle ways that individuals are judged, relationships are formed, and
products are chosen and promoted over others.

[T]aste [is] one of the most vital stakes in the struggles fought in the field of
the dominant class and the field of cultural production (Ibid., p. 11)

In the next section, I will look at how my workers in the UK film industry
discursively position women's taste and how this discourse is used to
account for the lack of women screenwriters.

THE CURRENCY OF TASTE IN THE UK FILM LABOUR MARKET

[Y]ou have to feel in some way confident in your taste and creative instinct.
(Nick, employer)

In analysing my interviews with screenwriters and their employers, I
observed frequent references my participants made to 'taste', and the associations made between gender and taste. Many of my participants made
reference to their own tastes and those of others, for example:

I learnt and I know my taste, my skills, my taste as a producer was very much
formed there. (Jo, employer)

> I wasn't terribly taken with the script, and she took it very personally, thought I was challenging all of her taste. (Frank, employer)

> And it isn't really my taste either. (Frankie, screenwriter)

> My own taste isn't like that. (Laura, employer)

> If you look at the BBC, or Film 4 or the BFI. It's the same people with the same taste. (Jay, employer)

Often taste was closely associated with power and money, such as in one employer's comment that '[I]f the tastemaker, the financier, disagrees, it's irrelevant' (Eloise, employer). Here, being a film financier appears to be synonymous with having the power of making judgements based on taste. In fact, her use of the term 'tastemaker' echoes Bourdieu's (1984) own use of the word in reference to museum curators, whom he described as artistic guides to the elite. Eloise used the term in reference to powerful people who head up organizations that financially support film development and production, giving them the power to endorse their own tastes. These are still predominantly men. Men have the dominant habitus in the film industry, are therefore perceived to have more worthwhile ideas and more valuable stories than women.

> And he to this day can go in, even – amazing – two massive flops in a row and still walk into the studios and convince them. You show me a woman who could do that. (Colin, employer)

Many of my participants talked about taste in gendered terms, a discourse in which men and women were positioned as having different interests and instinctive understandings. For example:

> I think there's a perception that women are more interested in relationships and emotions and the hidden depths and complexities of human drama, human life, quite rightly, okay? (Rob, employer)

> [I]nstinctively when you meet a male writer you think he has a better understanding of genre and therefore of audience than a female writer does (Kate, employer)

A dominant discursive pattern can be identified in which women are seen as interested in relationship dramas, whilst men are viewed as naturally inclined to write genre films full of action and special effects. This discourse has an effect in limiting employment prospects for women screenwriters whether they want to write these films or not. Gendered taste was clearly linked to employment opportunities for screenwriters by the employers:

[F]rom my point of view I know that there are female screenwriters that I'll go to for drama, male screenwriters I'll go to for genre (Frank, employer)

So, there's a book that we've optioned recently which is absolutely a woman's story. It's about a female friendship and mothers and daughters and relationships, so I'm looking for a writer now and I'd ideally like to find a woman to write it. (Vanessa, employer)

More worryingly, and without any reference to data or evidence, several of my participants made a connection between women screenwriters' association with drama and the reasons why they may have trouble getting their films made. For example, here are some of the answers I received to the question 'Why do you think there are so few women screenwriters?'

[B]ecause the female screenwriter is writing drama (Frank, employer)

Um – so it's what's perhaps left on the shelf are the more character-driven pieces written by more intuitive, character-interested female writers (Nick, employer)

[T]hings that one might imagine women would write, more drama led, might be tougher to get made (Vanessa, employer)

In this discourse, taste is presented as conforming to very stereotypical gendered roles that echo the public/private dichotomy. Women are positioned as being interested in people and relationships whereas men are all about action and adventure. These types of stories are then in turn given different economic values, without taking into account other influencing factors, such as production and marketing budgets. Indeed, the one genre recognized to be both 'for women' and commercial—the romantic comedy—was often described in disparaging terms. Romantic comedies were described as 'sappy', 'soppy', and 'half-baked' in my discussions.

In this extract from my conversation with Nick, it is clear that he is having to do discursive work in order to explain to me his understanding of gendered differences in taste without sounding sexist. He gets himself into uncomfortable corners and is not very successful in navigating his way out.

> [T]eenage boys who grow up to be young adolescents they want – again, generally speaking – they want the brash loud thriller things, they want *The Fast and the Furious* and the superhero movies and um – loads of explosions and car chases. You know I'm sure there have been countless studies exploring the relationship between violent movies and testosterone levels and pre-adolescent and men and what can you do about that? So it's no surprise that those young boys who do turn out to be writers, who pursue that as a career, grow up to be writers who write the sort of thing that they were drawn to when they were younger, you know. It's certainly not the reverse that girls grow up to be female writers who only write sappy romantic comedies or *Tinkerbell* movies, you know. I think, generally speaking, female writers can be more versatile in the market place as much as anything because you know the big tent pole movies or the mainstream films their first point of access for the audience tends to be male-skewed. (Nick, employer)

Nick starts by trying to establish a natural link between boys and men and action-packed films. He even uses the discursive technique of drawing on 'experts', although the 'studies' he refers to are most likely ones trying to judge whether violent films and video games *increase* aggression in boys' behaviour (Anderson and Bushman 2001). These studies are looking for causality and influence on behaviour, but Nick's comment 'and what can you do about that?' seems designed instead to make the association appear inevitable and rooted in biology. However, once he moves to extend his argument to why men screenwriters are drawn to write this type of material, he quickly realizes that he is potentially limiting what women screenwriters are allowed to write and so then contradicts himself whilst at the same time reinforcing the sexist idea that young girls prefer to watch romantic comedies and films about fairies. It ends with a suggestion that women potentially have more opportunities as they 'can be more versatile', an extraordinary reversal of what actually happens in the film labour market.

What is missing from this discourse of gendered preferences is some awareness that screenwriters do not often get to choose the projects that they work on (McCreadie 2006).

The reason I was commissioned was because they thought I would be able to write the women, the relationships between the four women at the centre. (Catherine, screenwriter)

[O]ne of them said 'you can't write about a housing estate in Brixton, you've never been to one'. Well actually I have been to a housing estate in Brixton and no I don't actually live on one, sorry, but I have this thing called an imagination, it's amazing. And I just think, you'll take Guy Ritchie writing about East End gangsters? I can assure you he hasn't been near the East End. But they're like, 'you're a woman, you don't know about fighting'. (Emily, screenwriter)

People don't give me war movies or Sci-Fi's but I'm not interested so it's not that surprising. And certainly I do get sent 'oh this is supposed to have a strong female character in it' etc. etc. so I suppose there is that. (Rachel, screenwriter)

Certainly in my conversations with women screenwriters, few of them felt that their skills or interests were limited to women characters and romantic relationships. I asked all the screenwriters, men and women, whether there were any subjects or genres of film that they felt they either could not or would not be interested in writing. Very few expressed any kind of limit on their abilities or interests, and many who did then added a caveat that they probably could depending on the story within the broader genre. Overall the genres that were specified as uninteresting were very similar for men and women. The women screenwriters mentioned horror (four writers) and crime (two writers) but also kitchen-sink dramas (one writer), children's films (one writer), and 'chick flicks' (one writer). The men screenwriters also mentioned horror (two writers) but also science fiction (three writers), romantic comedy (two writers), drama (one writer), and 'women's issues' films (one writer). Sometimes the same people who didn't limit themselves had no problem suggesting limits on others. Most notably Jack, who answered my question as to why he thought there are fewer women screenwriters thus:

Well, I can see how the traditional genres, things like thrillers, superhero movies, horror are boys natural comfort zone, um – so many films do lean towards teenage boys, you know action, all that stuff, that's got to be part of it.

Then *my very next question* was about his own tastes and abilities and he answered without any apparent awareness of the parallels:

> Yes. Horror. I have absolutely no interest in writing that. Um – big action movies, you know I don't have the experience for that. I'm more interested in character relationship movies compelled by a strong narrative.

However, Catherine echoed the gendered perceptions of her employer suggesting she has taken on these gendered associations in her own habitus:

> But what I thought I can't do is, I thought I can't do the action, the car chases, I can't do the heist bit. I can do the plotting, I can't do the crime. I can't do all the technical things. Oh but yes I'm a woman and I can do all that emotional stuff.

Although she also went on to contradict herself:

> I suddenly just got completely carried away with all the action and I was really excited about shooters and people were going to be hanging off hooks in the – and everybody just suddenly stopped and looked at me and I suddenly realized that I had assimilated, completely, the world that I thought was actually not my domain. So I suppose what I'm trying to say by that is I'm not sure that, there may be gender perceptions of what we're good at but I don't think they actually hold true.

Catherine's initial comment may also imply that many of the women screenwriters who have found some success in the UK may be those who conform to the expectations of commissioners about what women can write, as Rachel's comment earlier also suggests.

Some of the biggest box office successes of all time illustrate clearly that women can and *do* write films that are full of action and heroics and appeal to broad audiences. For example, *The Lord of the Rings* (Jackson 2001), written by Fran Walsh and Philippa Boyens; *The Hunger Games* (Ross 2012), written by Suzanne Collins based on her own novel—the fastest-selling non-sequel ever (McClintock 2012); *The Empire Strikes Back* (Kershner 1980) written by Leigh Brackett—recently voted the best film ever (Daily Mail Reporter 2014). These sorts of examples are not the majority, but they do trouble the notion that women's tastes and talents are limited. Indeed, the success of women screenwriters was also repeatedly framed as being due to their ability to write like men, or to write so that their gender is not obvious, much the way American director Kathryn Bigelow has had success:

> I mean the point, in fact the celebration, of her by audiences, by critics, is that you wouldn't know she was a woman, because she can direct a war film. (Yvonne, employer)

There were repeated references by my participants during our conversations to Jane Goldman writing *Kick Ass* and *X-Men* (Vaughan 2010, 2011), Kelly Marcel writing *Terra Nova* (2011) and *Mad Max* (Miller 2015), and Lucinda Coxon writing *Crimson Peak* for Guillermo del Toro (2015) as signs that women screenwriters were becoming more successful. Little or no mention was made of Laura Wade writing *The Riot Club* (Scherfig 2014), Misan Sagay writing *Belle* (Asante 2013), Abi Morgan's screenplay *Suffragette* (Gavron 2015), or even another of Kelly Marcel's scripts, *Saving Mr Banks* (Hancock 2013), which was being released at the time of my interviews. It's worth noting that three of these four screenplays were made into films with women directors, reflecting my observations on directors' choice of projects discussed in the previous chapter. Women's screenwriting success then is often defined by the UK industry as women writing films that men like. This clearly conflicts with the sort of films that the employers believe women want to write and indeed frequently commission them to write. If we are going to be able to include stories by and about women on the big screen, decision makers and powerful financiers need to understand that their taste is subjective, constructed, and not necessarily shared by significant portions of the audience.

Currently, in the UK film industry, white, heterosexual, able-bodied men's taste is dominant and anyone who does not share these tastes risks having their creative preferences judged as less valuable and even distasteful by those with the power to finance films, most of whom are still rich white men. Women screenwriters are associated with less commercial stories simply because of their gender and can find themselves restricted to writing films that predominantly revolve around relationships and the pursuit of love, despite evidence that they can very successfully write big, funny, action-packed box office hits. Indeed, it may only be when they find a way to write such films that they are seen as having real talent enough to compete for jobs alongside men screenwriters.

In recent years, the 'surprise success of *Wonder Woman*,[4] *Get Out*[5] and *Hidden Figures*[6]' (Wilkinson 2017), for example, has proven that films by and about both women and black men can break box office records and attract large audiences. Yet critical and commercial success around these films is repeatedly dismissed as a surprise (as above), a fluke, an exception, as unexplainable (for example, McClintock 2012). Are film critics, 78 per cent of whom are men (90 per cent in film industry trade publications) (Lauzen 2013) and 82 per cent white (Choueiti et al. 2018), subject to gender and other biases? It is starting to seem very likely. Lauzen reports that women film critics were more likely to review films written and/or directed by women, and men film critics were more likely to review films written and/or directed by men, which certainly indicates a preference for gendered stories and sensibilities which may be in part down to a perception of value through their own embodied experiences.

When films by and about women get made, there still seems to be a concern that they might be viewed by audiences as inferior. In 2013, the poster campaign for *Bridesmaids* (Feig 2011), written by Kristen Wiig and Annie Mumolo, led with the headline: 'Chick Flicks Don't Have to Suck!' (Deiseroth 2014), clearly trying to suggest that this film was the exception and therefore worth seeing. Ros Gill has highlighted the problematic nature of 'women's media' (2007a), which can offer genuine pleasures to women at the same time as reinforcing gendered preoccupations and placing women's concerns as 'other' to a man's norm. While film scholars continue to debate the existence of a 'female sensibility' (McCreadie 2006; Seger 2003), the reality is that women's voices continue to be sidelined in the film industries. From my analysis of my interviews, I argue that women shouldn't be restricted to writing certain *types* of stories or genres, but their approach to any story or genre may offer a different perspective because of their lived experience. In this, I do not mean to overgeneralize or treat women as a homogeneous group; indeed, we need to hear all sorts of women's voices and perspectives on all kinds of stories as well as a wider variety of men's voices in terms of class, race, sexuality, and other forms of embodied subjectivities. In this way, we can start to offer new ways of looking at the world, and new ways of understanding those we perhaps view as not so much like ourselves. At the very least, we can find some new approaches to telling stories, which perhaps even some white men might appreciate…

So it's like four men which is slightly predictable in itself, but because it's four men the first week all the ideas were hookers and strippers, hookers and strippers, and I was literally screaming at them by the end 'there are no hookers and strippers in this thing!' not because I'm banging the table for some feminist agenda, but because it's corny, we've seen it before. Until the point where they were going 'what about fat hookers?' (Ed, screenwriter)

A feminist appropriation of Pierre Bourdieu's study of the social construction of taste provides a way to understand why those with power fail to recognize the value of women's stories. Just as the dominant *class* constructs its tastes and preferences as naturally superior (Bourdieu 1984), the dominant *gender* (men) is considered to have superior and more universal tastes and preferences than the dominated (women). This point of view can of course be taken on and accepted by women critics as well as men, as they are likely to have been socialized to reproduce accepted discourses to survive in the field of film criticism. However, it is possible that the embodied and lived experiences of gender can allow women critics to see value in women's stories where men critics cannot.

When women write successful films about women's experiences, it is most often chalked up as an anomaly or sidelined into a specialist 'for women' category. Rarely is the success followed up with copycat films or sequels. I have argued that the construction of gendered taste plays a significant role in this as men critics, financiers, and audiences often find women's tastes frivolous and distasteful. This distaste has very real consequences in upholding the lack of opportunities for women screenwriters, as these judgements of taste appear natural and meritocratic rather than constructed and contentious. Women screenwriters are disadvantaged in a way that is self-fulfilling and difficult to circumnavigate. They are perceived as having innate gendered taste, which is considered less commercial and resulting in films that only women will watch. They are shut out from the biggest budgets and the most action-packed genres. These films are then made by and targeted at men and boys and often do not show a nuanced understanding of women as characters or include their views of the world. Indeed, this can mean women are more likely to want to watch films that *do* contain women characters and perspectives. If women wish to pursue a career in screenwriting, they are likely to be influenced by the films they grew up watching. However, these films are not valued by the industry, even when they succeed, making it difficult for women screenwriters to sustain a career. Conversely, should they wish to shrug off the shackles of stereotyped gendered taste, or break new boundaries, they are likely to be considered less knowledgeable and therefore less trustworthy than their men colleagues.

Jo observes that it's about 'what do we define as scale and what do we define as interesting?' Until these definitions are understood as subjective and not universal, it's difficult to see how inequality of opportunity will be addressed in the UK film industry. One senior UK employer that I interviewed believed it was important for women filmmakers to have a detailed knowledge of the 'canon' of film history:

> I say 'get out there, watch a lot the stuff because you can bet all those nerdy boys are and they know their stuff' you know, you can't just become a filmmaker, you've got to know your onions and I tend to say that men tend to be more sort of cinephile types than women. (Martha, employer)

However, she was not willing to make any allowances for women based on the lack of available films with a women's sensibility, worldview, or protagonist, despite the difference this might have in engaging young girls and women, or allowing them to see films as 'for them':

> I kind of think you have to grow up and if you're a woman filmmaker and interested, you've got to be interested in everything. You've got to learn from the great masters, and I use the word 'masters' in the very obvious sense of the word. You know, look at why Hitchcock works, look at why Walter Hill works, you know, look at how Michael Mann works, what I'm sort of saying is you can't say I'm not going to study how film works because I'm not seeing myself represented. (Martha, employer)

This is a simplistic view that downplays the experience of being asked to repeatedly engage with a protagonist whose concerns and preoccupations are so unlike your own. My research provides ample evidence that men financiers find this difficult to do, so why should it be any different for young women, whose own habitus, tastes, preferences, and experiences have not been explored with any consistency in film history? The idea that women should be able to see beyond this and feel equal excitement and engagement with the medium as men is another clear form of inequality. Whilst film school syllabi or published lists of the 'best films' (Berger 2015) still continue to include less than a handful of women filmmakers, the required foundation for a career in film remains unequal. White men are able to tap into and be inspired by a rich cinematic history of stories by and about those who share their habitus and life experiences in a way that women and black, Asian, and minority ethnic (BAME) filmmakers are not. Women creative workers in the UK film industry seem aware of this difference but find it hard to articulate:

> I think you can't separate the gender from your point of view. I don't think it means women can only write about women and men can only write about men. At all. Um – but I do think that it has to matter at some kind of DNA level that we may not necessarily clearly articulate every time we write a story. (Jo, employer)

> Women differ massively from woman to woman but there is a common experience that is probably based on – genetics, although I'm very sceptical about genetics, definitely society and how you're treated and what opportunities you have and all that comes through in the way you write but not necessarily in an obvious way. (Kate, employer)

Habitus allows an understanding of how men and women may indeed write about the same subject in a different way, as may Africans or Europeans, heterosexual and lesbian writers, CIS-gender or transgender individuals, and so on. Habitus is a way to understand experience as both constructed and lived so that the individual cannot help but bring a unique perspective to creative work. This is a strong argument for why it matters that the majority of screenwriters are white, rich, CIS-gender, heterosexual men. Even if they do create stories *about* poor, BAME, lesbian, disabled women, they will most likely be unable to provide the same perspective on those experiences as a diverse range of women screenwriters could. As one black woman employer clearly understood:

> [It's] about having been on the receiving end of something and how when you're telling a story the different nuances that say being a Muslim woman writing, or being a Muslim man writing, as opposed to being a white man writing. (Esther, employer)

Notes

1. Science, Technology, Engineering, and Mathematics.
2. Fletcher (2008).

3. Winick (2009).
4. Jenkins (2017).
5. Peele (2017).
6. Melfi (2016).

REFERENCES

Aldrich, Robert. 1967. Director: The Dirty Dozen. Screenwriters: Nunnally Johnson, Lukas Heller and E.M. Nathanson (novel). Metro-Goldwyn-Mayer.
American Film Institute Archives. 2002. Nora Ephron's favourite scene in sleepless in Seattle. Cheideo.com. https://www.chideo.com/chideo/afinora-ephron-favorite-sleepless-in-seattle-scene. Accessed 21 Apr 2018.
Anderson, Craig A., and Brad J. Bushman. 2001. Effects of violent video games on aggressive behavior, aggressive cognition, aggressive affect, physiological arousal, and prosocial behavior: A meta-analytic review of the scientific literature. *Psychological Science* 12 (5): 353–359.
Asante, Amma. 2013. Director: Belle. Screenwriter: Misan Sagay. British Film Institute.
Bailey, Ryan. 2015. Remember BBC's Italia 90 opening credits? Here's the incredible story behind them. The 42. http://www.the42.ie/italia-90-bbc-opening-credits-philip-bernie-2140805-Jun2015/. Accessed 21 Apr 2018.
Barnes, Brooks. 2013. Save my blockbuster! *New York Times.* https://archive.nytimes.com/www.nytimes.com/interactive/2013/06/28/movies/BLOCKBUSTER.html. Accessed 21 Apr 2018.
Berger, Laura. 2015. BBC lists top American films of all time; only 3 female directors make the cut. *Indiewire.* http://www.indiewire.com/2015/07/bbc-lists-top-100-american-films-of-all-time-only-3-female-directors-make-the-cut-203082/. Accessed 21 Apr 2018.
Bielby, Denise D., and William T. Bielby. 2002. Hollywood dreams, harsh realities: Writing for film and television. *Contexts* 1 (4): 21–27.
Bourdieu, Pierre. 1984. *Distinction: A social critique of the judgement of taste.* Cambridge, MA: Harvard University Press.
Butler, Judith. 1990. *Gender trouble: Feminism and the subversion of identity.* New York: Routledge.
Choueiti, Marc, Stacy L. Smith, Katherine Pieper and Ariana Case. 2018. Critic's choice? Gender and race/ethnicity of film reviewers across 100 top films of 2017. USC Annenberg Inclusion Initiative. http://assets.uscannenberg.org/docs/cricits-choice-2018.pdf. Accessed 14 June 2018.
Christopherson, Susan. 2009. Working in the creative economy: Risk, adaptation, and the persistence of exclusionary networks. In *Creative labour: Working in the creative industries,* ed. Alan McKinlay and Chris Smith, 72–90. Hampshire: Palgrave Macmillan.

Cobb, Shelley, Linda Ruth Williams, and Natalie Wreyford. 2018. Calling the Shots: Women directors and cinematographers on British Films since 2003. https://s25407.pcdn.co/wp-content/uploads/2018/02/Calling-the-Shots-Report-Feb-2018-Women-directors-and-cinematographers.pdf. Accessed 26 Mar 2018.

Creative Skillset. 2012. Employment census of the creative media industries. http://creativeskillset.org/assets/0000/5070/2012_Employment_Census_of_the_Creative_Media_Industries.pdf. Accessed 24 Apr 2018.

Daily Mail Reporter. 2014. "Empire Strikes Back is number one film: Star Wars beats The Godfather to be named greatest movie of all time. *The Daily Mail.* http://www.dailymail.co.uk/tvshowbiz/article-2643379/Empire-Strikes-Back-number-one-film-Star-Wars-beats-The-Godfather-named-greatest-movie-time.html. Accessed 21 Apr 2018.

de Beauvoir, Simone. 1949. *The second sex.* New York: HM Parshley.

Deiseroth, Sarah. 2014. Chick flicks don't have to suck. Women in Comedy. https://sarahdeiseroth.wordpress.com/2014/12/11/its-womans-world/. Accessed 21 Apr 2018.

del Toro, Guillermo. 2015. Director: Crimson Peak. Screenwriters: Giullermo del Toro, Matthew Robbins and Lucinda Coxon (uncredited). Double Dare You.

Elias, Ana Sofia, Rosalind Gill, and Christina Scharff, eds. 2017. *Aesthetic labour: Rethinking beauty politics in neoliberalism.* Hampshire: Palgrave Macmillan.

Ephron, Nora. 1993. Director: Sleepless in Seattle. Screenwriters: Nora Ephron, David S. Ward and Jeff Arch. Columbia Tristar.

Feig, Paul. 2011. Director: Bridesmaids. Screenwriters: Kristen Wiig, Annie Mumolo. Universal Pictures.

Fletcher, Anne. 2008. Director 27 Dresses. Screenwriter: Aline Brosh McKenna. Fox 2000 Pictures.

Francke, Lizzie. 1994. *Script girls: Women screenwriters in Hollywood.* London: British Film Institute.

Frascella, Lawrence. 2012. On the front lines with Nora Ephron. *Rolling Stone.* https://www.rollingstone.com/movies/news/on-the-front-lines-with-nora-ephron-20120626. Accessed 21 Apr 2018.

Friedan, Betty. 1963. *The Feminine Mystique.* New York: Dell.

Furness, Hannah. 2012. BIC ridiculed over 'comfortable' pink pens for women. *The Telegraph.* https://www.telegraph.co.uk/news/newstopics/howaboutthat/9503359/BIC-ridiculed-over-comfortable-pink-pens-for-women.html. Accessed 19 Apr 2018.

Gavron, Sarah. 2015. Director: Suffragette. Screenwriter: Abi Morgan. Pathé.

Gill, Rosalind. 2007a. *Gender and the media.* Cambridge: Polity Press.

———. 2007b. Postfeminist media culture: Elements of a sensibility. *European Journal of Cultural Studies* 10 (2): 147–166.

Hancock, John Lee. 2013. Director: Saving Mr Banks. Screenwriters: Kelly Marcel and Sue Smith. Walt Disney Pictures.

Hesmondhalgh, D., and S. Baker. 2015. Sex, gender and work segregation in the cultural industries. *The Sociological Review* 63 (1_suppl): 23–36.

Irigaray, Luce. 1985. *This sex which is not one.* New York: Cornell University Press.

Jackson, Peter. 2001. Director: The Lord of the Rings: The Fellowship of the Ring. Screenwriters: J.R.R. Tolkien (novel), Fran Walsh, Philippa Boyens and Peter Jackson. New Line Cinema.

Jenkins, Patty. 2017. Director: Wonder Woman. Screenwriters: Allan Heinberg, Zack Snyder, Jason Fuchs, William Moulton Marston (Wonder Woman created by) and Harry G. Peter (Wonder Woman created by). Warner Brothers.

Kershner, Irvin. 1980. Director: Star Wars: Episode V – The Empire Strikes Back. Screenwriters: Leigh Brackett, Lawrence Kasdan and George Lucas (story by). Twentieth Century Fox.

Lauzen, Martha M. 2013. Gender @ the movies: On-line film critics and criticism. San Diego State University Centre for the Study of Women in Television and Film. https://womenintvfilm.sdsu.edu/files/2013_Gender_at_the_Movies_Exec_Summ.pdf. Accessed 21 Apr 2018.

Lawler, Steph. 2004. Rules of engagement: Habitus, power and resistance. *The Sociological Review* 52 (s2): 110–128.

Mangold, James. 1999. Director: Girl, Interrupted. Screenwriters: Susanna Kaysen (book), James Mangold, Lisa Loomer and Anna Hamilton Phelan. Columbia Pictures.

Marcel, Kelly, and Craig Silverstein. 2011. Creators: Terra Nova. 20th Century Fox Television.

McCarey, Leo. 1957. Director: An Affair to Remember. Screenwriters: Delmer Daves, Leo McCarey, Mildred Cram (story) and Donald Ogden Stewart. Twentieth Century Fox.

McClintock, Pamela. 2012. Box office shocker: Hunger Games third-best opening weekend of all time. *The Hollywood Reporter.* https://www.hollywoodreporter.com/news/box-office-hunger-games-jennifer-lawrence-josh-hutcherson-liam-hemsworth-twilight-304028. Accessed 21 Apr 2018.

McCreadie, Marsha. 2006. *Women screenwriters today: Their lives and words.* Connecticut: Praeger Publishing.

Melfi, Theodore. 2016. Director: Hidden Figures. Screenplay: Allison Schroeder, Theodore Melfi and Margot Lee Shetterly (based on the book by). Fox 2000 Pictures.

Miller, George. 2015. Director: Mad Max: Fury Road. Screenwriters: George Miller, Brendan McCarthy, Nick Lathouris, George Miller (uncredited), Byron Kennedy (uncredited) and Kelly Marcel (uncredited). Warner Brothers Pictures.

Moi, Toril. 1991. Appropriating Bourdieu: Feminist theory and Pierre Bourdieu's sociology of culture. *New Literary History* 22 (4): 1017–1049.

O'Mara, Eileen. 2014. How can we better tackle the gender imbalance in technology careers? *Huffington post.* https://www.huffingtonpost.co.uk/eileenoamara/how-can-we-better-tackle-_b_6179346.html. Accessed 19 Apr 2018.

Oliver, Mark. 2007. Nessun Dorma and Italia 1990 were the greatest. *The Guardian.* https://www.theguardian.com/news/blog/2007/sep/06/nessundormaan. Accessed 21 Apr 2018.

Peele, Jordan. 2017. Director: Get Out. Screenwriter: Jordan Peele. Universal Pictures.

Puccini, Giacomo. 1926. Turandot. Librettist: Giuseppe Adami and Renato Simoni. Premiere 25th April 1926, Teatro alla Scala, Milan.

Ross, Gary. 2012. Director: The Hunger Games. Screenwriters: Gary Ross, Suzanne Collins, Billy Ray and Suzanne Collins (novel). Lionsgate.

Scherfig, Lone. 2014. Director: The Riot Club. Screenwriter Laura Wade. Film 4.

Seger, Linda. 2003. *When women call the shots: The developing power and influence of women in television and film.* Lincoln: iUniverse.

Sinclair, Alice, Emma Pollard, and Helen Wolfe. 2006. Scoping study into the lack of women screenwriters in the UK. A report presented to the UK Film Council. UK Film Council. http://www.bfi.org.uk/sites/bfi.org.uk/files/downloads/uk-film-council-women-screenwriters-scoping-study.pdf. Accessed 26 Mar 2018.

Smith, Stacy L., and Chrystal Allene Cook. 2008. Gender stereotypes: An analysis of popular films and TV. Annenberg School for Communication and The Geena Davis Institute on Gender in Media. https://seejane.org/wpcontent/uploads/GDIGM_Gender_Stereotypes.pdf. Accessed 20 August 2018.

Strauss, Elissa. 2018. Why girls can be boyish but boys can't be girlish. *CNN.* https://edition.cnn.com/2018/04/12/health/boys-girls-gender-norms-parenting-strauss/index.html?no-st=1524507332. Accessed 22 Apr 2018.

Vaughan, Matthew. 2010. Director, Kick-Ass. Screenwriters: Jane Goldman, Matthew Vaughn. Lionsgate.

———. 2011. Director, X-Men: First Class. Screenwriters: Ashley Miller, Zack Stentz, Jane Goldman, Matthew Vaughn, Sheldon Turner, Bryan Singer. 20th Century Fox.

Wilkinson, Alissa. 2017. Hollywood's ideas about audiences are outdated. Wonder Woman's record-smashing debut proves it. *Vox.* https://www.vox.com/culture/2017/6/5/15739284/wonder-woman-box-office-records-female-director-get-out-hidden-figures. Accessed 21 Apr 2018.

Winick, Gary. 2009. Director: Bride Wars. Screenplay: Greg DePaul, Casey Wilson and June Diane Raphael. Fox 2000 Pictures.

CHAPTER 8

Conclusion: Moving Beyond Numbers to Make Change Happen

And I never went back to him and said: 'You were wrong. Everyone thought your writing was absolutely diabolical, apart from you. You thought you're the best thing ever.' (Vicky, employer)

Whilst I was in the process of finishing this book, the conversation about women in film continued to amplify worldwide. High-profile revelations of sexual harassment and assault, huge pay inequality, and campaigns by a growing number of organizations have kept the subject in the news and on the agenda for film festivals, film bodies, and financiers. Despite this—and some individual success stories—the overall participation of women in key roles in the film industry remains unchanged, according to the latest data, as I have shown. As I argued in my introduction, these numbers are important because they identify the problem, and there is a pressing need to continue monitoring the diversity of the film workforce to ensure change happens, as past initiatives have so far failed to produce meaningful results. However, it is also now time to move beyond the numbers in order to understand why, despite an increased awareness of inequality and an appetite for change, women remain underemployed in key roles in the UK film industry. This book provides an understanding of what lies behind the low numbers for women screenwriters, with clear implications for other filmmaking roles too. I identify where and how gender is invoked and inequality upheld, as well as the ways that the employment processes and working practices need to change if we are to ever see more equality of opportunity in the UK film industry and elsewhere.

© The Author(s) 2018   193
N. Wreyford, *Gender Inequality in Screenwriting Work*,
https://doi.org/10.1007/978-3-319-95732-6_8

In January 2013, as part of my research, I attended a BAFTA 'Masterclass' at the *Institut Français* in London entitled 'Why don't more women write for TV?' (BAFTA Masterclass 2013). I was disappointed to hear the usual post-feminist, neoliberal arguments being made by members of the onstage panel of women screenwriters, such as women needed to work harder, make their own opportunities, and were perhaps *choosing* not to write for *Dr Who* and other programmes dominated by men writers. Then audience member Greg Brenman, a very senior and experienced television producer,[1] stood up and said this:

> Everything we do is about looking for quality, and we often lament that there aren't enough women writers. I think there would never ever be a moment where we would turn down a woman who was of top quality or as good as any men. There would never be any prejudice, ever, in our company. And we actively look for women writers and we would love there to be more women writers and more women directors. I don't see the barrier. I don't know where it is. (Greg Brenman, producer)

I was struck, and more than a little shocked, that he found this an acceptable statement to make, particularly in a room full of mostly women—many of them screenwriters. When I began this research, I had been focused, like Brenman, on where the missing women were, desperate to see more films written by women. But my anger and outrage at his suggestion that good women screenwriters are just so hard to find helped me understand that I had come to view the problem very differently.

I have gathered evidence that successful films involving women in key creative roles have been repeatedly written off as anomalies and that women are less likely to see their screenplays get made into films than men. Brenman's claim to be without prejudice, whilst making what seemed to me to be a sexist comment, echoed what I'd heard in my interviews, and whilst working in the film industry. Now I believed that the women *were* there—as they were in that theatre—but older, white men employers, like Brenman, simply were not recognizing their ability and the value of their stories. Indeed, it is hard for young women to even see themselves in the role of screenwriter, in an industry where the senior roles, the directors, the highest paid actors, and the imagined audience are still predominantly men.

In this chapter, I draw together the central arguments of the book, summarize my findings, and suggest areas for future research that arise from my results. I finish with some suggestions for addressing inequality in screenwriting and other creative professions. My research is unusual in creative labour studies in that the empirical data included the experiences and opinions of employers as well as the creative labourers themselves. My own experience working in the British film industry gave me unprecedented levels of access to both senior figures and to those struggling to be visible. In addition, simply by talking to many of my participants, I helped to raise consciousness of gender inequalities in the film industry, and many have remained interested to hear my findings, as indeed have others that I didn't interview. A significant contribution and focus of this book is not simply documenting inequality but *accounting for the lack of change*. Ros Gill's (2014) timely call for more nuanced understandings of sexism in practice has, I hope, begun to be unpacked here with regard to the main social, educational, and environmental dimensions of creative work.

I have shown how the very talk of film workers contributes to limiting possible embodiments of the screenwriter subject position and, in particular, how men are positioned as more inherently suitable to screenwriting work. Screenwriters need to be 'tough' to cope with the 'brutality of the film world', which was likened to the military or a game of rugby where the writer is 'king' but never 'queen'. Screenwriting was consistently deemed to require an innate and magical quality possessed exclusively by special individuals, something that can be recognized by an obsessive drive to write that takes precedence over other aspects of a more 'normal' life, such as having a family, a social life, or indeed sleeping and eating. It was common to find the linked idea that success or failure in screenwriting is heavily influenced by 'how much you want it', that is, your ambition, commitment, and priorities. This all-consuming, obsessive notion of the creative individual excludes those with other responsibilities or demands on their time and ignores the fact that many men screenwriters have children but aren't required to be their primary carer. In my interviews, women were frequently framed as having more important things to do, thus dismissing the writing ambitions they may have found curtailed by these gendered expectations that they will do more than their fair share of childcare and housework. Men were described as more selfish, a subtle and clever form of sexism, which apparently flatters women on the surface but conveniently dismisses any further need to justify the lack of inclusion of women in screenwriting work.

I have also demonstrated how discursive work limits opportunities for women screenwriters and the stories they are expected—and indeed allowed—to tell. This is closely linked with the entrenched idea that the film business is a meritocracy, where only the most deserving people succeed. Women are blamed for choosing to write stories that have less market value, even though, as demonstrated, they were much more likely to be *commissioned* to write this sort of work and yet showed no natural preference for particular types of stories any more than men did. Indeed, women are often dissuaded from writing in more overtly commercial genres, which are very much perceived as 'boys' territory, although at the same time women screenwriters were apparently only viewed as succeeding if they did write stories for and about men in genres that they were considered to be less naturally gifted at writing.

On the other hand, I have also been able to disrupt and problematize these established discourses and offer some alternative readings of screenwriting work, which could provide more opportunities and recognition for women. For example, I have shown that some contributions to the collaborative process of writing a screenplay are considered more important than others. Whilst academic writing consistently demonstrates that creativity is a process and that creative work grows from collaboration and company, the film industry maintains a belief and a worship of individual genius. Perhaps this is beginning to crumble in a post-Weinstein world, where so many heroes of the film world are revealing themselves to be extremely flawed (Gilbey 2018), but we still have a long way to go.

When it comes to the actual employment processes for screenwriters, I have demonstrated that they need to be in either a personal or professional relationship with one of the key financiers or production companies to access the most lucrative work, and the role homophily plays in achieving this, meaning that once again, white men have the advantage. I have identified the continued reliance on nepotism, homophily, and ideas of 'trust' in the recruitment of screenwriters. I describe the triple disadvantage of motherhood—assumptions about its impact on women workers, the continued positioning of women as the 'default parent', and the disproportionate sacrifices women are still more likely to have to make or even consider in order to become parents. Despite all this, I also observed a common disarticulation of gender and racial inequality by even those suffering most from prejudice, although people felt more able to speak of the continued class and financial inequality in the film industry. This was particularly surprising, given the prevalence of privately educated and independently wealthy individuals thought by my participants to make up a majority of film industry workers in the development sector. This also reflects the profound precarity and wage insecurity felt by a huge majority of film workers, whatever their background.

Finally I applied Bourdieu's work on class and taste to argue that taste is also constructed along gendered lines. Women's taste is considered inferior to, and is therefore dominated by, men's taste. This impacts on the type of work women screenwriters are employed to do, and the status of that work. It also has a profound effect on audiences, since men can feel discomfort, disinterest, or even distaste at the idea of going to see a film with a woman protagonist or themes, locations, and storylines that are socially constructed as feminine. Whilst the equivalent 'men's' genres, characters, and themes are considered 'universal' and therefore less problematic for women audiences, men's stories and concerns continue to dominate in production and at the box office. This explains why even after films by and about women have huge financial and critical success, the percentage of women protagonists, or women screenwriters and directors remains stagnant and grossly unfair. It also offers a way to address this inequality at one of the root causes rather than trying to promote more women filmmakers through initiatives that simply feed the same dynamic. I now discuss three areas that I argue are similarly key to successfully addressing gender inequality in screenwriting work, before suggesting some possible future directions for research.

THE SCREENWRITER SUBJECTIVITY

Through this book, I have identified some key discourses about creative workers. These highlighted the entrenched view by film workers that their industry is a meritocracy where special creative individuals can reasonably expect to have a successful career if they are born with the talent and remain committed. Film workers believe that both the talent and commitment of these special individuals can be demonstrated by their willingness to devote every possible minute to the pursuit of their screenwriting art, prioritizing it over other aspects of life, as if inevitably driven to create. The discursive work done by this talk is to exclude from screenwriting anyone who has commitments that might prevent them from showing such devotion, most notably women with caring responsibilities. Chapter 5 demonstrated how women are still perceived as the most natural caregivers of children, and frequently do have primary responsibility for the majority of childcare and associated labour. However, whether they wish to become mothers or not, motherhood was positioned discursively as an essential aspect of all women's nature. Then women were perceived to make a choice for motherhood over a career, leaving little room for discussion about the difficulties of combining both, or whether men should take equal responsibility for childcare and other domestic and caring responsibilities.

Studying screenwriters has raised questions for me about the way that motherhood is the preferred explanation for why women do not succeed in a variety of professions. Many of my participants believed the characteristics of screenwriting work—such as the freedom to work where and when you chose—allow more accommodation of caring responsibilities than other film roles, particularly those involved in film production such as the director. Indeed, for those with the economic resources and familial support, it can be possible to consider a screenwriting career, although this still makes it difficult for a large proportion of women. More critically, by suggesting that creativity is an innate quality of certain individuals and then positioning women as naturally nurturing whist men are driven and 'pig-headed', men are seen as more inherently suited to screenwriting work. However, motherhood alone cannot account for the dismally low participation of women in screenwriting work and I have identified some other key areas where discrimination and inequality are reawakened and reinforced.

HOMOPHILY AND HABITUS

Screenwriters and employers frequently describe a reliance on homophily and the importance of collaboration. Evidence of homophily—the tendency to want to work and associate with those most like yourself—was a theme throughout, contributing to my discussions of employment processes in Chap. 4 and judgements of creative material in Chap. 6. It is also vital to understanding how the myth of the special creative individual masks and therefore upholds inequalities of access to screenwriting work. Although collaboration is a recognized and widely discussed undertaking in the filmmaking process, it is still the individual genius that is perceived as the key to the best creative output. The employers I spoke to were particularly quick to recognize the importance of collaboration—reflecting perhaps their own input in the creative process—but by then distancing themselves from the act of creation, they are able to hold others accountable for the success or failure of the product (most notably, the screenwriter in the development process and the director in the filmmaking process). Both employers and screenwriters also acknowledged the way that homophily could often make collaboration a more pleasant and uncomplicated process. However, homophily also plays a role in concealing subjectivity in taste and the selection of both people and creative products. This proves critical when discussing the role of directors and financiers in choosing which films actually get made. In Pierre Bourdieu's words, 'taste is a match-maker' (1984, p. 238). By failing to acknowledge the full reliance on homophily in collaboration, or how fundamental collaboration is to the creative process, the idea of meritocracy can be upheld. A hierarchy is created where some contributions are considered to be more valuable than others—with corresponding remuneration and respect. As I argue, the screenwriting role is frequently positioned as more suitable for men, whilst the less valued development role is similarly positioned as for women. Although women do write and men do hold development positions, women are often seen as naturally having the skills and disposition to nurture men screenwriters, and men who hold development positions are often given senior roles and more recognition. This echoes Elisabeth Kelan's study of ICT workers (2009), where men who exhibit the traits more regularly attributed to women such as good communication skills are given more credit and recognition because these aspects of their role are viewed as not naturally occurring in men as they are in women.

Screenwriters are commonly considered to be superseded by the director as the author of a film. During the creation of the screenplay, however, their authorship is unquestioned, despite input from a range of others, and can only be diluted by other screenwriters. Many of the employers I spoke to illustrated a desire and some actual attempts to turn to screenwriting themselves, sometimes borne out of a frustration with handing over their ideas and skillsets for little recognition. However, success in crossing over from another position in the film industry into screenwriting was also shown to be heavily gendered, with men once again far more likely to succeed. The discourses of creativity and meritocracy used by film industry workers fail to recognize the social, educational, and environmental dimensions of creativity. They assume a level playing field for anyone wishing to pursue a screenwriting career. But while the roles of producers, executive producers, directors, and other valued positions remain dominated by men, it is impossible for women to have the same chances of finding homophily in their employers and collaborators.

The social and informal nature of finding and securing work in the UK film industry means that homophily plays a key role for anyone seeking to build a career as a screenwriter. Nepotism, social and educational capital are frequently referenced by film workers as aiding entry to film work, but acknowledgement of these benefits conceals evidence of disadvantage due to gender or race. My research data are peppered with references to social occasions and ongoing personal relationships whereby similar and like-minded people identify and befriend each other, a widely practised recruitment process in the film industry. Creative roles in film were discursively positioned as requiring the worker to have a personal, emotional, and often instinctive response to the project. As a result, it was seen as important to work with others who understand and share your sensibilities. It eases communication and helps to avoid creative conflicts. Bourdieu's conception of the habitus is critical to understanding how this process works. Habitus acts like a shorthand and enables people to identify those with whom they are most likely to share similarities of taste and background. I problematize this by drawing attention to the fact that the most powerful positions in film work are dominated by people with very similar habitus compared with the population as a whole. I also illustrate the way that gendered habitus leads to fewer opportunities for women in screenwriting. I argue that it is critical to understand that those with the dominant habitus can fail to recognize the value of those unlike themselves. In culturally influential industries like film, this frequently leads to stories and storytellers of the dominant habitus being the most valued and therefore most frequently seen by audiences. This in turn upholds the perception of these stories and characters as more important and more valuable than others.

Women, those from lower socio-economic backgrounds and those of Black, South and East Asian origin are unable to break into the creative roles in the UK film industry in great numbers because the dominant habitus of those already inside the industry is that of wealthy white men. To even take part in the field of the UK film industry is difficult for anyone with a different habitus, since the habitus is not a choice, but the sum of a person's social position, experiences, and upbringing. An individual's habitus, expressed through the minutiae of their appearance, interests, preoccupations, and other gathered and embodied signifiers, is read by potential employers in social situations, in recruitment processes, and in the creative work itself. Since an individual's capital is embodied in the habitus through an elaborate and lengthy learned process of tiny details, it is difficult for anyone who isn't white, rich, or a man to replicate or acquire the necessary symbols of taste and belonging, even if they are prepared to conform to the dominant preferences. In this way, undesirable new entrants—and indeed those who achieve a degree of success—are more likely to be excluded from the most lucrative employment opportunities as much for their tastes and preferences as for their appearance and connections. The film workers I spoke to described ways that they used social and educational capital and altered their dress and appearance to try to fit in, but they still face barriers to success if they attempt to introduce projects or characters that the dominant habitus does not recognize or value.

Outsiders may find a way to be accepted if they convincingly play the game—by making films for and about men, for example, like Kathryn Bigelow (2008), still the only woman director to win an Academy Award for directing. Often, however, this is only possible with access to a surplus of other forms of capital—in particular, economic and social.[2] Exceptions are possible, but they are frequently held up as just that—exceptional, and ignored as a proven business model by men practitioners and investors. The romantic notion of the artist discussed in Chap. 2 is also at work here, facilitating the idea that individual genius is a rare commodity and concealing the processes of luck, hard work, advantage, and forms of capital which may have played a part in someone's success.

THE SYMBOLIC VIOLENCE OF GENDERED TASTE

Pierre Bourdieu's work on taste production and cultural capital can also facilitate an understanding of how dominant players maintain the perception that their own preferences are 'naturally' better than others in a way that discriminates against those of working class origin. Those in possession of greater cultural capital show 'strong degrees of disgust or revulsion' (McRobbie 2005, p. 128) towards those who do not share their tastes. My arguments in this book contribute to the growing body of evidence showing how Bourdieu's theories are applicable to gender. Women's tastes and preoccupations, which can be generalized as different to men's only as the lived consequences of socialized gender construction, are misunderstood and marginalized by the predominantly white male film industry. Whilst women, already encouraged to be other-oriented, learn by omission to engage with stories of the preoccupations of a men's habitus, 'women's films' are apparently of limited interest to men cinema audiences. As I demonstrate in Chap. 7, women are consigned to a small niche, expected to write smaller stories focused on human relationships, predominantly exploring the pursuit of romantic (heterosexual) love, the principal point at which women's lives intersect with heterosexual men's lives. Rarely do they get the chance to explore other aspects of their existence through the cinematic experience, whether central to women's experience, like motherhood, or central to the human experience, like survival. In addition, the cinema women are allowed to participate in is simultaneously devalued as frivolous, small in scope, and overly emotional.

Those who hold power cannot admit that their cultural competences and symbolic capital have in fact been 'learnt' through socializing and then upheld as having greater value purely by the recognition of their peers. Acknowledging the constructed nature of judgements of taste and superiority would make it much harder to lay claim to the limited resources available for film production. I had initially hoped that by interviewing key intermediaries they would interpret and therefore reveal the prejudices of others. But as I have shown, the confidence of the dominant habitus is such that they actually saw no problem in reproducing their own socially constructed and gendered ideas of what constitutes good or important work. Women were seen as able participants when they proved themselves capable of writing stories that fit with the dominant view—stories perceived to be for an audience of men and about men characters. Universal human concerns like relationships and parenting, which are attached particularly to women and girls through a process of socialized learning, are constructed rather than innate and not relevant to all women at all times in their lives. However, these socialization processes are also likely to produce a very different way of experiencing the world, different perspectives, and some different preoccupations. The habitus allows us to understand why it isn't sufficient to have men tell stories about women, or white people tell stories about women of colour, or to continue to see the white straight man's viewpoint as the gold standard to which others must learn to conform if they want success.

We must diversify the workforce creating the product, not just what is seen onscreen. Increasing the number and variety of women's voices as screenwriters—and directors—can only help complicate the view that women are all the same. When women are so scarce, any position they hold or product they make is often held up as representative of all women. We desperately need not just more women, but a range and diversity of women's voices in order to deconstruct the category of women, their tastes, and interests. Just as it has become unacceptable to say we don't 'see race', it is no longer possible to suggest that a good writer will be recognized regardless of their gender. There is no way to not 'do gender', in life and in writing. We cannot make the playing field level by trying to take gender out of the equation. This leads to women only having real success when they can behave like men, for example, by not having babies or writing films about men soldiers. Equal opportunities law understands that different people may require different approaches and assistance in order to provide a *real* equality of opportunity. Whilst the work that women do—in the workplace and at home—is not considered to be as valuable as that of men, we cannot hope to eradicate inequality.

WHAT NEXT?

This book is, to my knowledge, the first detailed study of gender inequalities in a particular filmmaking profession. My focus on the employers of screenwriters is particularly unique in creative industries research and provides much-needed discussion of the recruitment processes—both overt and unconscious—to which creative professionals are subject. One clear indication of my analysis is a pressing need for research into the creative managers themselves: who holds these positions and how these professions come to be gendered. Indeed, I propose that there is an urgent need to examine all the gatekeepers to creative professions such as screenwriting. Agents, producers, creative writing courses, and other well-trodden paths that lead to screenwriting, such as playwriting, need to be examined for further evidence of gendered practices and gendered assumptions.

However, the key creative role that my research points to as in desperate need of fine critical examination is that of the film director. Using Bourdieu's theories of taste and embodied capital, I have shown that the desire for a film director to respond personally and instinctively to a piece of screenwriting can substantially disadvantage women screenwriters whilst the percentage of women directors remains around 7 per cent. It is therefore extremely important to understand—and remove—the barriers to women directors. Although I would expect such a study to draw many similar conclusions to my own examination of screenwriters (some of my participants were indeed directors as well as screenwriters), this would only strengthen arguments and provide more evidence of the critical points where change might happen (see the final section later).

Indeed, I would argue that more research is needed across all film roles as to their gendered assumptions and practices. Patterns are observable across the current available studies of gender in creative professions. Ros Gill's (1993) radio workers suggested that women had a lack of interest in applying for jobs in a way that is very similar to my participants' assertions that women are too sensible to pursue a screenwriting career. Stephanie Taylor and Karen Littleton (2012) observe the same conflicts between caring and creative work in the art world that I found and that Mark Banks and Katie Milestone (2011) argue also exist for new media workers. The reluctance of Christina Scharff's (2015) classical musicians to actively promote their abilities echoes the positioning of women as more naturally taking up the shadowy position of nurturing men creative workers. Adding to this growing body of work can only strengthen our understanding of new and old forms of discrimination in practice and eventually permit some bolder claims across professions and industries about mechanisms that uphold inequality.

I believe there is an urgent need for research into the position of screenwriters marginalized by their race and a focus on the role that class plays in screenwriting careers. I have demonstrated how both of these are particularly problematic in the UK film industry and yet very little is known about the dynamics of these axes of inequality. I also propose that some consideration is given to the extension of Bourdieu's theories to an understanding of continued racial inequality in creative work. Neither race nor class is directly comparable to gender in the way that inequalities are produced and reinforced, but they share the position of dominated to a dominant taste and habitus. An examination of the similarities between these different forms of inequality would be helpful as well as a deeper understanding of the ways in which they are different and indeed the implications at the points of intersection (Crenshaw 1989).

This book is part of a growing body of work on the continued gender inequalities at work, and particularly in creative professions, such as those that I have mentioned. After being submerged in the film industry for so many years as a worker, I began this study thinking that the film industry was lagging behind other professions in achieving gender equality. Sadly, I have been led to an increased awareness of the prevalence of gendered assumptions and consequential discrimination in many labour markets, and particularly in creative professions. Thankfully, data are very slowly beginning to emerge to highlight the extent of these inequalities, as it did for me in film, and hopefully this book will inspire similar empirical studies. It is clear that there are continued gender biases and discriminatory practices in industries such as publishing (Franklin 2011), popular music (Negus 2002), gaming (Sarkeesian 2015), theatre (Hemley 2017), and the intersection with other forms of inequality, such as the lack of black women dancers in professional ballet companies (Goldhill and Marsh 2012). Each of these fields—and more—deserve focused attention to understand the particular mechanisms at play, as well as the shared cultural assumptions that need to be recognized if they are ever to be challenged.

What Can Be Done?

During the course of my interviews, one recurring discourse was a firm belief that things were getting better for women screenwriters in the UK film industry. I argued in Chap. 2 that the rhetorical function of this is to release the speakers from feeling any guilt, or actively taking responsibility for change. However, it is also clear from the growing body of available data that this is not the reality of the situation, as can be seen in the latest reports from Calling the Shots, The Writer's Guild of Great Britain, Directors UK, and many more. Although more detailed and nuanced research is needed, particularly on other key roles, my study has highlighted particular ways that inequality is perpetuated in creative professions.

I hope this book can inform film industry practitioners, particularly those with a responsibility for employing screenwriters. Screenwriters may feel frustrated that the focus is less on what they can do, as I believe a turn away from neoliberal discourses of individual responsibility and choice is fundamental to real change. My eyes are on the employers, and on the structural and discursive mechanisms that currently do not allow change to happen. Film workers of all roles and responsibilities must become aware of their own subjective judgements and be prepared to open up to alternative ways of working and talking about creative jobs that allows a greater diversity of people to participate. This is particularly true at the very top of the tree, where powerful white men are going to need to relinquish their power.

With homophily so key in recruitment processes and creative collaborations, it is vital that women have as large a pool to choose from as men do. It is not a new idea to advocate for more women in senior and powerful positions, but my research highlights the need for caution when assessing candidates for even these roles, which are often subject to the same judgements of taste and merit. Just like screenwriters, it is likely that homophily and shared habitus are playing a key part in these appointments. It is important for all involved to have an awareness of subjective judgements, a commitment to overcome personal bias, and most crucially to enable a process of taking risks and hiring beyond comfort zones. This is a practice that could be adopted in all recruitment practices in the film industry. One of my participants told me that she is frequently contacted by colleagues in other companies who are hiring development personnel, for example, and who express doubts about a potential employee's 'taste'. However, by only hiring personnel who share their taste, employers are potentially restricting the recognition of projects that may have huge value for those unlike themselves, including large sections of a cinema audience, and they are certainly likely to be discriminating on the basis of gender, class, and race.

Women are not a homogeneous group, and I write this book, I am aware of Judith Butler's warnings of even treating 'women' as a subject since it reinforces a gender binary, which is both constructed and exclusionary. However, because there are a smaller number of women directors and financiers, and an even smaller number of those openly identifying as gender queer, it is much harder for any of these individuals to find others who might understand their stories and characters. This recommendation to diversify the employers is a good example of how the arguments in this book may also be applicable to different types of discrimination. There is clearly a similar need for a larger number and variety of collaborators and enablers from a range of gender identities, class backgrounds and ethnicities, sexualities, and differing abilities too. It is time for wealthy white men to relinquish their dominance of the most powerful positions. Indeed, there is an argument for those organizations funded with public money to actively seek to redress the gender imbalance in the private sector by ensuring that their funds are *completely* controlled by women. Past evidence has shown this to be effective in increasing opportunities for women, even though women in these positions are still required to collaborate with men co-financiers (Steele 2013).

Those that work in the film industry have a responsibility to reflect on the impact of believing that they exist in a meritocracy and to try to understand the ways that these working conditions are actively excluding people. Deeply held assumptions about creativity and audiences seem to thrive even in the face of contrary evidence and function more to uphold the status quo than to serve the creative and commercial ends they profess to. This is not a trivial matter. Film workers are in the business of creating narratives and subject positions through which viewers can reflect on their own lives and possibilities. How can we continue to justify the exclusion of women's voices, women characters, and women's agency from having equal footing in this process? I appeal to decision makers to question the objectivity of their judgements and to understand that their tastes are not always universal or shared by large sections of potential audiences. The evidence exists to challenge myths and long-standing beliefs if we are prepared to listen.

I believe this research has implications for an audience that is wider than the employers of screenwriters, or indeed the film industry. A wider cultural change would help to improve the situation for women screenwriters, and so, this last paragraph is directed to anyone who wants to help creative women, to improve gender equality more generally, or to increase the diversity of available films in cinemas. Much of it is about challenging gendered assumptions and segregations, from birth, through toys and education and into the workplace. It is about men taking equal responsibility for taking care of their children, and employers making that easier for all parents. Indeed it is society recognizing the need for new generations so that even those who choose *not* to have children understand the fairness of making allowances for those who do, in the knowledge that they are raising future taxpayers, doctors, bankers, road sweepers, and story tellers. More specifically, it is vitally important to make it more acceptable for men and boys to show interest in women and girls and anything that has become culturally labelled as feminine or female. It is essential that men see stories about women as frequently as women see stories about men. It's also important that we break down the binary by seeing stories about and by those who identify as everything outside and in between. Men need to relearn the early childhood perspective of seeing girls and women as people just like them. This will help establish women as an accepted point of empathy, acknowledge shared concerns and universal themes through women characters, and engender genuine interest in unfamiliar preoccupations caused by gendered habitus. My hope is that this will be a crucial tipping point that begins a process whereby women are allowed equal opportunities as screenwriters, film audiences, and human beings.

Notes

1. Greg Brenman's Wikipedia page says that he is an award-winning film and television producer, with over 400 hours of TV drama to his name as former head of British production company *Tiger Aspect.*
2. It is interesting to note that such is Bigelow's social capital that when she won the Academy Award for Best Director in 2010, one of her four fellow nominees was her ex-husband, James Cameron.

References

BAFTA Masterclass. 2013. Why don't more women write for TV? *Institut Français*, London. Recording available: http://guru.bafta.org/craft-master-class-why-dont-more-women-write-for-tv-podcast. Accessed 2 Apr 2018.

Banks, Mark, and Katie Milestone. 2011. Individualization, gender and cultural work. *Gender, Work & Organization* 18 (1): 73–89.

Bigelow, Kathryn. 2008. Director, The Hurt Locker. Screenplay by Mark Boal. Voltage Pictures.

Bourdieu, Pierre. 1984. *Distinction: A social critique of the judgement of taste.* Cambridge, MA: Harvard University Press.

Crenshaw, Kimberle. 1989. Demarginalizing the intersection of race and sex: A black feminist critique of antidiscrimination doctrine, feminist theory and antiracist politics. *University of Chicago Legal Forum* 1989 (1), Article 8: 139–167.

Franklin, Ruth. 2011. A literary glass ceiling? *New Republic.* https://newrepublic.com/article/82930/vida-women-writers-magazines-book-reviews. Accessed 2 Apr 2018.

Gilbey, Ryan. 2018. The end of the auteur? *The Guardian.* https://www.theguardian.com/film/2018/mar/23/the-end-of-the-auteur?CMP=Share_iOSApp_Other. Accessed 2 Apr 2018.

Gill, Rosalind. 1993. Justifying injustice: Broadcasters' accounts of inequality in radio. In *Discourse analytic research: Repertoires and readings of texts in action*, ed. Erica Burman and Ian Parker, 75–93. London: Routledge.

———. 2014. Unspeakable inequalities: Post feminism, entrepreneurial subjectivity, and the repudiation of sexism among cultural workers. *Social Politics: International Studies in Gender, State & Society* 21 (4): 509–528.

Goldhill, Olivia, and Sarah Marsh. 2012. Where are the black ballet dancers? *The Guardian.* https://www.theguardian.com/stage/2012/sep/04/black-ballet-dancers. Accessed 2 Apr 2018.

Hemley, Matthew. 2017. Women directors face gender gap at top theatres 'sobering' report claims. *The Stage.* https://www.thestage.co.uk/news/2017/male-directors-outnumber-women-at-75-of-english-theatres-sobering-report-claims/. Accessed 2 Apr 2018.

Kelan, Elisabeth. 2009. *Performing gender at work*. Hampshire: Palgrave Macmillan.
McRobbie, Angela. 2005. *The uses of cultural studies: A textbook*. London: Sage.
Negus, Keith. 2002. The work of cultural intermediaries and the enduring distance between production and consumption. *Cultural Studies* 16 (4): 501–515.
Sarkeesian, Anita. 2015. Gender breakdown of games showcased at E3 2015. *Feminist Frequency*. https://feministfrequency.com/2015/06/22/gender-breakdown-of-games-showcased-at-e3-2015/. Accessed 2 Apr 2018.
Scharff, Christina. 2015. Blowing your own trumpet: Exploring the gendered dynamics of self-promotion in the classical music profession. *The Sociological Review* 63 (1_suppl): 97–112.
Steele, David. 2013. *Succès de plume?* Female screenwriters and directors of UK films, 2010–2012. *BFI*. http://www.bfi.org.uk/sites/bfi.org.uk/files/downloads/bfi-report-on-female-writers-and-directors-of-uk-films-2013-11.pdf. Accessed 2 Apr 2018.
Taylor, Stephanie, and Karen Littleton. 2012. *Contemporary identities of creativity and creative work*. Oxfordshire: Routledge.

Index[1]

[1] Note: Page numbers followed by 'n' refer to notes.

211